Something and Nothingness

The Fiction of
John Updike & John Fowles

John Neary

Southern Illinois University Press

Carbondale and Edwardsville

Copyright © 1992 by the Board of Trustees,
  Southern Illinois University
All rights reserved
Printed in the United States of America
Edited and designed by Melissa L. Riddle
Production supervised by Natalia Nadraga

95 94 93 92   4 3 2 1

Library of Congress Cataloging-in-Publication Data

Neary, John, 1952–
    Something and nothingness : the fiction of John Updike and John
Fowles / John Neary.
    p. cm
    Includes bibliographical references and index.
    1. Updike, John—Criticism and interpretation. 2. Fowles, John,
1926– —Criticism and interpretation. 3. Literature, Comparative—
American and English. 4. Literature, Comparative—English and
American. I. Title.
PS3571.P4Z785 1992
823'.91409—dc20   90-25137
ISBN 0-8093-1742-7   CIP

The paper used in this publication meets the minimum requirements of
American National Standard for Information Sciences—Permanence of
Paper for Printed Library Materials, ANSI Z39.48-1984. ∞

For Laura, Kevin, and Kyle

Contents

Acknowledgments

I wish to thank the following publishers who have given permission to use extended quotations from copyrighted works. *The Centaur* (1963), *Couples* (1968), *Assorted Prose* (1965), *Midpoint and Other Poems* (1969), *A Month of Sundays* (1975), *Rabbit, Run* (1960), *Roger's Version* (1986), and *S.* (1989) by John Updike are reprinted by permission of Alfred A. Knopf, Inc. and Andre Deutsch, Ltd.

Permission has been granted by Little, Brown and Company and by Anthony Sheil Associates, Ltd. to quote from the following works by John Fowles: *The Collector* (copyright © 1963 by John Fowles, Ltd.), *The French Lieutenant's Woman* (copyright © 1969 by John Fowles, Ltd.), *A Maggot* (copyright © 1985 by John Fowles, Ltd.), *The Magus: A Revised Version* (first edition copyright © 1965 by John Fowles; revised edition copyright © 1977 by John Fowles, Ltd.). The first British publisher of Fowles's novels was Jonathan Cape, Ltd. Permission has also been granted by Little, Brown and Company and by Anthony Sheil Associates, Ltd. to quote from *The Tree* by John Fowles and Frank Horvat, text and English translation copyright © 1979 by the Association for All Speech Impaired Children (AFASIC). And permission has been granted by the Ecco Press and by Anthony Sheil Associates, Ltd. to reprint the poem "A Tree in the Suburbs" (copyright © by John Fowles), from *Poems,* first published by The Ecco Press in 1973, reprinted by permission.

Portions of chapter 1 appeared in *Essays in Literature,* Volume 15.1 (Spring 1988): 46–62. Reprint permission granted by *Essays in Literature,* Western Illinois University, Macomb, Illinois. Portions of chapter 2 appeared in *Religion and Literature,* Volume 21.1 (Spring 1989): 89–110. Reprint permission granted by *Religion and Literature,* University of Notre Dame, Notre Dame, Indiana. Portions of chapter 3 appeared in *Renascence: Essays on Values in Literature,* Volume 38.4 (Summer 1986): 228–44. Reprint permission granted by *Renascence: Essays on Values in Literature,* Marquette University, Milwaukee, Wisconsin.

I wish to thank Ken Zahorski, St. Norbert College's Director of Faculty Development, and the St. Norbert Faculty Development Committee, for two generous summer grants that permitted me to do concentrated work on this project. I am also thankful to Morton Kelsey, who taught me most of what I know about theology, and James McMichael, who introduced me to the work of Alain-Fournier, Denis de Rougemont, and Emmanuel Levinas. In addition, I want to thank Curtis Clark and Melissa Riddle, acquisitions editor and manuscript editor at Southern Illinois University Press, for their civil, gracious treatment of me and my manuscript. And I am indebted to Jill Landes, who helped me prepare the book's index.

Something and
Nothingness

1

Introduction

In their attempts to capture a valid vision of human existence, writers of English-language fiction have tended to waver between literary versions of what theologians call the *via negativa* and the *via affirmativa.* Although the act of writing in itself may seem to assert the possibility of saying something about something, it is more than ever true in this age of postmodernist deconstructing that many writers—and, according to some, the only self-conscious and compelling ones—are akin to the religious followers of the *via negativa* in the way they use language: breaking it down, and hence pointing toward the unspeakable, the darkness behind being. But other writers, who are included in what is clumsily called the realistic tradition, follow an affirmative way; they are more interested in capturing existence, in using language not to deconstruct but precisely to construct a world of things. Sometimes such writers *are* unselfconscious, concerned only with photographing phenomena without ever considering whether these pheonomena have any value or even reality; but others, the great creators of substantial worlds, see things, content, and imagery as a positive revelation—about some substantive human nature or even cosmic order.

In the theology of spirituality, the two *viae,* the negative and the affirmative, are ways specifically of approaching God. The *via negativa* is the way of the "apophatic" mystical tradition, which asserts that nothing, no thing, can approximate the divine, who is beyond all thingness; the "kataphatic" tradition, on the other hand, which embraces the *via affirmativa,* "uses terms from our own experience to describe God and his qualities" (Kesich 254). But these two mystical traditions do not just have differing notions of God; their theologies lead to differing orientations toward the world, toward the human imagination, and toward language, which make them emblematic of the two literary *viae* that I wish to introduce. In his book *Christian Mysticism,* Harvey Egan, S.J., explains that the *via negativa* leads to a stripping away of attention

1

to the world, an elimination of content from consciousness: "The apophatic tradition, the *via negativa,* emphasizes the radical difference between God and creation. God is best reached, therefore, by negation, forgetting, and unknowing, in a darkness of mind without the support of concepts, images, and symbols." In apophatic theology, Egan suggests, language itself must negate, not posit: "God is 'not this, not that'" (31). For those following the negative way, the deepest and most authentic experience is an experience of absence, darkness, silence. The *via affirmativa,* on the other hand, is a way to God that is predicated not on absence but on presence; according to followers of this route, the world of things and the images that arise within consciousness can be revelations of God. As Egan puts it, "Kataphatic mysticism, the *via affirmativa,* emphasizes the similarity that exists between God and creatures. Because God can be found in all things, the affirmative way recommends the use of concepts, images, and symbols as a way of contemplating God" (31). The kataphatic tradition, therefore, affirms the value of a world with texture, with substance—a somethingness rather than a nothingness.

These two religious attitudes have existed in an uneasy tension for many centuries. In a book on Christian meditation, Morton Kelsey contrasts the two *viae* as they have affected actual religious practices; he asserts that the quest for "Union with the Imageless State," in which "physical matter, symbols, ritual are all forgotten" (the *via negativa*), is Eastern and Neoplatonic in origin (133), while an embracing of concrete images (the *via affirmativa*) affirms God's incarnation in the human world and is therefore quintessentially Christian (137). Egan reports, however, that "some contemporary writers hold the thesis that 'pure' mysticism exists only in the apophatic tradition and relegate the kataphatic tradition to an inferior position" (32), while he himself asserts that "both are orthodox ways of mystically reaching God, and one type of mysticism always contains elements of the other type" (31).

A similar tension has existed in the literary tradition between the negative and affirmative ways of using language and presenting the world, between what I am loosely calling postmodernism and realism. And although the gap between these two orientations has become particularly glaring in the twentieth century (it is difficult to believe that a self-consciously negative writer like Samuel Beckett, who mutters "I can't go on, I'll go on" [414], is even working in the same genre as a fact-oriented practitioner like James Michener), it has been with the English-language novel since its earliest days. Daniel Defoe, for instance, was the novelist-of-things par excellence, while in the same century, Laurence Sterne wrote a lengthy masterpiece about the inability to tell stories about any-thing. Furthermore, the tension between the two literary *viae* often exists within one work, as in Samuel Richardson's *Clarissa*. This is a magnificent piece of realism (the concrete particulars that flood a character's mind have perhaps never been recorded more meticulously), but its very length and obsessiveness give it a deconstructive quality; eventually it seems, as much as Sterne's *Tristram Shandy,* to be a meditation on the limitations of dis-course itself.

John Updike and John Fowles are literary opposites in just these terms—Updike tends to be a social realist, and Fowles tends to be a postmodernist, metafictional experimenter. A book on the two writers, therefore, is inevitably an attempt to discuss these poles of contemporary English-language fiction. But any two writers from these poles—Pynchon and Styron, say, or Barth and Cheever—would serve equally well to illustrate this contrast. There are some striking similarities between Fowles and Updike, though, that highlight this large literary/philosophical contrast in a remarkable way. Updike and Fowles are nearly the same age, and their respec-tive careers are marked by a series of novels that parallel each other structurally and thematically. And throughout their fiction the writers reveal similar intellectual influences: romanticism and especially existentialism.

Both are also distinctly interested in theological issues, and their integration of the theological and the literary suggests that the relation between the literary and the religious *viae* is not merely analogical but essential. On the face of it, this is not obvious. It would seem, for instance, that theological language would be particularly irrelevant to a discussion of those who follow the negative literary path, those who use language to negate. Fowles, like many postmodernists, is an avowed atheist, while those who follow the mystical negative way, at least within the Christian tradition, are in quest of an unmediated experience of God. As Kelsey puts it, apophatic mysticism negates matter, language, and images because "the only things that matter are the person and the immediate perception of the divine" (133). But I suggest that Fowles's atheism is a very specific sort—a *religious* atheism, so to speak. God's absence is, for Fowles, the ground of all possibility. Indeed, Fowles flirted with Zen for a time, a venerable Eastern form of apophatic mysticism. And Fowles's religious athe-ism may, if theologian Mark C. Taylor is correct, point toward the religious interests that actually undergird much of deconstruction and postmodernism. Taylor claims that Jacques Derrida himself is a kind of theologian, "profoundly influenced by Lurianic Kabbalism" (xx), and I propose that there are variations on strict Derridean deconstruction that are even more explicitly theological. "Followers of Derrida," Taylor says, "have preferred to overlook the theological and religious aspects of his thought, no doubt suspecting that they represent a vestige of the nostalgia which he criticizes so relentlessly. But Derrideans who disregard such theological issues risk superficiality, just as theologians who ignore Deconstruction risk irrelevance. . . . Despite its overt atheism, postmodernism remains profoundly religious" (xx).

So ultimately I am comparing the writers' presentations of philosophical/aesthetic visions that have decided, though decidedly different, existentialist and theological foundations. Fowles's existentialism is that of Sartre, an atheistic celebration of nothingness-as-freedom; his books, therefore, are founded on absence (of God, of substantive human selves). Updike's, on the other hand, is that of Kierkegaard, a Christian celebration of faith beyond nothingness; and his books are founded on presence (of God, of substantive selves). These two writers, therefore, clearly reveal the dissimilar approaches to the real—one the literary *via negativa* and the other the *via affirmativa*—that underlie their forms of fiction. And whatever our contemporary preference for gaps and absences, Fowles's commitment to the negative road is neither philosophically more sophisticated nor aesthetically more daring than Updike's commitment to the affirmative. In fact, if I risk the inappropriate by talking about the atheist Fowles in religious terms, I take an equal risk here by talking about the Christian Updike as a sort of affirmative postmodernist. It is not only Fowles to whom I ascribe the activity of deconstructing; I also suggest that sometimes Updike's fiction performs deconstructive strategies as well. Fowles's and Updike's works ultimately demonstrate that the literary *via negativa* and *via affirmativa* can in certain ways merge. Indeed, in a discussion of Denys the Areopagite, Andrew Louth asserts that such merging also takes place between the theological *viae:* "Both symbolic and cataphatic theology then point beyond themselves to a state where symbols and concepts are transcended and God is known by unknowing. This is apophatic theology, the theology of rest" (188).

In showing this bridge between the *viae,* I hope also to effect some reconciliation between traditionalism and postmodernism, which are these days battling for control of literary theory. In the chapters that follow, I examine the impressive way in which Updike constructs a real, substantial world that is integrally, morally related to the world we humans really live in, but I also show how he sometimes accomplishes this goal precisely by *decon-*

structing the conventional and that he often dwells in darkness, relativity, absence. I also argue that Fowles writes to *un*write, to deconstruct, in order to open up a radical absence, and yet that a theological interest (even a trace of faith, especially in Fowles's later novels) seems to underlie this activity. Coming to grips with this tension between traditional faith and radical skepticism is, as Mark Taylor has noted, a project that has been too rarely undertaken by either theologians or literary theorists. Does deconstruction, for instance, dismantle traditional assertions of meaning to espouse utter meaninglessness? Or does it, as J. Hillis Miller (invoking William Carlos Williams) suggested in his 1986 MLA presidential address, bring "the hidden spark or spirit back into the open" (282)? I do not pretend that I can reconcile such issues definitively, but I do take them seriously.

I compare Updike and Fowles by looking at several pairs of similar novels. Chapters 2 and 3 sketch out each writer's basic vision by looking at two early, rather schematic books: Fowles's *The Collector* and Updike's *Rabbit, Run* (the third chapter also briefly touches on the other Rabbit novels). Though each of these chapters focuses on only one of the writers, the two chapters together establish my ccomparative strategy: it turns out that the tensions in each of these very schematic books, as well as the repetitive structures, are remarkably similar, and yet the resolutions of the tensions and the purposes of the repetitions are quite different. In chapter 4, I begin comparing the writers more directly; I discuss Fowles's and Updike's biographies and philosophical orientations, primarily by examining autobiographical pieces by each, which, somewhat uncannily, both use trees as the central metaphor. Chapter 5 compares the writers' respective *Bildungsromane,* Updike's *The Centaur* and Fowles's *The Magus,* which both use Greek myth in allegorical ways. In this chapter, I discuss the dialectic of the self and the other in the works of the two writers; for the Christian Updike, the self confronts a substantive other—and, by analogy, an ontologically real God—while for the atheistic Fowles, the other vanishes, leaving the self absolutely alone, absolutely free. The remaining chapters compare Updike's *Couples* and Fowles's *The French Lieutenant's Woman* as novels that use sex to deconstruct nineteenth-century fictional conventions, and Fowles's *Mantissa* and *A Maggot* and Updike's *Roger's Version* and *S.* as experimental texts that look directly at the issue of religion. In addition, these last four novels have Fowles and Updike almost reversing their positions: these books reveal, most strikingly, the ambiguity of the differences between the two *viae.* In *A Maggot,* especially, Fowles seemingly negates his own negations, and although he does not suddenly find a substantive God in the existential darkness, he does seem to present a vision of some ineffable goodness beyond the self. Updike, on the other hand, so pushes God beyond the human in these later books that he seems—for a while, at least—to be asserting that an absolute darkness, an essential nothingness, surrounds the human world. Still, despite this ambiguity, my contrast between the two authors, and between the literary *viae,* remains valid and instructive: for all his skepticism, Updike ends up, even in these novels, calling back the world of ordinary thingness after all, while Fowles's ultimate truth always remains bathed in mystery and darkness—as it is for even the most devoutly theistic followers of the religious *via negativa.*

This complicated interplay between realism and postmodernism, and atheism and theism, makes John Fowles and John Updike fascinating literary allies/adversaries, and it also makes them important exemplars of issues that are at the forefront of current literature and literary theory.

2

Rebellion and Repetition
in
The Collector

Most critics have seen John Fowles's *The Collector* as a schematic statement of some of Fowles's major ideas; indeed, in his introduction to the revised edition of *The Aristos*, a collection of philosophical aphorisms, Fowles himself describes the book as a "parable" analyzing the confrontation between the "Few" and the "Many" (a confrontation analyzed more explicitly in the philosophical text). On these terms, the novel is a kind of philosophical dialogue examining this particular intellectual issue. Or, rather, it is a pair of monologues: roughly half the book is narrated by its young heroine, aspiring artist Miranda Grey, who sees the world from the viewpoint of the Few (Fowles's Heraclitean elite — "aristoi, the good ones"), and the other half is narrated by Miranda's kidnapper, the twisted anti-hero Frederick Clegg, who represents the Many (the "unthinking, conforming mass — *hoi polloi* [*Aristos* 9]).

Unquestionably the book is schematic. Clegg's and Miranda's social, intellectual, and emotional differences, along with their opposing roles within the prisoner-versus-imprisoned plot, set the characters' respective narratives in ideological contrast. Nonetheless, exclusive concentration on the "Few versus Many" polarity, which assigns to Miranda all of the novel's "potential good" (in Fowles's words) and to Clegg all its "actual evil" (*Aristos* 10), obscures some of the text's novelistic richness, what Shyamal Bagchee calls the "profoundly ironic view of the absurd that escapes the notice of readers interested only in broad thematic generalities" (220). Bagchee argues that, rather than thoroughly clashing, the narratives of Miranda and Clegg "rhetorically illuminate each other" (222). Both characters, for example, espouse an atheistic philosophy that matches Fowles's own (Bagchee 222–23), and both experience "nearly epiphanous moments" of a tranquility and harmony that exists between them, despite the obviously ghastly nature of their relationship (227–28). Indeed, Bagchee argues that Clegg's forcible domination of Miranda is partially counterbalanced by Miranda's own desire to "play a mild verion of the godgame" with Clegg (233).

Although I admire Bagchee's unusual reading of the book, I do not think that it goes far enough. After virtually turning Miranda's and Clegg's generally accepted roles topsy-turvy, Bagchee draws only the vaguest, most modest conclusion: "My point," he says, "is simply that Fowles's imagination, even in *The Collector,* is more paradoxical than antithetical." This is not, he maintains, "a *roman á thése*" (234). What Bagchee neglects to do is point out that it is only when we look beneath *The Collector*'s obvious polarity between good and evil, *aristoi* and *hoi polloi*, that we truly understand some of the novel's most quintessentially Fowlesian themes.

Clegg's evil, for example, is at least somewhat softened by Fowles's biological view of the human situation. Human beings, for Fowles, are simply organisms like any other, and organisms—even *thinking* organisms—are merely complex machines. Fowles enunciates this position in a discussion, in *The Aristos,* of the human brain:

> 39 There is no thought, no perception, no conscious-
> ness of it, no consciousness of consciousness, that
> cannot be traced to an electrochemical event in
> the brain. 'I have an immortal and immaterial soul'
> is a thought or statement; it is also a recording of
> the activity of certain cells by other cells. . . .
>
> 41 Machines are made from 'dead' matter; brains are
> made from 'living' matter. But the frontier between
> 'dead' and 'living' is confused. One could not con-
> struct a machine as complex as the brain out of
> 'dead' matter; but part of the complexity (as proved
> by its actual inconstructability) of the brain is that
> its machinery is made of 'living' matter. Our inabili-
> ty to construct mechanical yet fully human brains
> shows our scientific and technological inadequacy,
> not any real difference between mechanical func-
> tions and supposedly 'spiritual' thoughts. (37–38)

This equation of human nature with biology and mechanism is a crucial part of Fowles's rigorously atheistic philosophical position, which is, he has claimed, heavily indebted to Darwinism. Fowles rebels against the religious notion of a spiritual self or soul or of the kind of deity that such a soul might traffic with; as we will see, absence—of substantive selves and, most fundamentally, of a god—is central to Fowles's writings. God is *not,* Fowles asserts, and the universe is a random collection of matter in which "hazard" rules with sublime impartiality. In the section of *The Aristos* entitled "Atheism" he writes: "I live in hazard and infinity. The cosmos stretches around me, meadow on meadow of galaxies, reach on reach of dark space, steppes of stars, oceanic darkness and light. There is no amenable god in it, no particular concern or particular mercy" (28).

Frederick Clegg embodies the most blindly deterministic aspects of such a worldview, and it is this fact, ironically, that to a large degree makes his actions forgivable. Again and again the character tells us, and he at least partially convinces us, that he has stumbled into his involvement with Miranda by a series of accidents—by hazard—rather than by real choice. It "happened suddenly," he maintains; "it wasn't something I planned" (14). Fowles himself, moreover, in his introduction to *The Aristos,* validates Clegg's claim, saying, "Clegg, the kidnapper, committed the evil; but I tried to show that his evil was largely, perhaps wholly, the result of a bad education, a mean environment, being orphaned: all factors over which he had no control" (10).

But, of course, scientific determinists are not the only, or even the principal, thinkers who have used biological imagery to represent the workings of the human world. Such imagery has much more commonly been linked with romanticism, and romantic thinkers have generally set biological organicism in absolute opposition with mechanical determinism. Coleridge's distinction between the organic and the mechanic is one of the prototypal romantic statements: "The form is mechanic when on any given material we impress a predetermined form, not necessarily arising out of the properties of the material, as when to a mass of wet clay we give whatever shape we wish it to retain when hardened. The organic form, on the other hand, is innate; it shapes as it develops itself from within, and the fulness of its development is one and the same with the perfection of its outward form" (432–33). And, Coleridge maintains, Nature, "the prime genial artist," generates its forms organically, not mechanically: "Each exterior is the physiognomy of the being within, its true image reflected and thrown out from the concave mirror" (433). John Stuart Mill, Utilitarianism's born-again romantic, makes the distinction between organicism and mechanism even more succinctly, and—using the common romantic metaphor of a tree—he applies it specifically to *human* nature: "Human nature is not a machine to be built after a model, and set to do exactly the work prescribed for it, but a tree, which requires to grow and develop itself on all sides, according to the tendency of the inward forces which make it a living thing" (59).

Fowles has very strong leanings toward this romantic version of an organicist philosophy, incompatible as it may seem with his mechanistic materialism. In the nonfictional book called (fittingly) *The Tree,* he describes the suprascientific vitality of consciousness in words that seem to echo and expand on earlier organicist statements such as Coleridge's and Mill's:

> Ordinary experience, from waking second to second, is in fact highly synthetic (in the sense of combinative or constructive), and made of a complexity of strands, past memories and present perceptions, times and places, private and public history, hopelessly beyond science's power to analyze. It is quintessentially 'wild' . . . : unphilosophical, irrational, uncontrollable, incalculable. In fact it corresponds very closely—despite our endless efforts to 'garden', to invent disciplining social and intellectual systems—with wild nature. Almost all the richness of our personal existence derives from this synthetic and eternally present 'confused' consciousness of both internal and external reality, and not least because we know it is beyond the analytical, or destructive, capacity of science. (36–37)

The romantic Fowles, in other words, dislikes positivistic science, which analyzes away the "wild," individual human consciousness, at least as much as the deterministic Fowles dislikes religion. In *The Tree,* Fowles links science with materialistic society and suburbia; he considers these things deadening forces that deprive human beings of their natural autonomy. This romantic Fowles, therefore, is a romantic *rebel:* he rebels against both analytical science and mass society, which always try to "garden" the wildness of human experience. And, like their rebellious creator, the heroes of Fowles's novels struggle to escape from mechanistic oppressors, often by withdrawing into a hidden, natural place, a green world.

So Fowles is a rather unusual intellectual hybrid. He combines a romantic devotion to organic nature with an atheistic, mechanistic Darwinism. He frequently seems, therefore, to be at odds with himself: as a rebel against scientific rationalism, he condemns mechanistic explanations of the world, while as a rebel against religion, he subscribes to them. As Peter Conradi describes it,

Fowles's work "tends to split between a behavioral determinism, often borrowing from evolutionary metaphor, and idealism" (31).

The poles of this split, however, are at least partially mediated by existential rebellion itself, which, in the words of Albert Camus (an existentialist whom Fowles admires), "is founded simultaneously on the categorical rejection of an intrusion that is considered intolerable and on the confused conviction of an absolute right which, in the rebel's mind, is more precisely the impression that he 'has the right to . . .' " (*Rebel* 13). Both Fowles's romanticism and his deterministic atheism are spurred by a rejection of intrusion—an intrusion on the one hand by science and mass society and on the other by a deity—in order to proclaim the self's right of sovereignty.

And Fowles's two categories of intrusion—science/society and God—correspond to the two things that, according to Camus, the "metaphysical rebel" protests against: "Metaphysical rebellion," Camus says, "is the movement by which man protests against his condition"—an imprisonment in a limited (mechanistic, materialistic) world—"and against the whole of creation"—and its purported Creator (23). Camus's description of metaphysical rebellion and its aims is relevant to Fowles and his novelistic characters, and it is worth quoting at some length; comparing the metaphysical rebel to the rebellious slave, Camus says:

> The slave protests against the condition in which he finds himself within his state of slavery; the metaphysical rebel protests against the condition in which he finds himself as a man. The rebel slave affirms that there is something in him that will not tolerate the manner in which his master treats him; the metaphysical rebel declares that he is frustrated by the universe. For both of them, it is not only a question of pure and simple negation. In both cases, in fact, we find a value judgment in the name of which the rebel refuses to approve the condition in which he finds himself. (23)

For both the slave and the metaphysical rebel, Camus maintains, an "act of rebellion . . . seems like a demand for clarity and unity. The most elementary form of rebellion, paradoxically, expresses an aspiration to order" (23).

So Fowles's rejections of God and of scientific and social materialism are of a piece. Both are radical existential acts, attempts to clear away a space—a nothingness—for the individual, conscious, free self. It is by seeking such space, by pursuing the presence of absence, that each of Fowles's rebel-heroes makes a demand for clarity, unity, order—for what is clearer, more unitary, and more free of disorder than *nothing?* The absoluteness of these quests for nothingness is what makes many of Fowles's fictions, for all their maker's espoused atheism, seem strongly mystical, even sacred. The Fowles world is very paradoxical indeed.

The original—and, perhaps, the most schematically clear— Fowles hero (*The Collector* was the first of Fowles's published novels, if not the first written) is, I suggest, Frederick Clegg. In making this claim, I am, I realize, going out on a limb. Clegg does not seem terribly heroic, for one thing. And furthermore, although most critics would grant that Clegg embodies one pole of the Fowlesian worldview—determinism, the omnipotence of "hazard"—they might balk at the notion that he also embodies romanticism and metaphysical rebellion. Indeed, on the surface it would seem that it is Miranda who is, in Camusian terms, the novel's rebellious slave (and, at least metaphorically, a metaphysical rebel), while Clegg is merely a repressive master. I will demonstrate, however, the extent to which Clegg himself is an underdog, one with surprisingly romantic characteristics, who perversely but genuinely demands "clarity and unity" by kidnapping Miranda. Fowles, in his characterization of Clegg, sketches out his own philosophical/theological/aesthetic position with startling precision; Clegg is a volatile combination of both tensely joined halves of Fowles's thought: romanticism as well as atheistic determinism. And Miranda, in so many ways Clegg's opponent, ends up supplementing rather than contradicting this sketch. In addition, the novel itself, in its generic tension (is this a horrific thriller or a romance?), is an image of that same Fowlesian dichotomy between determinism and romanticism, between mechanical repetition and mystery. I agree, in other words, that *The Collector* is a schematic novel, but its schema is not reducible to a tension between the *aristoi* and the *hoi polloi.*

Clegg the Romantic

Apart from his slips into a number of sadistic statements (and even sadism, as we will see, can be a form of Camusian metaphysical rebellion), Frederick Clegg is established in the opening pages of his initial first-person narrative as a kind of fairy-tale hero, an ugly stepson who contains a hidden, beautiful self. This is not simply a naturalistic portrayal of a working-class psychopath. Rather, Clegg seems in part to be a modern-day combination of characters from two great postromantic novels: Pip and Augustin Meaulnes, from *Great Expectations* and *Le Grand Meaulnes* respectively (books, Fowles claims, that had a significant influence on the creation of *The Magus* but that seem equally relevant to *The Collector*). Like Pip, Clegg dreams of bettering himself socially; like Meaulnes, he is drawn not—as Pip is—toward the city but rather into a secluded "*domaine*" in the country. And like both characters, Clegg has embodied his dream in the person of a beautiful, and seemingly unattainable, young woman. Frederick Clegg, in other words, is a character with great aspirations, if not expectations ("I always had higher aspirations" [13]), a member of that species of romantic quester which Fowles claims to be central to the history of the novel: "Every novel since literary time began," Fowles says in *The Tree,* "since the epic of Gilgamesh, is a form of quest, or adventure" (60). So Clegg is a distinct portrait of the Fowles hero as a young man.

Like most of Fowles's central characters, Clegg is an orphan (or essentially so: his father died when he was two, and his mother "went off" soon after his father's death [9]). And his childhood is strikingly similar to that of another orphan, Dickens's Pip. Though the woman who raises him is an aunt rather than a sister, she is as shrewish as Pip's Mrs. Joe; indeed, Miranda at one point actually refers to her as "Mrs. Joe," thereby directly invoking the Dickens novel and all its romantic associations. And Clegg's aunt has been married to a man, "Uncle Dick," who is a kind of stand-in for Joe Gargery: "Aunt Annie and Mabel used to despise my butterflies when I was a boy, but Uncle Dick would always stick up for me. He always admired a good bit of setting. . . . When I won a hobby prize for a case of Fritillaries he gave me a pound on condition I didn't tell Aunt Annie. Well, I won't go on, he was as good as a father to me" (9–10). Fowles's Pip, however, does not have his Joe for long; Uncle Dick dies when Clegg is fifteen. But, before dying, Dick gives Clegg a romantic alter-ego: it is Dick who bestows on him the name Ferdinand—"Lord Ferdinand Clegg, Marquis of Bugs" (37).

His romantic identity remains a secret, though. Now that he is a young man, he is an object of ridicule for his co-workers at the Town Hall Annexe, where he works as a clerk. They do not understand his hobby, butterfly collecting (and, considering the intelligent way that he has been discussing butterflies in these opening pages, it is clear that Clegg is actually a legitimate entomologist, a young version of Joseph Conrad's Stein), so they tease him about it mercilessly:

> "Fred's looking tired—he's been having a dirty week-
> end with a Cabbage White," he [Crutchley, a co-worker]
> used to say, and, "Who was that Painted Lady I saw you

> with last night?" Old Tom [another co-worker] would
> snigger, and Jane, Crutchley's girl from Sanitation, she
> was always in our office, would giggle. (10)

Of course, these joking suggestions that butterfly collecting is a
kind of sexual activity carry a heavy irony in light of the story's
imminent developments. But they also establish Clegg as a poignant underdog, a misunderstood Cinderella picked on by gangs
of nasty stepsisters. It is true that Clegg himself often sounds rather
sour ("I always hated vulgar women, especially girls," he snaps,
after mentioning Crutchley's Jane), and most readers—especially
if they know where the plot is leading—probably assume that
Clegg is more sinning than sinned against. In these early pages,
however, there is surprisingly little to support such an inference.
When Clegg calls himself a "lone wolf" (10), he is linking himself
less with Jack the Ripper than with Pip (and any number of other
Dickensian child-heroes) and Meaulnes, and—projecting into the
literary future—with Fowles's own Nicholas Urfe, Charles Smithson, and Daniel Martin.

And like all of these romantic dreamers, Clegg has an ideal
woman. Critics have noted that, from his very first observation of
Miranda, Clegg sees her as a scientific specimen rather than as a
real human being. Barry Olshen puts it this way: "The voyeur
observes her as he would a butterfly, reducing her free and vital
nature in his mind's eye to the status of an object, a 'specimen' in a
collection. This life-destroying power of the collector, this objec-
tification of another human being, is manifest from the beginning
in the language of Clegg's narrative" (17). Olshen's analysis is
absolutely correct, and I take up this destructive, "necrophiliac"
(28) aspect of Clegg's character later. But what Olshen and others
seem to have missed is the genuinely lyrical quality of Clegg's early
descriptions of Miranda. Yes, he records his observation of her
with an "X" in his butterfly collector's "observations diary," but he
also finds elegantly simple, poetic phrases to describe her. "I
watched the back of her hair in a long pigtail. It was very pale, silky,
like Burnet cocoons" (Olshen uses this statement to show how
Clegg reifies the young woman [17], but in itself this is a precise,
lovely image); "[her loosened hair] took my breath away it was so
beautiful, like a mermaid"; "She didn't think at all about the men
when she moved. Like a bird"; "hearing her voice turned her from a
sort of dream person to a real one. . . . She spoke like she walked, as
you might say" (7, 15, 16). These similes aren't exactly Shakespearean, but they do give this record of the young man's obsession
a note of touching dreaminess that resonates uncannily with his

more grisly, violent comments. Perhaps most uncanny of all is Clegg's sweet, ominous description of the domestic fantasies he has entertained about Miranda: "She drew pictures and I looked after my [butterfly] collection (in my dreams). It was always she loving me and my collection, drawing and coloring them; working together in a beautiful modern house in a big room with one of those huge glass windows" (8).

Clegg's fantasy is remarkably similar to another literary dream, more lushly poetic than Clegg's, but similarly structured:

> He recalled a dream, a vision, rather, which he had had as a small child, and of which he had never spoken to anyone: one morning, instead of awaking in his bedroom, where his trousers and coats were hanging, he had found himself in a long green room with tapestries that looked like foliage. The light streaming into this room had been so soft that it seemed as if one could taste it. He had seen a young girl sewing near the first window, apparently waiting for him to awake.

The dreamer in this case is hardly a psychopathic monster; he is a bona fide romantic quester, Augustin Meaulnes in *Le Grand Meaulnes* (Alain-Fournier 48–49). Indeed, the similarities between Clegg's and Meaulnes's respective sexual obsessions go far beyond these brief fantasies. The initial description of Yvonne, the young woman with whom Meaulnes falls in love—"a tall, slender blond girl in a charming dress ... a face whose features, though not pronounced, were drawn with almost heartrending delicacy" (65–66)—has the same conventionally romantic tone as Clegg's first descriptions of Miranda. And Meaulnes's pursuit of this girl, before he has even met her, is as compulsive and uncontrollable as Clegg's stalking of his human butterfly:

> without knowing how, Meaulnes found himself aboard the same boat as [Yvonne]. As he stood on deck, leaning his elbow against the railing and keeping one hand on his hat to prevent the strong wind from blowing it away, he looked at the young girl, who had sat down in a sheltered spot. ...
>
> Meaulnes set off along a lane, ten paces behind the young girl. He found himself beside her before he had time to think. (66–67)

Like Clegg, who feels "clumsy and awkward" in comparison with the cultured Miranda (*Collector* 77), Meaulnes is socially inferior to his upper-class lady love and painfully aware of that fact. His first words to Yvonne are not a grand, chivalrous speech but are only two plain words, "You're beautiful"—and Meaulnes is mortified: "Meaulnes sharply reproached himself for what he called his clumsiness, his crudeness, his stupidity" (67). The eventual relationship between Meaulnes and Yvonne, different as it is from that of imprisoner Clegg and the imprisoned Miranda, has the same desperate end for very much the same reason. Meaulnes, as much as Clegg, cannot abide a real, flesh-and-blood version of his ideal. He finds himself (the narrator surmises) tempted "to shatter immediately, irremediably, the miraculous prize he had won" (169)—something that could surely be said of Clegg as well. Meaulnes ends up as responsible for Yvonne's death as Clegg is for Miranda's.

At first, though, Clegg does differ in one essential way from the romantic quester Meaulnes, who pursues his ideal as relentlessly as Ahab pursues Moby-Dick: Clegg has little of Meaulnes's energy, his Camusian capacity for "metaphysical rebellion"—for actively protesting "against his condition and against the whole of creation" (*Rebel* 23). And then something happens. It happens, as it must in the Fowlesian world, not through the workings of a benevolent, or even malevolent, God, but as a product of pure chance, of "hazard." Clegg wins a fortune in the football pools. He now has the wherewithal to attack his "shattered world in order to demand unity from it" (*Rebel* 23–24). And he seeks this unity, as Meaulnes does, in the typical romantic location: away from the bland suburbs, in the country, where there are secret places and butterflies.

The newspaper advertisement that Clegg answers might well be describing a resort for Fowles heroes: "Old cottage, charming secluded situation, large garden, 1 hr. by car London, two miles from nearest village" (17). The ad also describes a more modest version of the house of Les Sablonnieres, which, even more than Yvonne, embodies Meaulnes's secret fantasy in *Le Grand Meaulnes*—and which certainly embodies for Fowles the seductive mysteries of Alain-Fournier's novel. In the Afterword that he wrote for a paperback edition of *Le Grand Meaulnes*, Fowles links the book (which he says is "like a secret garden") with secluded country houses:

> Only last October I was traveling down a remote byroad
> in a part of France not very far from where *Le Grand
> Meaulnes* is set. We passed a dilapidated gateway. I
> made my wife, who was driving, stop and walk back
> with me. I said nothing. A rusty iron grille, one side ajar,
> through which we walked a few steps: a long drive, a

> dense avenue of ancient trees, and in the autumnal dis-
> tance the facade of a seventeenth century manor-house.
> Silence, the gray, silent house and the dim trees. My wife
> murmured, "That book." She didn't have to say the title.
> (208–9)

The newspaper ad draws Clegg to a similar, if simpler, house; it draws him, therefore, even more deeply into "that book."

If *Le Grand Meaulnes* is, for Fowles, a garden, it is perhaps the sort of garden that adjoins Clegg's prospective house: "It was a nice garden," Clegg tells us; "it runs back to a field which had lucerne then, lovely stuff for butterflies" (19). (So butterflies are directly linked here with gardens.) And both house and garden are as isolated, as secret, as they could be: "The field goes up to a hill (that is north). East there are woods on both sides of the road running up from the valley towards Lewes. West there are fields. There is a farmhouse about three-quarters of a mile away down the hill, the nearest house. South you have a fine view, except it was blocked by the front hedge and some trees" (19–20). Isolation, a garden, a screen of hedges and trees: these are potent images of the romantic withdrawal of the self into its own natural, wild privacy, and such images will emerge as a recurring motif in the Fowles corpus. But in itself this setting is not enough for Clegg. He wants a special house, and at first he thinks he has not found it; as he tours this place with a somewhat pompous realtor, it seems all too ordinary. And then, just as Clegg is about to leave in disappointment—he hasn't yet articulated to himself why he even wants to buy a house, but he knows that this one will not do—the realtor says, "well, that's the lot, bar the cellars" (18).

If its location gives the house some of the aura of an Alain-Fournier *domaine perdu,* the cellar (it is actually a cellar beneath the cellar) is the lost domain of the lost domain. Indeed, the realtor explains that precisely because the house is "so on its own," it was equipped with an extra room, either for something as benign as food storage or for such surreptitious activities as Roman Catholic services or smuggling. In any case, the room is, in the root sense of the word, occult, and Clegg's comment about it is as canny as that of a trained Freudian or Jungian: "It was two worlds. It's always been like that. Some days I've woken up and it's all been like a dream, till I went down again" (19). Fortified with the energy of this hidden world, this secret place, Clegg's infatuation with Miranda takes on a sense of purpose that allows Clegg to become a kind of Camusian rebel rather than a passive slug: "I read in the paper the other day (Saying of the Day)—'What Water is to the

Body, Purpose is to the Mind.' That is very true, in my humble opinion. When Miranda became the purpose of my life I should say I was at least as good as the next man, as it turned out" (20). So the put-upon clerk is ready to rebel against his groveling condition, to create, in Camus's terminology, a unity that has so far been lacking in his life.

Of course, it can be objected that I have interpreted the first dozen or so pages of *The Collector* entirely from Clegg's point of view, without acknowledging that he is a foolish, insidious, grossly unreliable narrator. And that is precisely what I have done. I am aware that the text is ironic. The irony could hardly be more obvious (it might even be called heavy-handed); as Simon Loveday says, in his fine analysis of Fowles's romanticism, this novel is "a savage parody of the romance form" (27). But there is an irony beneath the irony, showing that Fowles's portrayal of Clegg has an existential/romantic resonance that makes the book's eventual parodic romantic paradigm, Shakespeare's *The Tempest* (the book's heroine is named Miranda, and Clegg himself is nicknamed both Ferdinand and Caliban), less ironic—or even more ironic—than it superficially seems. The book, after these introductory pages, seemingly turns away from any resemblance to lyrical romances like *Le Grand Meaulnes* and toward the genre that Fowles most explicitly wanted to play with here: the suspense/horror tale. Written just two years after the release of the film *Psycho*, Fowles's story of a soft-spoken clerk who does secret, terrible things to a beautiful young woman whom he has kidnapped is surely a sort of *hommage* to such Hitchcock thrillers. But even after the novel has taken its horrific turn, Clegg has more than a few truly, jarringly charming moments, moments that seem to make him more Ferdinand than Norman Bates.

Even after Clegg has kidnapped Miranda, for example, in a scene that occurs shortly after she has dubbed him "Caliban," Clegg reveals a trace of Ferdinand-like emotion. He takes Miranda out into the garden and a scene ensues that, though qualified by an almost comic ghastliness (the romantic heroine is gagged and handcuffed), is somehow genuinely sweet. Clegg describes the scene, saying, "It was a funny night, there was a moon behind the cloud, and the cloud was moving, but down below there was hardly any wind. . . . I took her arm respectfully and led her up the path between the wall that ran up one side and the lawn. . . . I really would have liked to take her in my arms and kiss her, as a matter of fact I was trembling" (59). Clegg's inarticulateness (the best word he can find to describe the night is "funny") and his prudishness— qualities that most critics use simply to debase him to that category of the Many—actually give this passage its poignancy. And they lead us, as Clegg proceeds to make one of his longest speeches, to believe that his declaration of his own emotional depth is, if twisted, valid and even admirable:

> You wouldn't believe me if I told you I was very happy, would you, I said. Of course she couldn't answer.
>
> Because you think I don't feel anything properly, you don't know I have deep feelings but I can't express them like you can, I said.
>
> Just because you can't express your feelings it doesn't mean they're not deep. All the time we were walking on under the dark branches.
>
> All I'm asking, I said, is that you understand how much I love you, how much I need you, how deep it is. (59)

There is a passion here worthy of Meaulnes himself, and perhaps it even carries the force of an existential rebellion against the uneducated, inarticulate self that fate has assigned to Clegg.

If the emotional profession in the garden is one of Clegg's longest verbal statements, his most touching of all is a model of brevity, and it disarms even Miranda. He makes this statement at the end of a long scene, contained at the exact center of Miranda's narrative, in which Miranda questions him about his upbringing and learns its Dickensian mistreated-orphan details. Responding, perhaps, to Clegg's sad, storybook childhood, Miranda tries to weave her own fairy tale. "Once upon a time," she tells Clegg, "there was a very ugly monster who captured a princess and put her in a dungeon in his castle" (174). To call Miranda's wordy, heavy-handed tale (it ends, of course, with the monster being transformed into a handsome prince after he frees the princess) an allegory is far too generous. Even she is embarrassed, at least dimly aware that she has strained to romanticize her own situation after watching Clegg effortlessly and unselfconsciously metamorphose into Dickens's Pip. "I knew," she tells us, "it was silly as I was saying it. Fey" (174). She refuses to let the game stop, though, and she asks Clegg to reciprocate by telling another fairy story. His response is as succinct as it could be: "He just said, I love you" (174).

It is impossible not to realize that Clegg reveals a good deal more integrity here than Miranda does. Miranda herself is made to admit that "yes, he had more dignity than I did then and I felt small, mean" (174–75); she even acknowledges that a "most peculiar closeness" has developed between them (175). Even Robert Huffaker—who has perhaps most eloquently put forward the popular

theory that Clegg is a personification of "undistilled evil ...
literature's first convincing villain since Conrad's Gentleman Brown"
(73, 75)—grants that this scene "shows Clegg as human" (79). But
Clegg's three-word "fairy story" is actually more potent than
Miranda and Huffaker (and all of those other critics and readers
who have judged Clegg to be a simple villain) seem to realize.
Clegg's words very nearly overturn the novel linguistically. In a
novel structured as two self-contained, dissimilar, essentially incompatible systems of verbal discourse, this fairy-tale contest (I'll
tell mine, then you tell yours) is probably the clearest face-off
between these two voices. And, whatever "Few versus Many"
jargon is spouted within the text by Miranda, and outside the text
by critics and by Fowles himself, the winner of this contest—both
morally and aesthetically—is Clegg. With his simplicity and sincerity (two highly romantic attributes), Clegg makes Miranda's
verbose and artificial tale seem empty. Indeed, Clegg's fairy story
shines a light on all of his other discourse and makes one question
whether it really is, as Huffaker has alleged, just a collection of
"schoolbook morality and working-class clichés" (89). Especially
in relation to the discourse of the socially and intellectually
"superior" Miranda, Clegg's is frequently clear, interesting, and true.

Critiques of *The Collector* are littered with lists of words that
Clegg twists and abuses or uses naively or prudishly. He calls
Miranda not his prisoner but his "guest"; he refers to anything
connected with sex with words like "nasty" or "the obvious" or
some other euphemism; he offers to serve tea by saying "shall I be
mother?" This aspect of Clegg of course absolutely exasperates the
intelligent, self-consciously modern and artistic Miranda, and she
complains, "You know what you do? You know how rain takes the
colour out of everything? That's what you do to the English
language. You blur it every time you open your mouth" (64). But
an underlying linguistic tendency within the novel—epitomized,
as we have seen, in the trade-off of fairy tales—upends Miranda's
criticism: in many ways it is she, with her middle-class snobbish-
ness, who takes the color out of language, and Clegg who has the
richer, more surprising pallet of linguistic paints.

Indeed, Clegg uses one particularly effective dab of color
immediately before recording Miranda's allegations about his col-
orlessness. First he describes a rampage that Miranda went on
during her imprisonment: suddenly, without warning, she began
shrieking, and then, laughing, she explained casually, "I just felt
like a good scream." And then Clegg comments on the incident
with a three-word paragraph that resonates with linguistic ambiguity. "She," he says, "was unpredictable" (64). On the most

superficial level, that laconic statement indicates a shocking emotional flatness, an inability to appreciate the existential extremity
that has driven Miranda to employ a kind of primal-scream therapy.
And Miranda's complaint about Clegg's tendency to take the color
out of language, recorded in the very next paragraph, seems to
underline such a reading. But in context, Clegg's remark does not
seem flat or bland at all; it seems more like a wry understatement
that very wittily undercuts Miranda's theatrics. Even if this is
inadvertant wit or Fowles's clever use of an unwitting narrator, that
would indicate only that Clegg is unselfconscious; his words are
still, however spontaneous and unplanned (like those of a Wordsworthian rustic, for instance), exactly right. There is evidence in
the sequence of paragraphs, though, that Clegg is more self-
conscious than we may have thought: although there is no chrono-
logical connection between Miranda's "unpredictable" scream and
her criticism of Clegg's colorless language, Clegg places the two
incidents together in his narrative. So he knows that "unpredictable" is exactly one of those words that Miranda would have
complained about.

This inverted way of looking at Clegg's flat use of language
opens up his three narrative sections in a rather startling way. From
this perspective, Clegg is almost poetic in his verbal simplicity, a
kind of natural Hemingway, who wages a linguistic war against
Miranda's verbal pretensions. In the following exchange, for example, it seems perfectly reasonable to assert that Clegg's speech is a
good deal less hackneyed than Miranda's:

> [Miranda said,] "You're the most perfect specimen
> of petit bourgeois squareness I've ever met."
> Am I?
> "Yes you are. . . . Do you know that?"
> I don't know what you're talking about, I said. (72)

And in her own narrative section, Miranda reveals even more
strikingly—though, of course, inadvertantly—Clegg's freedom from
cliché relative to hers: "Another thing I said to Caliban the other
day—we were listening to jazz—I said, don't you dig this? And he
said, in the garden. I said he was so square he was hardly credible.
Oh, that, he said. Like rain, endless dreary rain. Colour-killing"
(152). One wonders, now that "don't you dig this?" has become a
laughably outdated bit of slang, who it is who really kills language
in this exchange. Indeed, Miranda's narrative is a compendium of
upper-middle-class British colloquialisms that have dated very
badly—"lame-duck" (as a verb), "unwithit," "hero-pash." And her
dogmatic little list of things that her mentor (or Magus), G. P., has

taught her is Fowlesian philosophy reduced to the level of a Boy Scout handbook: "If you are a real artist, you give your whole being to your art. . . . You don't gush. . . . You *have* to be left politically. . . . You *must* act, if you believe something. Talking about acting is like boasting about pictures you're going to paint. The most *terrible* bad form" (134).

Clegg's gaucherie, his *terrible* bad form, is refreshing compared with this. And, in his modest way, Clegg is—as we have already seen—even capable of some genuine bursts of poetry. This particularly lovely passage, for example, sounds even more honest when juxtaposed with Miranda's high-flown jargon:

> It was like we were the only two people in the world. No one will ever understand how happy we were—just me, really, but there were times when I consider she didn't mind in spite of what she said, if she thought about it. I could sit there all night watching her, just the shape of her head and the way the hair fell from it with a special curve, so graceful it was, like the shape of a swallowtail. It was like a veil or a cloud, it would lie like silk strands all untidy and loose but lovely over her shoulders. (61)

And he immediately adds, without a trace of coyness (though the reader certainly finds the statement ironic): "I wish I had words to describe it like a poet would or an artist."

Much more could be said about the ways in which the novel presents Clegg as a genuinely, disconcertingly romantic figure, but I will merely add to my treatment of the topic a discussion of a final, striking issue: Clegg's varied collection of names.

The character's given name, Frederick, is a kind of foundation of ordinariness upon which Fowles has constructed his fictional creation. As Frederick or Fred, Clegg is easily reducible to a representation of any dull young man, of the "Many." And in relation to this ordinariness, his assumed name, Ferdinand, is most obviously a bit of cutting Fowlesian satire. As the story of Ferdinand and Miranda, *The Collector* is, of course, a distorted re-envisioning of Fowles's favorite Shakespeare play (and perhaps the grandest of all theatrical romances), *The Tempest*. From this perspective the novel does seem, as Simon Loveday puts it, to be a "savage parody" (27)—not just of Shakespeare's play in particular, but of the romance form in general. And Clegg, when he uses the name Ferdinand, seems to be a grotesquely parodic romance hero.

I certainly would not deny that this assumed name does, to a large degree, operate parodically; I must point out, however, that there are ways in which the parody is softened and problematized. First of all, the nickname "Ferdinand" was given to Clegg, as I have already mentioned, by the novel's most unambiguously kind character, Clegg's Uncle Dick. The name, then, was originally bestowed not sarcastically but lovingly: "Lord Ferdinand Clegg, Marquis of Bugs" is an affectionate rather than cruel name. And since Clegg has had this nickname for many years before his involvement with Miranda, it is not entirely bound to the novel's Shakespearean Miranda-Ferdinand dialectic. More importantly, though, Clegg himself seems to be aware, at least marginally, of the parodic analogy between his story and Shakespeare's play. After Clegg tells Miranda that his name is Ferdinand, he adds quickly, "It's just a coincidence" (37); the coincidence, presumably, is that he and she have the names of a famous pair of Shakespearean lovers. So despite his lack of education, he knows about the Shakespearean parallel, and he is perhaps even using it consciously. (The impact of the name and its connotations on Miranda—"vile coincidence!" she writes in her journal [116]—indicates that Clegg has indeed struck a nerve.) Fowles, therefore, is not just making fun of Clegg by generating a parodic literary parallel behind his character's back. He has allowed Clegg to be an ally in the creation of the parody, and in the process, he has forced us to wonder to what degree it really is a parody after all. Is it possible that this is not just a fiercely satirical look at the gap between Frederick and Ferdinand, but rather is at least partially a story (dare I call it a romance?) about the conscious desire of Frederick to become Ferdinand?

Clegg's most ambiguous nickname, however, is not Ferdinand but Caliban, though on the surface its significance may seem to be spelled out quite straightforwardly within the text. It is Miranda who gives Clegg this name, and in her own mind it is not ambiguous at all; it simply indicates her contemptuous feeling of superiority to Clegg. She decides to rename him after complaining about his abominable taste:

> I couldn't stand the orangeady carpet any more and he's brought me some Indian and Turkish rugs. Three Indian mats and a beautiful deep purple, rose-orange and sepia white-fringed Turkish carpet (he said it was the only one "they" had, so no credit to his taste).
>   . . . I've broken all the ugly ashtrays and pots. Ugly ornaments don't deserve to exist.
>   I'm so superior to him. . . .
>   He is ugliness. But you can't smash human ugliness. . . .

> I have to give him a name. I'm going to call him Cal-
> iban. (122)

And as her narrative progresses, "Calibanity" becomes a kind of catchword for Miranda. In her criticism of the dull English masses, she rants about "the great deadweight of the Calibanity of England" (152); discussing the hated "New People" ("the new-class people with their cars and their money and their tellies and their stupid vulgarities and their stupid crawling imitation of the bourgeoisie"), she asks with exasperation, "why *should* we tolerate their beastly Calibanity?" (191).

For Miranda, in other words, the nickname "Caliban" indicates that Clegg is a personification of mediocre, almost sub-human humanity. But the name acquires a resonance within the novel that complicates its meaning. Fairly late in the book, Miranda pulls out her Shakespeare, reads *The Tempest,* and remembers that the original Caliban was not a simple monster: "Reading *The Tempest* again all the afternoon. Not the same at all, now what's happening has happened. The pity Shakespeare feels for his Caliban, I feel (beneath the hate and disgust) for my Caliban" (223). This direct reference to the play which so thoroughly operates as the novel's subtext jars readers, reminding them that Shakespeare's funny, poignant, horrible Caliban possesses not a trace of the kind of colorless dullness that Miranda has named "Calibanity."

So the novel hints that there is another, more positive meaning to the name Caliban. And Fowles himself, in his clearest romantic statement, *The Tree,* suggests an alternate meaning that goes to the heart of his romantic philosophical framework. He discusses, in this book, the "long and damaging doubt" that made Westerners, before the Romantic Movement, fearful of untamed nature. Nature, he says in a telling passage, "remained a potential dissolver of decency, a notion that the endless chain of new discoveries about the ways of more primitive man—*the nearer nature, the nearer Caliban*—did nothing to dispel. It remained essentially an immense green cloak for Satan . . ." (68, my italics). In this book, in other words, Shakespeare's Caliban is Fowles's representation of all that "civilized" Europeans have found distasteful, even evil, about nature. Fowles, however, describes nature's wildness not as something evil but as an analogue of the wild richness of human consciousness—of the "greener, more mysterious processes of mind" (76). And a connection with the wildness is, he maintains, essential for human sanity: "The return to the green chaos, the deep forest and refuge of the unconscious is a nightly phenomemon, and one that psychiatrists—and torturers—tell us is essential to the human mind. Without it, it disintegrates and goes mad" (76). Fowles's references to Caliban and to torturers in these key passages inevitably remind us of Clegg, and they link him with the romantic mysteries of what Fowles calls the "wild, or green man, in our psyches" (51).

Of course, this undercurrent of meaning within the novel radically subverts the notion that Miranda represents the noble "Few" attacked by the mediocre "Many." Rather, it seems that in labeling Clegg as "Caliban," Miranda allies herself with blind civilization cutting itself off from the natural, mysterious wildness of the psyche. (It is significant that, at times, she describes Clegg as an impenetrable mystery: "Oh, you're like mercury. You won't be picked up," she tells him at one point [71], and in both her narrative and Clegg's, we hear her call him "a Chinese box" [91, 213].) I am not suggesting, however, that this "subversive" reading of the novel is absolutely, finally correct, that Frederick Clegg possesses no trace of the mediocre dullness which Miranda labels "Calibanity." But I am suggesting that there are dimensions to this Caliban which Miranda is unaware of, and that this Ferdinand is more than a mere parody. Even Simon Loveday—who, as we have seen, considers *The Collector* not a romance but a grisly parody of the romance form—admits that the book generates real pathos in its depiction not of Miranda but of Clegg, who possesses "the paradoxical dignity of the inarticulate" (28).

The Collector

I have been romanticizing the character of Clegg—quite literally, in fact. I wanted to show the extent to which Clegg, far from being a thoroughgoing personification of evil, has at least some of the force of a legitimate romantic hero: the resonances within the novel of *Great Expectations* and *Le Grand Meaulnes,* the underlying sincerity and poetry of Clegg's use of language, and the ambiguity of his varied names suggest that Fowles is doing more here than caricaturing England's *hoi polloi.* Indeed, these romantic strands in Clegg's characterization are a remarkably clear blueprint of the side of Fowles's art that is generally labeled organicist or romantic or idealistic.

But this is certainly only half of the story. My reading of the novel would be shamelessly perverse, and it would give a distorted picture of the Fowlesian aesthetic and moral schema, if I neglected to discuss Clegg's anti-organicist, materialistic, grimly destructive "collector" side—and to discuss the significance of collecting within the body of Fowles's published work. Frederick Clegg does indeed possess a strain of Meaulnes-like lyricism that makes him seem at least partly to be a rebel against his dull, restrictive upbringing, searching for a green *domaine perdu* in which a beautiful unity reigns. But Clegg's specific action — "collecting" a beautiful young woman as if she were a specimen to be studied — reveals not the vital organicism associated with Fowles's romantic "green chaos" (*Tree* 76) but rather a cold, mechanical materialism.

In *The Tree,* Fowles specifically links collecting with the mechanistic, Linnaean-scientific tendency to classify — and kill — organic reality:

> A great deal of science is devoted to this . . . end: to providing labels, explaining specific mechanisms and ecologies, in short for sorting and tidying what seems in the mass indistinguishable one from the other. Even the simplest knowledge of the names and habits of flowers or trees starts this distinguishing or individuating process, and removes us a step from total reality towards anthropocentrism; that is, it acts mentally as an equivalent of the camera view-finder. Already it destroys or curtails certain possibilities of seeing, apprehending and experiencing. . . .
>
> I spent all my younger life as a more or less orthodox amateur naturalist; as a pseudo-scientist, treating nature as some sort of intellectual puzzle, or game, in which being able to name names and explain behaviourisms — to identify and to understand machinary — constituted all the pleasures and the prizes. I became slowly aware of the inadequacy of this approach: that it insidiously cast nature as a kind of opponent, an opposite team to be outwitted and beaten; that in a number of very important ways it distracted from the total experience and the total meaning of nature. . . . I came to believe that this approach represented a major human alienation, affecting all of us, both personally and socially. . . .
>
> Naming things is always implicitly categorizing and therefore *collecting* them, attempting to own them. . . .
>
> All this is an unhappy legacy from Victorian science, which was so characteristically obsessed with both the machine and exact taxonomy. (26, 28–30, my italics)

In other words, collecting is antagonistic to the primitive wildness that is one of the qualities suggested by Clegg's nickname "Caliban." Nonetheless, this Caliban is a collector in exactly the alienating, deadening way that Fowles condemns in this passage from *The Tree*. Indeed, such an interpretation of the activity of collecting is precisely articulated in the novel's text, voiced by Miranda (Clegg's first human collectible); on this subject, she speaks intelligently and persuasively, with hardly a trace of the jargon that mars many of her other pronouncements. Fairly early in her narrated section she puts it this way: "I could scream abuse at him all day long; he wouldn't mind at all. It's me he wants, my look, my outside; not my emotions or my soul or even my body. Not anything *human*. "He's a collector. That's the great dead thing in him"(150–51). Later she elaborates on her insight, describing the collector phenomemon clearly and graphically:

> I am one in a row of specimens. It's when I try to flutter out of line that he hates me. I'm meant to be dead, pinned down, always the same, always beautiful. He knows that part of my beauty is being alive, but it's the dead me he wants. He wants me living-but-dead. I felt it terribly strong today. That my being alive and changing and having a separate mind and having moods and all that was becoming a nuisance.
>
> He is solid; immovable, iron-willed. He showed me one day what he called his killing bottle. I'm imprisoned in it. Fluttering against the glass. (188– 89)

Collecting, however, is only one facet of Clegg's destructive materialism. His interest in photography, for example, reveals the same sort of mental disposition. Miranda describes photographs as "dry and dead" ("when you draw something it lives and when you photograph it it dies" [52]), and, whether or not this is a fair assessment of all photographs, it certainly sums up Clegg's reason for liking his shots of the drugged Miranda: "They didn't talk back at me," he says of them (98). But I refrain from supplying a litany of Clegg's perversities. Instead I will examine a single additional example of his devotion to inanimate matter: his obsessive concern about his little prison's security system. This particular obsession reveals the mechanical nature of Clegg's materialism, and it is also directly relevant to the Fowlesian theme of secret places.

Usually rather laconic, Clegg is downright effusive when he describes the measures he has taken to design a foolproof prison, a place that is impenetrably secret:

> [The door to the cell] was two-inch seasoned wood with sheet metal on the inside so she couldn't get at the wood. It weighed a ton and it was no joke getting it

hung, but I did it. I fixed ten-inch bolts outside. Then I
did something very clever. I made what looked like a
bookcase, only for tools and things, out of some old
wood and fitted it with wooden latches in the doorway,
so that if you gave a casual look it just seemed that it
was just an old recess fitted up with shelves. You lifted
it out and there was the door through. It also stopped
any noise getting out. I also fitted a bolt on the inner
side of the door which had a lock too down to the cellar
so I couldn't be disturbed. Also a burglar alarm. (22)

Perhaps aware that all this may sound rather excessive, narrator
Clegg adds, somewhat apologetically, that the burglar alarm is
"Only a simple one, for the night." But the apology merely rein-
forces our sense of excess, of a mind engulfed by mechanical
minutiae. And although the very design of the prison is obsessive, it
is not until we see the prison in operation that we realize how
absolute its system is. We repeatedly observe Clegg's dogged
attention to mechanical details, but perhaps nowhere better than
in Miranda's funny, unnerving description of the complicated
procedure he goes through simply to fetch her a bottle of Worcester sauce: "Incident. Today at lunch I wanted the Worcester sauce.
He hardly ever forgets to bring anything I might want. But no
Worcester sauce. So he gets up, goes out, undoes the padlock
holding the door open, locks the door, gets the sauce in the outer
cellar, unlocks the door, repadlocks it, comes back. And then looks
surprised when I laugh" (130). Spontaneity is not one of the
qualities of Clegg's secret place.

These aspects of Clegg's character, his love of mechanical
details and of dead specimens, have been thoroughly and ably
discussed in other critiques of the novel, the examples of which
need not be presented again. Barry Olshen sums up Clegg's perversity as well as anyone:

In terms of abstract psychological types, Fowles has . . .
depicted the distinctive features of what Erich Fromm
calls the necrophiliac, the type attracted to all that is
unalive, sick, or mechanical. Hating life, his activities are
largely destructive. He is boring; he kills liveliness in social discourse; he seemingly possesses the capacity to
transform all that he touches into something dead. . . .
This is what Fowles has so concretely and economically
embodied in the figure of the Collector. (28)

I disagree with only one clause of Olshen's analysis: I do not find
Clegg boring. Even this most dreadful, necrophiliac side of Clegg
has a kind of fierce passion. Indeed, it is this necrophiliac dimension of Clegg's character, rather than his more appealing, Meaulnes-like romanticism, that most strikingly makes him seem to be a
Camusian rebel. Camus's description of a lover's desire for total
possession of the beloved—which he considers a prototype of the
rebellious demand for absolute order and unity—could be a gloss
on *The Collector*, an analysis of Clegg's demand that Miranda
become a dead butterfly to be added to his collection rather than a
living, unpredictable woman:

> The desire for possession is only another form of the de-
> sire to endure; it is this that comprises the important
> delirium of love. . . . On the pitiless earth where lovers
> are often separated in death and are always born di-
> vided, the total possession of another human being and
> absolute communion throughout an entire lifetime are
> impossible dreams. . . . In the final analysis, every man
> devoured by the overpowering desire to endure and
> possess wishes that those whom he has loved were ei-
> ther sterile or dead. This is real rebellion. (261)

Even as a collector, in other words, Clegg is a kind of existential
hero/anti-hero (when discussing existential rebellion, the categories blur). And his obsession with creating a sealed world that is
precisely, mechanically systematized makes Clegg a modest reincarnation of Camus's most fierce—and fiercely negative—metaphysical rebel, a historical figure who looms large in Fowles's
works, filled as they are with manipulative magi: the Marquis de
Sade.

It was Sade, Camus says, who launched "the first coherent
offensive" in the war against God and the universe that constitutes
metaphysical rebellion (36). Camus's Sade, in other words, is much
more awesomely Satanic than Fowles's mousy clerk; Sade's destructiveness, the "absolute negation," is for Camus downright apocalyptic:

> Sade denies God in the name of nature—the ideological
> concepts of his time presented it in mechanistic form—
> and he makes nature a power bent on destruction. For
> him, nature is sex; his logic leads him to a lawless uni-
> verse where the only master is the inordinate energy of
> desire. This is his delirious kingdom, in which he finds
> his finest means of expression: "What are all the crea-

tures of the earth in comparison with a single one of our
desires!" The long arguments by which Sade's heroes
demonstrate that nature has need of crime, that it must
destroy in order to create, and that we help nature create from the moment we destroy it ourselves, are only
aimed at establishing absolute freedom for the prisoner,
Sade, who is too unjustly punished not to long for the
explosion that will blow everything to pieces. (38)

It would be hard for anyone to muster such passion in a discussion
of Clegg. Nonetheless, the world that Camus's Sade creates for his
fictional victims is really just a grandiose version of Clegg's secret
place in the country. Sade's dream is to have power over the entire
universe; in reality, however, he knows that he can create his
rebellious unity only in a controlled microcosm:

The law of power never has the patience to await complete control of the world. It must fix the boundaries,
without delay, of the territory where it holds sway, even
if it means surrounding it with barbed wire and observation towers.
   For Sade, the law of power implies barred gates, castles with seven circumvallations from which it is impossible to escape, and where a society founded on desire
and crime functions unimpeded, according to the rules
of an implacable system. (42)

Absolutely secure and absolutely systematized, Sade's prison-
castles might well be the archetypes from which Clegg's house is
derived. Like the Collector, Sade has to destroy any trace of the
organic in his sealed world: "The heart, that 'weak spot of the
intellect,' must be exterminated; the locked room and the system
will see to that. . . . Objects of enjoyment must . . . never be allowed
to appear as persons" (42–43). In place of the organic, which Sade
detests ("I abhor nature," he says [44]), is the mechanical, to which
Sade is passionately devoted. For Camus's Sade, people must be
nothing more than machines: "If man is 'an absolutely material
species of plant,' he can only be treated as an object, and as an
object for experiment" (43). And the system of a Sade castle
becomes, like that of Clegg's house, obsessively mechanistic: "In
Sade's fortress republic, there are only machines and mechanics.
The system, which dictates the method of employing the machines, puts everything in the right place" (43). "Everything in the
right place": that describes Clegg's foolproof, exhaustingly complicated security system as precisely as it describes Sade's castles.

So even the terrible, necrophiliac aspects of Clegg's character, which seem utterly damnable from the novel's "romantic" perspective (that side of the book which evokes the green, forest world of *Le Grand Meaulnes*), have an existential significance. If Clegg is a kind of mini-Sade—and I think he is—then his dead, mechanistically determined world is, like Sade's, founded on an absolutely negative form of rebellion: a thoroughgoing rejection of God and of a divinely managed cosmos. Sade's atheistic characters, Camus says, "suppose, on principle, the nonexistence of God for the obvious reason that His existence would imply that He was indifferent, wicked, or cruel. Sade's greatest work [*Justine*] ends with a demonstration of the stupidity and spite of the divinity" (37). And Clegg does indeed voice a similarly blasphemous creed. Early in the novel, he says that God's existence or nonexistence simply does not matter (56). Later, however, he eloquently espouses an atheistic worldview that could stand as a succinct statement of a "Collector Philosophy": "Because what it is, it's luck. It's like the pools—worse, there aren't even good teams and bad teams and likely draws. You can't ever tell how it will turn out. Just A versus B, C versus D, and nobody knows what A and B and C and D are. That's why I never believed in God. I think we are just insects, we live a bit and then die and that's the lot. There's no mercy in things. There's not even a Great Beyond. There's nothing" (250).

Clegg's very construction of his sealed, mechanical, dead world has been a kind of rebellious proclamation, throughout the entire novel, of this rejection of a providential God. It has, in other words, been a stark embodiment of what I have called the deterministic, atheistic half of Fowles's own philosophical schema.

A Repetition

So Clegg, like his creator, is to a certain degree divided against himself. He is a kind of Meaulnes, in rebellion against an oppressively ordinary society, and he is also a kind of Sade, a mechanical materialist in rebellion against God and all transcendent ideals. And although the concept of rebellion itself may at least partially mediate this opposition, the tension between dreamer and destroyer remains powerful throughout the book. What this rebel's story cries out for is an ending, the sort of novelistic synthesis that is, according to Camus, the passionate desire of everyone who rebels: "Man ... tries in vain to find the form that will impose certain limits between which he can be king. . . . "What, in fact, is a novel but a universe in which action is endowed with form, where final words are pronounced, where people possess one another completely, and where life assumes the aspect of destiny?" (262–63).

It seems, for a short time, that Clegg will earn such a formally satisfying ending, an ending that will merge the necrophiliac collector with the romantic idealist. Miranda has died, allowing Clegg to forget the ways in which her living, breathing humanity subverted his dreamy ideals and—to his mind, at least—forced him to collect (and implicitly murder) her: "I forgave her," he says, "all the other business. Not while she was living, but when I knew she was dead, that was when I finally forgave her. All sorts of nice things came back" (248). It is, of course, grimly ironic that the kidnapper-torturer should be the one who thinks he needs to grant forgiveness, but it is also understandable. As horrible as Clegg's treatment of Miranda was, she did something to Clegg that, from his perspective, was more thoroughly—even metaphysically— unforgivable: she made his dream (*his* dream, a dream he thought he owned) have the unpredictability of flesh-and-blood otherness. But now she is dead; her behavior has become as certain as that of a photographed image. And this new certainty teaches Clegg how to give his own story the kind of ending that would unite necrophilia with transcendent romance. An inevitable idea occurs to him: "All I had to do was kill myself. . . . We would be buried together. Like Romeo and Juliet. It would be real tragedy. Not sordid" (249–50). In the glow of this idea, Clegg finds the eloquence to make the blasphemously rebellious proclamation previously quoted ("There's nothing."); he is, at this moment, quite grand. He ends this penulti-mate section of the novel with a real aesthetic flourish: "She was waiting for me down there. I would say we were in love, in the letter to the police. A suicide pact. It would be 'The End' " (250). His love of death and dead things seems, at this moment, to have been wholly (if unnervingly) integrated with his most lyrical, romantic aspirations.

The reader, of course, knows that this is not "The End." The novel has a fourth section that adds an ironic twist to this portrayal of a very twisted lover. The ending of Part 3, however, has an importance in its own right, apart from the ultimate ironic under-cutting. This description of a planned suicide, combined with the rather articulate blasphemy which accompanies it, represents the apotheosis of both sides of Clegg's rebellion: his idealistic rebel-lion against a limited world and his materialistic, death-courting rebellion against God. In this first of the novel's two endings, Clegg overcomes the mundane, "sordid" particulars of his life in order to give it a formal shape and destiny, but he does this by opting not for higher things but for lower, for death. Having withdrawn, at the beginning of the book, to a hidden house in the country, his version of Meaulnes's *domaine perdu*, Clegg now manages to give his life the kind of dramatic design human beings often long for when they escape—literally or metaphorically—to the "secret place." He merges his quest for a secret place with his attachment to the inorganic: there is no more hidden, inscrutable *domaine* than the one Clegg has decided to find for himself.

If we rush, therefore, immediately from Part 3 to Part 4—if we do not allow "The End" to be, temporarily, a real end—we overlook the ways in which this first ending is almost a genuine summation of the novel. On the face of it, this conclusion is merely conventional (psycho kills lover, then self); but by carefully gathering together the book's two strands, romantic idealism and necrophilia, this ending transforms the conventional into something compellingly right. In this sense, it is reminiscent of the second, published ending of that Dickens novel which has had a good deal of impact on the Fowlesian corpus: *Great Expectations*. In that novel's final version, the union of Pip and Estella is Dickens's concession to romantic convention, but it occurs within an episode—Pip meets Estella in the moonlight amid the ashes of Miss Havisham's house—which is such a lyrical culmination of the book's themes and images that it transcends its own conventionality.

As interesting as it is, however, the ending of the third section of *The Collector* is not quite transcendent. We do well to remind ourselves that the "suicide" ending is not just a trick but is a vividly rendered potential ending—but it is also important to note that it is not the actual ending. Integrating mechanistic materialism with lyrical romanticism is not what Fowles is up to. Having first toyed with a kind of nihilistic synthesis of romanticism and materialism in the "Romeo and Juliet" ending, he proceeds to wrench apart these two impulses after all, to allow them, in the real ending, again to gape.

The real ending begins after the formally designed conclusiveness of the aborted ending with a return of mere mechanical chance (Fowlesian "hazard") without a trace of romantic idealism. "As it happened," Clegg says, "things turned out rather different" (253). Before killing himself, Clegg decides to take "a last look through her things," and he chances upon her journal—"which shows she never loved me, she only thought of herself and the other man all the time" (253). The plot is wrenched, in other words, by a chance event, an event that seems as forced and heavy-handed as the positioning of the rug to gobble up the letter that Tess tries to give to Angel Clare in Thomas Hardy's *Tess of the d'Urbervilles.* In both cases, we initially feel manipulated and cheated until we realize that we are in novelistic worlds—one dominated by "hazard," one by "Hap" (this similarity between Fowles's and Hardy's worlds is, as we will see, significant)—in which feeling cheated is the point. Impersonal, unprovidential mechanism does feel like an affront.

Throughout *The Collector*'s brief final section we are affronted precisely by mechanism, by the spectacle of a machine spinning; Clegg seems to have become a wind-up Jack the Ripper rather than either a romantic hero or an anti-hero. The ludicrously coincidental discovery of the journal (if it were so easily found, Clegg surely would have discovered it much earlier) is followed by another, more important coincidence:

> That morning in Lewes, it was a real coincidence, I was just driving to the flower-shop when a girl in an overall crossed the crossing where I stopped to let people over. For a moment it gave me a turn, I thought I was seeing a ghost, she had the same hair, except it was not so long; I mean she had the same size and the same way of walking as Miranda. I couldn't take my eyes off her, and I just had to park the car and go back the way she was where I had the good fortune to see her go into the Woolworth's. Where I followed and found she works behind the sweet counter. (253)

After a meticulously mechanical description of the burial of Miranda ("I did it scientific. I planned what had to be done and ignored my natural feelings" [254]), the first teeth of that same old spinning gear, the gear that drives Clegg to collect, appear again: "I have not made up my mind about Marian (another M! I heard the supervisor call her name), this time it won't be love, it would just be for the interest of the thing and to compare them and also the other thing, which . . . I would like to go into in more detail and I could teach her how. And the clothes would fit. Of course I would make it clear from the start who's boss and what I expect" (254–55). This second, final ending is not an ending at all, but a repetition.

Critics, philosophers, and psychologists have found various kinds of significance in the appearance of repetition in literature, and in his book *Fiction and Repetition,* J. Hillis Miller has devised a neat, if imperfect, framework for describing all of the forms that these literary repetitions can take. Using categories first set forward by Gilles Deleuze, Miller has theorized that there are two essential modes of repetition: the Platonic and the Nietzschean. Miller's Platonic mode is straightforwardly mimetic; the repetition repeats a clear, substantial first term. This form, Miller says, "is grounded in a solid archetypal model which is untouched by the effects of repetition. All the other examples are copies of this model. ... The validity of the mimetic copy is established by its truth of correspondence to what it copies" (6). The Nietzschean mode, on the other hand, exists in a world in which there is no substantial archetype to be repeated; it is a world "based on difference. Each thing, this other theory would assume, is unique, intrinsically different from every other thing." Repetitions within the latter mode are "ghostly": "It seems that X repeats Y, but in fact it does not, or at least not in the firmly anchored way of the first sort of repetition" (6). The two dissimilar things resonate with each other and create an "image" (9), but it is an image that exists only within a gap of difference; it has no substantive grounding.

As impressed as I am with Miller's idea, however, I would modify it by saying that there are repetitions of absence (the most "ghostly" examples of Miller's "Nietzschean" repetition, in which the X and Y cancel each other out, generate a kind of nonimage rather than an image) but also repetitions of presence that are not Platonic in the reductive, mimetic way which Miller describes. For example, we will see in John Updike's fiction that repetition carries a Kierkegaardian suggestion of gratuitous grace, of a gift re-endowed without warrant. As a gift, it is new, surprising, in just the way that Miller's Platonic repetition—based on a familiar, conventional model—cannot be; but as a gift, it is also substantial, a real presence, not a mere ghost. And, in these terms, Clegg's is very much a repetition of absence. The repetition at the end of *The Collector* is precisely a denial of the possibility of grace; if it is affirmative at all, it is an affirmation of blind mechanism in the place of grace.

The world that delivers up Miranda's journal to Clegg in such a coincidental way is controlled by a blind, materialistic antiprovidence. And the Clegg who, like one of Pavlov's dogs hearing a dinner bell, salivates at the mere sight of a random young woman at Woolworth's seems precisely to be a human machine. This is not to say, however, that this conclusion lacks all traces of the dreamy idealism that has run through the novel. Clegg's romantic dream is still present, in a sense; Clegg, having lost one personification of the dream, is setting off on another quest, just as Meaulnes goes off again at the end of *Le Grand Meaulnes*. But, given the grotesquely mechanical nature of this final segment of the novel, the dream is present only as a kind of absence. It is still shaping the narrative structure, but it is displaced by the utterly reductive materialism of the actual prose.

This displacement creates the kind of gap between ideal and actual (which were thoroughly unified in the initial ending) that is, according to Fowles, extremely fruitful for a writer. In an essay called "Hardy and the Hag"—an analysis of Thomas Hardy's *The Well-Beloved,* a novel that perhaps even more than *Le Grand Meaulnes* or *Great Expectations* looms over Fowles's fiction— Fowles describes the fruitfulness of such a gap. *The Well-Beloved* is quite explicitly a novel about the repetitions generated by a separation of the ideal from the actual: the book's hero, Jocelyn Pierston, is driven by an inner Hardyan fate to move from one doomed love relationship to another in a vain attempt to find a flesh-and-blood incarnation of his perfect woman, his "Well-Beloved." Fowles sees this repetitive activity as a metaphor for the novelist's attempt to incarnate his or her own dream in words and to repeat this attempt again and again because it again and again fails. And he finds Hardy's conclusion to *The Well-Beloved*—in which the Ideal vanishes altogether and the hero is left in a grimly ordinary world, as spiritless as the machine in which Clegg is a cog in *The Collector*'s final pages—to be more satisfying than a more conclusive, unifying ending. The happy ending, he claims, "is in this light mere wish-fulfillment, childish longing of the kind re- flected in the traditional last sentence of all fairy stories" (35). Such an ending—the kind of formal consummation of ideal and actual that Clegg contemplates in his own novel's initial, aborted conclusion—is sterile for a writer, Fowles thinks, because it "re- solves not only the story, but the need to embark on further stories" (35). And, indeed, Fowles claims to have realized that his interest in the kind of repetition represented by *The Well-Beloved* is exactly what led him to end *The Collector* as he did: "I have only quite recently, in a manner I trust readers will now guess, under- stood the real meaning of my ending ... the way in which the monstrous and pitiable Clegg (the man who acts out his own fantasies) prepares for a new 'guest' in the Bluebeard's cell beneath his lonely house" (38). This is a rather striking statement by Fowles himself that Clegg is not a portrait of "undistilled evil" but is an embodiment of his own artistic endeavors.

But what kind of embodiment is he, after all? What Clegg are we left with? Throughout the novel we have seen Clegg as a kind of Camusian rebel, simultaneously in the romantic tradition of Dick- ens and Alain-Fournier (protesting against his constrictive social background by escaping into a secret, ideal world) and in the materialistic, nihilistic tradition of Sade (protesting against God by worshipping all that is decidedly not ideal: the mechanical, the inorganic, the dead). These alternative personae—romance hero and psycho killer, Ferdinand and Norman Bates—are a volatile combination throughout the novel. And just when they seem to have achieved the kind of formal novelistic unity that Camus considers the goal of all rebellion—arriving at a true, integrative ending in which "final words are pronounced" and heroes "complete things that we [mortals] can never consummate" (262–63)—the unity is wrenched apart. We are left with an unresolvable conflict: the force of absolute determinism eternally confronts the force of infinite idealism. Or rather we are left with the gap between these forces, which turns out to be a kind of unity after all (a vacuum certainly cannot harbor multiplicity), though not the substantially satisfying unity that Camus describes.

And Clegg himself is an embodiment of this conflict. He ends up being the gap between the motif of the sadistic enslaver and that of the dreamy aspirer. What really happens in that final section is that Clegg simply cancels himself out. He thoroughly justifies one of Miranda's most hopeless statements about him: "He's not human; he's an empty space designed as a human" (205).

Nothingness and Freedom

Although my concluding analysis of Clegg seems to portray him as more absolutely abhorrent than even the "drooling horror-film monster" that Miranda frequently considers him to be (188), that is not my intention at all. It is rather to stand by my original claim that Clegg is not as demonic as many critics consider him. By virtue of his very blankness he is a permanent *tabula rasa* on which the philosophical extremes of the Fowlesian world—ranging from the determinism of *The Aristos* to the romanticism of *The Tree*—can be dabbed and immediately erased. He is, therefore, an extremely "fruitful" character in Fowles's own terms, since he uses up nothing; he leaves room for infinite repetition.

Ironically, it is his nothingness that allows him, despite his role within the plot as an imprisoner, to be the sort of hero who can open up space for the central existential concept—freedom—that slips into the Fowlesian world in that gap between biological determinism and romantic idealism. And Miranda, walled in by Clegg the imprisoner and worshipped by Clegg the dreamer, is the personification of this freedom, a freedom which is depicted in terms that must remind us of the poet of nothingness, Jean-Paul Sartre.

From the beginning, Miranda (not surprisingly, considering her situation) makes it clear that freedom is her be-all and end-all. When Clegg first tells her that he is "going into the shops," and that she can have anything she wants, her response is simple and clear: "I just want to be set free" (33). Indeed, even her most tiresome clichés—Clegg, she maintains, would never imprison her if he only knew something about art (41)—are rendered as somewhat tolerable because they are counterbalanced by poignant reaffirmations of the value of freedom. When she talks about the superiority of her own taste to Clegg's—that is, when she self-consciously exemplifies the Fowlesian "Few"—Miranda is difficult to tolerate. But when she puts herself forward simply and passionately as a self, constituted by freedom, when she affirms life itself, she is quite moving. From the earliest pages of her narrative, she indicates that Clegg himself has strangely created the space in which she can affirm such a self: "I don't want to die, I love life so passionately, I never knew how much I wanted to live life before. If I get out of this, I shall never be the same" (112). Somewhat later Miranda reveals a spark of genuine artistic insight when she describes a painting that she will do when she is free. It is a vision of the Fowlesian secret place, the hidden garden; it is, in other words, precisely constituted by aspects of Clegg's self and world: "I've been making sketches for a painting I shall do when I'm free. A view of a garden through a door. It sounds silly in words. But I see it as something very special, all black, umber, dark, dark grey, mysterious angular forms in shadow leading to the distant soft honey-whitish square of the light-filled door. A sort of horizontal shaft" (146). This could be a painting of Clegg himself, of the tension between Clegg's romantic self (the garden) and his mechanically constricting self (the door). The two, in a sense, cancel each other out and allow Miranda to be the opening, the shaft of light, the nothingness-that-is-freedom which pierces through the gap.

In Sartrean terms, then, Miranda is the pinprick of freedom which slips into the wedge of nothingness that is created—or, as Sartre puts it, "nihilated"—by the intersection of Being-in-itself, the unconscious world (which corresponds to that part of Clegg's world that is mechanical, dead), and Being-for-itself, consciousness (the secret, romantic world of Clegg the dreamer). The "nihilation" of the one by the other creates the space of nothingness which is, Sartre says, freedom itself:

> Freedom in its foundation coincides with the nothingness which is at the heart of man. Human-reality is free ... because it is perpetually wrenched away from itself and because it has been separated by a nothingness from what it is and from what it will be. It is free, finally, because its present being is itself a nothingness in the form

of the "reflection-reflecting" [i.e. consciousness]. . . . Freedom is precisely the nothingness which is *made-to-be* at the heart of man and which forces human-reality *to make itself* instead of *to be*. . . . [F]or human reality, to be is to *choose oneself*; nothing comes to it either from the outside or from within which it can *receive or accept*. Without any help whatsoever, it is entirely abandoned to the intolerable necessity of making itself be—down to the slightest detail. Thus freedom is not *a* being; it is *the being* of man—i.e. his nothingness of being. (568–69)

This is not to suggest that *The Collector* is a straightforward allegory of Sartrean philosophy any more than it is a straightforward allegory of Camusian or Heraclitean philosophy. If it were an orthodox Sartrean tract, Being-for-itself, freedom, and nothingness would be essentially equated and set apart from Being-in-itself; but Clegg here is both Being-in-itself and Being-for-itself, a combination that Sartre considers impossible and even unimaginable. Clegg nihilates *himself,* in other words, and freedom is represented by a separate character altogether, Miranda. No, this is not pure Sartre. But it ends up with a kind of Sartrean vision, a vision of a nothingness—the "nothingness which is at the heart of man" to which no substantive thing can come "either from the outside or from within which it can *receive or accept*"—that is freedom.

I end my treatment of Miranda by quoting a particularly impressive passage, a passage in which Miranda most eloquently reveals the way her freedom, her self, requires the nothingness-world of Clegg:

> A strange thought: I would not want this not to have happened. Because if I escape I shall be a completely different and I think better person. Because if I don't escape, if something dreadful happened, I shall know that the person I was and would have stayed if this hadn't happened was not the person I now want to be.
>
> It's like firing a pot. You have to risk the cracking and the warping. (229)

In later novels, Fowles will find less destructive (though, in *The Magus* at least, not less sadistic) ways of creating this space of nothingness in which a human self can achieve freedom. But *The Collector* remains prototypal in that the creation of this space is, for Fowles, more important than the creation of substantive, ontologically solid characters. As a particular nineteen-year-old woman, Miranda Grey is not terribly interesting; but as a potentiality—a representation of the very possibility of freedom—she is

a successful artistic creation. Fowles himself seems to have under-
stood that this was the most successful aspect of his portrayal of
Miranda. Although, in the introduction to the revised edition of
The Aristos, he ostensibly declares that Miranda is a budding
aristos, he is really saying something about her ontological status
as a character; she is not "perfect," he says, but she represents a
potential good: "If she had not died she might have become
something better, the kind of being humanity so desperately
needs. "The actual evil in Clegg overcame the potential good in
Miranda" (10).

Miranda, then, is merely potential; but even Clegg, a possessor
of some actuality, is a possessor only of actual *evil,* which for
Fowles (as for many philosophers) is not a presence but an
absence. As we have seen, Clegg's dualities cancel each other out,
leaving an emptiness. Even this character, interesting as he is, is not
quite there. He reminds one of the invisible man: a reader can
easily picture his staid, dark suit—but he does not quite have a
face. In Updike's world, as we will see, there is a substantive God, an
Other, who can encounter substantive selves. But for Fowles,
substance is exploded, "nihilated," by the clash of determinism
and idealism that allows for freedom. There is no God in Fowles's
universe (" 'God' is present by being absent in every thing and
every moment" [*Aristos* 27]), and there is no substantive "I" either
("the myth of a separate consciousness partly arises because of the
loose way we use 'I' " [38]). And in his fiction, therefore, there are,
in the traditional sense, no characters.

Romance/Thriller

Clearly Fowles, for all the storytelling ability that pushes his
books onto bestseller lists, is a kind of antinovelist: he constructs
his characters and plots in order, ultimately, to deconstruct them.
Nevertheless his characters and plots are quite compelling; to be
paradoxical, I suggest that Fowles writes antinovels that are nonetheless very rich novels. (And I will argue that Updike—whose
work is like and unlike Fowles's in uncanny ways—writes novels
that are nonetheless daring antinovels.) I have already shown at
length how the Fowlesian tension between mechanical determinism and romantic idealism is played out in the characterization of
Clegg: the disparate aspects of Clegg remain irreconcilable, and
the gap, the nothingness, opens up (if only temporarily) a hole of
freedom for Miranda. And, since Clegg to a large degree defines his
novel's shape, it should be superfluous to state that *The Collector* as
a whole embodies this tension. So I end my discussion of the novel

by only briefly pointing out the ways in which this, the most formally traditional of Fowles's works, has elements of deconstructionist metafiction: with a dark playfulness, it dramatizes the self-canceling tension between two literary genres.

The book's two endings, which show the two ways a divided character like Clegg can be novelistically disposed of (the first ending synthesizes the division, while the second allows it to gape), also epitomize the two genres that fight for ascendency throughout *The Collector.* The first, the "Romeo and Juliet" ending, represents the book's romantic strain. This is a powerful strain throughout the novel. With his affection for wild nature, for secret places, and for Alain-Fournier, Fowles is without question a neoromantic writer, and *The Collector* has solid, not wholly ironic ties with fairy tales ("Bluebeard," "Beauty and the Beast"), *The Tempest, Le Grand Meaulnes, Great Expectations,* and other romantic works. Clegg's decision to become a suicidal Romeo, to offer up his most necrophiliac impulses on a pyre of romantic passion, powerfully consummates this romantic aspect of the novel. But the second ending, the grisly repetition of the urge to collect young women, reminds us that traditional romance has been battling here with another, more modern literary genre: the psychological thriller. Clegg may be a Meaulnes or a Ferdinand, but he is also a Norman Bates. The book, therefore, contains a large dose of *Psycho.* With this final section of *The Collector,* Fowles undercuts his own romantic tendencies by squeezing his novel into the constricted, reductive form of a psychological thriller. The last pages of the book jar us less because Clegg has backed away from his suicide fantasy than because, after more than two hundred pages of aesthetically and psychologically complex prose, *The Collector* ends with the sort of banal turn of the screw that concludes innumerable episodes of *The Twilight Zone* and *Alfred Hitchcock Presents.*

This generic dichotomy between romance and thriller corresponds well to the larger thematic dichotomy between idealism and determinism. Dominated as it is by the quest motif, romance is the genre that celebrates (or at least yearns for) the ideal, a surpassing of earthbound limitations—of all those aspects of the human condition that seem merely physical, mechanical, forced. And psychological thrillers, I think, frighten us with the opposite of this idealism. The villains in such stories tend to be machine-like rather than living (organic) human beings; they are driven by an inexorable force, a psychologically explainable fate, to reduce others to the level of inert matter by killing or torturing or doing other horrible things. The mechanical nature of such destroyers dooms them incessantly to repeat the destructive process: pre-programmed by sexual repression, Norman Bates in *Psycho* and the female protagonist in Roman Polanski's *Repulsion* are driven to kill again and again.

When Clegg sets off to victimize another random young woman in the last pages of *The Collector,* he joins this not very illustrious company. And the novel itself ends with a sardonic understatedness. Denying to himself that he really plans to kidnap "the girl in Woolworth's," Clegg coolly says: "it is still just an idea. I only put the stove down there today because the room needs drying out anyway" (255). This icy tone subverts the heated prose that ended Part Three, in which Clegg proclaimed his plans to become Romeo to Miranda's Juliet. Yet the tone of that prose—and, indeed, of the entire romantic portion of the novel—subverts, retroactively, this final reduction of the book to mechanistic thriller. Just as Clegg refused to become either simple hero or simple robot, so the novel refuses to settle comfortably into either of its potential genres. Though it seems, superficially, to be a traditional piece of pop fiction, lacking the self-reflexiveness of Fowles's later works, it is actually a kind of empty space generated by the play between two traditional fictional forms.

So *The Collector* is a great deal more than a novelistic embodiment of the "Few versus Many" social philosophy that is spelled out in *The Aristos.* Its main character, Frederick Clegg—who is often seen as simply a representation of the mediocre masses—is a volatile mixture rather than a fixed allegorical type. Furthermore, concerning thematic issues, the tension between romantic organicism and rationalistic materialism is more significant, and more quintessentially Fowlesian, than the tension between the *aristoi* and the *hoi polloi.* And the tension, whether presented through character, plot, or literary structure, is not resolved by a definitive either/or but rather by a both/and—or even by a neither/nor. Just as there is no substantive God in the Fowles world, so there is no substantive resting place in *The Collector,* thematically, narratively, or structurally. While reading this first of his published novels, we can very nearly watch John Fowles create the world of extreme existential freedom that will ultimately be inhabited—or not inhabited—by his later (anti)characters and (anti)novels. Even in this plain, seemingly straightforward thriller, we are already traveling on Fowles's *via negativa.*

3

Rebellion and Repetition
in
Rabbit, Run

I have argued that *The Collector* is the simplest, most schematic presentation of Fowles's existential worldview. Clegg is the embodiment of the Fowlesian world itself: half dreamer and half robot, Clegg is the self-canceling clash between the romantic Ideal and mechanistically determined matter. Miranda, then, is a portrait of the human being in this world: isolated, entrapped in the Clegg prison, and yet paradoxically free because this prison—a self-annihilating clash of dream and machine—is a nothing.

Miranda is the individual self that is imprisoned and yet free; Harry ("Rabbit") Angstrom is an individual caught in a net and yet still running. In other words, *Rabbit, Run* is Updike's version of *The Collector:* the most straightforward presentation of his existential vision of the individual in the world. But although Miranda's world is Clegg, and therefore nothing, containing no substantial reality transcending her own self ("God is not," says Fowles emphatically, and therefore his world is without any sort of providence), whether Rabbit's world contains nothing or something— some Thing, a real providential God—is precisely the question that the character and his novel directly address. That such a religious question can be seriously asked separates Updike from Fowles at the outset.

And yet the books are not dissimilar. Rabbit's plight as an entrapped individual matches, in a certain way, Miranda's; Fowles and Updike, existentialists both, are equally interested in the notion of freedom. And in his suburban ordinariness, Rabbit even more strikingly resembles Clegg. Miranda, reading Alan Sillitoe's *Saturday Night and Sunday Morning,* is disgusted by the book's protagonist, Arthur Seaton, because he reminds her of the mediocre Clegg; her description of Seaton could stand as Fowles's own description of Rabbit:

> I think Arthur Seaton is disgusting. . . .
> I hated the way Arthur Seaton just doesn't care about anything outside his own little life. He's mean, narrow, selfish, brutal. Because he's cheeky and hates his work and is successful with women, he's supposed to be vital. . . .
> It's the inwardness of such people. Their not caring what happens anywhere else in the world. In life.
> Their being-in-a-box. (*Collector* 211)

Miranda is appalled that Sillitoe considers it a valid literary endeavor to portray such a shallow character, especially since he seems to like Seaton. We can only imagine what Miranda would say about a novel which implicitly asserts that the sentences appearing during Rabbit's early drive to West Virginia are art: "On the radio he hears 'No Other Arms, No Other Lips,' 'Stagger Lee,' a commercial for Rayco Clear Plastic Seat Covers, 'If I Didn't Care' by Connie Francis, a commercial for Radio-Controlled Garage Door Operators, 'I Ran All the Way Home Just to Say I'm Sorry,' 'That Old Feeling' by Mel Torme, a commercial for Big Screen Westinghouse TV Set with One-Finger Automatic Tuning, 'needle-sharp pictures a nose away from the screen' " (33).

But however much Miranda (and even Fowles, in some moods) may despise him, Clegg economically synthesizes Fowles's interest in the romantic and the mechanistic; he is both an Alain-Fournier quester and a Sade necrophiliac. And Rabbit also contains both of these dimensions. He is a kind of Camusian rebel against his dead surroundings, a romantic dreamer in quest of a secret place, and he is also a destroyer, one who reduces living things to dead objects. Again like Clegg, he seems compelled to repeat both the romantic quest and the destructiveness over and over, establishing what critic Joseph Waldmeir considers the key Updikean dialectic: a conflict between "the two idealisms," transcendentalism (which corresponds to Rabbit's "romanticism") and pragmatism (which is a kind of earthboundness). It is a conflict that in many respects matches Fowles's own dichotomy between romanticism and mechanism.

This is the common ground that Updike shares here with Fowles. Almost as much as *The Collector, Rabbit, Run* can be looked at as a work of existential romanticism (or is it romantic

existentialism?). And—again, like *The Collector*—the novel presents its dialectic with a schematic clarity unmatched by other
works of its author; Waldmeir asserts that "the pragmatic-transcen-
dental battlelines are more clearly drawn here than in any other"
Updike book (18). So, as with Frederick Clegg, I will examine
Rabbit Angstrom (his name itself, of course, suggests his existential angst) as an exemplification of a Camusian metaphysical
rebel like Clegg, containing both the romantically heroic, Alain-
Fournier aspects of this rebellion and the destructive, Sade aspects.

There is, however, something else going on in the book that
reflects a fundamental difference between Updike and Fowles.
Where Fowles's existentialism harks back to that of Sartre and
Camus, Updike is a Kierkegaardian, as well as an admirer of the
Christian theologian Karl Barth. Romance and mechanism, spirit
and matter, for Fowles are mutually annihilating; they spring from
and create the vacuum that is God and that is the *sine qua non* of
freedom. But the God of Kierkegaard, and especially of Barth, is
surely *not* nothing. This God is a very particular and personal one,
whose story is told as precisely in the Bible as Clegg's is told in *The
Collector*. And Updikean pragmatism, therefore, ultimately takes
on a vitality and even a holiness that set it apart from Fowlesian
mechanism.

So although Updike's dialectic begins with a thesis and antithesis
that seem very similar to Fowles's, Updike's synthesis is founded on
a faith in, or at least a hope for, a personal Something. Creating
vacuums, carving out nothingness, is an intermediate goal of some
of Updike's characters (Rabbit, for instance), but it is not an
ultimate goal in the Updike world; perhaps that is why his books,
for all their romantic elements, remain resolutely realistic and
suburban rather than retreating to some romantic secret place.
And repetition for Updike is not finally a Hardyan compulsion to
circle around and around an absence; rather, it is what Kierkegaard
considers it to be—an unexpected gift, a providential surprise, the
second chance that Job did not make for himself but merely
received from the transcendent One Who Is.

In this chapter, then, I examine Rabbit Angstrom as another
exemplar of the metaphysical rebellion we saw in the previous
chapter (both heroic and destructive), but also as a character in
search of a substantial, personal God. And I conclude by showing
that Updike's Kierkegaardian use of repetition, in *Rabbit, Run*
itself and also in its sequels, helps to establish a fictional universe
precisely founded on some Thing—on substance rather than on
nothingness.

The Romantic Quest

Calling Rabbit Angstrom a romantic hero is not quite as outrageous as calling Frederick Clegg one. Indeed, in his Camusian jaunt through contemporary American fiction, *The Absurd Hero in American Fiction,* David Galloway claims that Rabbit is a Sisyphusian hero-rebel with a kind of romantic halo around his head: "Harry 'Rabbit' Angstrom rebels against the wasteland into which he is born. In consistently opposing the reality which he encounters, Rabbit becomes an absurd hero, and because of the highly spiritual devotion of this gesture against the world, he becomes a saint" (22). But few critics or readers have been so willing to canonize Rabbit. Many have condemned him—perhaps not as vigorously as most of Clegg's critics have condemned Clegg, but vigorously enough. Robert Detweiler, for example, rejects claims that Rabbit is a heroic, or even anti-heroic, rebel, "asserting his total freedom as he challenges the mores of his society." Rather, Detweiler sums Rabbit up this way: "Irresponsible, undependable, and gutless, Rabbit is the quintessence of the nonhero" (38). George Hunt, similarly, calls Rabbit a Nothing-man: "The Nothing-man is one who is fascinated with Nothingness or who confuses creation with Nothingness or who mimics and thus distorts goodness: Rabbit Angstrom" (46). And Rachael Burchard simply calls him "the moral derelict" (42–43).

But it is undeniable that Rabbit, like Clegg, has some attributes of the romantic hero. In each case, romantic heroism is at least half of the dialectic that composes the respective character's complete personality. There are four related areas in which Rabbit demonstrates his romantic idealism (the latter three are precisely the areas that show the more attractive side of Clegg, as previously discussed): his enthusiasm for immediate, unselfconscious experience; his rebellion against the stuffiness of the day-to-day world; his quest for a secret place; and his search for a Hardyan "Well-Beloved."

John Updike is lauded as a fine stylist, and perhaps the most striking stylistic device he uses in *Rabbit, Run* and its sequels is the present tense. I know of no literary work of a thousand pages or more other than the Rabbit series that employs the present-tense form throughout. (*Gravity's Rainbow,* at nearly nine-hundred present-tense pages, comes close—which startlingly suggests that Updike and Pynchon are literary kin.) And yet it is hard to imagine the Rabbit books in anything but the present tense. Updike has on several occasions explained that he used the present tense to accommodate the cinematic immediacy primarily of the introductory scene and secondarily of the entire novel (and, eventually, novel sequence):

> [*Rabbit, Run*] was conceived of as a movie. Originally, I had a short introductory section in italics talking about entering a theater; having entered the theater, the reader was presumably sitting down and watching the opening in which the kids are tossing the basketball around while the super-imposed title and credits rolled. And my use of the present tense was in some way to correspond to the continuous present of a movie. As the book went on, I think it lost some of its cinematic quality; and yet, picking it up again recently, I was struck by how speedily it moves—like a film. (Gado 95)

That very speedy opening, which makes readers feel not that they are being told about events but that they are watching them directly, establishes the first form of Rabbit's romanticism: a passion for pure immediacy.

The book's first paragraph is a mix of modes: straightforward description ("Boys are playing basketball around a telephone pole with a backboard bolted to it"), ragged sense impressions ("Legs, shouts"), thought ("He [Rabbit] stands there thinking, the kids keep coming, they keep crowding you up"). For several pages, the narrative never settles into any one of these modes. Rather, in a seemingly irrational and designless—but not graceless—way, it shoots one after another ("Eyeballs slide. . . . He takes off his coat. . . . It feels so right. . . .") at us as effortlessly as Rabbit, reliving his glory days as a high-school basketball star, shoots the ball: "the ball seems to ride up the right lapel of his coat and comes off his shoulder as his knees dip down, and it appears the ball will miss because though he shot from an angle the ball is not going toward the backboard. It was not aimed there. It drops into the circle of the rim, whipping the net with a ladylike whisper. 'Hey!' he shouts in pride" (10). Even the book's first word of dialogue—"Hey!"—is a mere grunt of emotion rather than a rational, meaningful signifier. And the scene ends with the kind of present-participial montage of sense impressions and thought that floods a person when he or she, as Rabbit so often does in this book, runs: "Running. . . . Running uphill. . . . The frame homes climb the hill like a single staircase. . . . The fronts are scabby clapboards, once white. There are a dozen three-story homes, and each has two doors. The seventh door is his. The wood steps up to it are worn; under them there is a cubbyhole of dirt where a lost toy molders. A plastic clown" (12).

Updike has come mightily close to capturing in language a pre-linguistic experiential immediacy, and it is this immediacy that Rabbit, in a sense, will run after throughout the rest of the novel.

It is similar to the kind of immediacy that Wordsworth, among other romantics, celebrated passionately:

> like a roe
> I bounded o'er the mountains, by the sides
> Of the deep rivers, and the lonely streams,
> Wherever nature led. . . .
> For nature then
> To me was all in all. — I cannot paint
> What then I was. The sounding cataract
> Haunted me like a passion; the tall rock,
> The mountain, and the deep and gloomy wood,
> Their colors and their forms, were then to me
> An appetite; a feeling and a love,
> That had no need of a remoter charm,
> By thought supplied, nor any interest
> Unborrowed from the eye.
> ("Tintern Abbey" ll. 67–83)

For Wordsworth, this immediate oneness with the natural has several qualities that make it very much like Rabbit's initial basket-ball game. First of all, the oneness is an utterly unconscious unity of self with other. The immediate sense experience has no added charm — or pain — that has been "By thought supplied." But it is, in addition, a unity that no longer exists for the adult Wordsworth: "that time is past," he goes on to say, "And all its aching joys are now no more, / And all its dizzy raptures" (ll. 83–85). Wordsworth has been separated from nature by grown-up self-consciousness just as surely as Rabbit has been separated from high-school basketball stardom by graduation.

Finally, Wordsworth has for five years ("five summers with the length / Of five long winters" [ll. 1–2]) yearned for a return to youthful passion, or at least a grown-up approximation of it, as an alternative to dreary, adult, urban life — "in lonely rooms, and 'mid the din / Of towns and cities" (ll. 25–26). Similarly, the second way that Rabbit displays romantic idealism is by rebelling against the dull ordinariness of his own adult situation.

Updike has commented that, despite its overall failure, the movie version of *Rabbit, Run* was loaded with just the right day-to-day details: "Certain things, like the furniture in the people's apartments, had been done with a richness that I had never even approached. I couldn't have imagined all those things they found to put in those sets: these identifying kinds of calendars, the style of furniture—all just for a few seconds on the screen" (Gado 94). Updike's attention to apartment furnishings in the filmed *Rabbit* is predictable, since the written *Rabbit* is so meticulously furnished. Immediately upon Rabbit's first entrance into his apartment, we are given a painstaking description of a 1950s middle-class living room, in which human life is all but crowded out by television: "The closet is in the living room and the door only opens halfway, since the television set is in front of it. He is careful not to kick the wire, which is plugged into a socket on the other side of the door" (13). In front of the television is parked Rabbit's pregnant wife Janice, half anesthetized both by an Old-fashioned and by a TV show. Updike all but drowns us in detail:

> She is watching a group of children called Mouseketeers perform a musical number in which Darlene is a flower girl in Paris and Cubby is a cop and that smirky squeaky tall kid is a romantic artist. He and Darlene and Cubby and Karen (dressed as an old French lady whom Cubby as a cop helps across the street) dance. Then the commercial shows the seven segments of a Tootsie Roll coming out of the wrapper and turning into the seven letters of "Tootsie." They, too, sing and dance. Still singing, they climb back into the wrapper. It echoes like an echo chamber. (14)

After hearing the Greek imperative "Know Thyself" reduced to banality by Jimmy the Mouseketeer ("Proverbs, proverbs, they're so true, . . . proverbs tell us what to do; proverbs help us all to *bee*— better—Mouse-ke-teers"), we are bombarded by a string of proper nouns that evoke middle-class America at its most oppressively tacky: the MagiPeel Peeler Company, Vitaconomy, the MagiPeel Method, Liberty scarf, Kroll's (a department store, we gather), Purply Paisley. By furnishing his set with such an overload of detail, Updike captures the dullness of the day-to-day in a way that, as we will see later, is paradoxically lyrical.

At the moment, though, it seems anything but lyrical to Rabbit. After the youthful, ecstatic basketball experience that opened the novel, his grown-up home and marriage seem to Rabbit—a true basketball player—to be a net that he must somehow swish through:

> It seems to him he's the only person around here who cares about neatness. The clutter behind him in the room—the Old-fashioned glass with its corrupt dregs, the choked ashtray balanced on the easy-chair arm, the

> rumpled rug, the floppy stacks of slippery newspapers,
> the kid's toys here and there broken and stuck and
> jammed, a leg off a doll and a piece of bent cardboard
> that went with some breakfast-box cutout, the rolls of
> fuzz under the radiators, the continual crisscrossing
> mess—clings to his back like a tightening net. (19)

Although Robert Detweiler and others refuse to see Rabbit as a
rebellious hero, Rabbit's rejection of this chaos and his pursuit of
"clarity and unity" do make him at least partially a Camusian rebel
(Camus 23). So he runs again (this time metaphorically—he is
driving a car), in search of Paradise, as Fowles's Clegg searches for
his house in the country, as Alain-Fournier's Meaulnes searches for
his secret *domaine.*

Rabbit's quest takes him south, away from his home in Mt. Judge,
Pennsylvania, away from dirty northern cities where "they live on
poisoned water, you can taste the chemicals": Rabbit wants to go
"south, down, down the map into orange groves and smoking
rivers and barefoot women. It seems simple enough, drive all night
through the dawn through the morning through the noon park on a
beach take off your shoes and fall asleep by the Gulf of Mexico.
Wake up with the stars above perfectly spaced in perfect health"
(29). And although he never gets even close to the Gulf of Mexico,
he does find a secret paradise in the dark and mysterious Other
World called West Virginia.

His radio first signals that he is in a kind of Twilight Zone: "The
music on the radio slowly freezes; the rock and roll for kids cools
into the old standards and show tunes and comforting songs from
the Forties. . . . Then these melodies turn to ice as real night music
takes over, pianos and vibes erecting clusters in the high brittle
octaves and a clarinet wandering across like a crack on a pond"
(36). He soon enters a diner that throughout the rest of the book he
will remember as a place of mermaids: "Growing sleepy, Rabbit
stops before midnight at a roadside cafe for coffee. Somehow,
though he can't put his finger on the difference, he is unlike the
other customers. They sense it too, and look at him with hard eyes,
eyes like little metal studs pinned into the white faces of young
men sitting in zippered jackets in booths three to a girl, the girls
with orange hair hanging like seaweed or loosely bound with gold
barrettes like pirate treasure" (36). But this is not Rabbit's secret
place; the diner is as enclosed and cramped as his apartment.
Paradise for Rabbit is in the diner's parking lot—outdoors, in a vast
vacuum containing nothing substantial: "Outside in the sharp air,
he flinches when footsteps pound behind him. But it is just two

lovers, holding hands and in a hurry to reach their car, their locked hands a starfish leaping through the dark. Their license plate says West Virginia. All the plates do except his. On the other side of the road the wooded land dips down so he can look over the tops of trees at the side of a mountain like a cutout of still paper mounted on a slightly faded blue sheet" (36).

Like most romantics—Meaulnes, for instance—Rabbit does not appreciate his secret place's full significance until he has lost it. Much later in the novel, he remembers the mermaid diner's parking lot as the site of a missed chance, an airy hole through which he could have escaped the oppressive social net:

> Out of all his remembered life the one place that comes forward where he can stand without the ground turning into faces he is treading on is that lot outside the diner in West Virginia after he went in and had a cup of coffee the night he drove down there. He remembers the mountains around him like a ring of cutouts against the moon-bleached blue of the night sky. He remembers the diner, with its golden windows like the windows of the trolley cars that used to run from Mt. Judge into Brewer when he was a kid, and the air, cold but alive with the beginnings of spring. He hears the footsteps tapping behind him on the asphalt, and sees the couple running toward their car, hands linked. One of the red-haired girls that sat inside with her hair hanging down like seaweed. And it seems right here that he made the mistaken turning, that he should have followed, that they meant to lead him and he should have followed. (214–15)

So Rabbit Angstrom, like Frederick Clegg, has a secret place. Rabbit's secret place, however, differs from Clegg's—the former is open and airy, the latter enclosed and confining—and this difference points toward one important incongruence between the idealism of Rabbit and that of Clegg. Although Clegg is concerned with secrecy, with mysteries hidden from his working-class peers, he is hardly a lover of freedom. That ideal is sought after in *The Collector* by Miranda, not by Clegg; and Clegg's nothingness creates the space in which, paradoxically, the imprisoned Miranda finds the freedom of self-possession. Rabbit, however, does seek freedom, and like John Fowles, he conceives of freedom in a Sartrean way, as something that requires space, nothingness. Therefore, the Grail that he pursues, like the secret place that he remembers so fondly, is a kind of vacuum: the hole in the net. So Rabbit, insofar as he is romantic, is in some ways more Fowlesian than Clegg is (despite the fact that Fowles may well detest the suburbanism of the Rabbit books). Oppressed by the "stuff" of his middle-class surroundings, Rabbit craves nothingness—the absence of such stuff.

This craving precisely explains his last and most obvious form of romanticism: his pursuit of a Well-Beloved. Although he sees it as neurotic rather than heroic, Robert Detweiler has neatly described this aspect of Rabbit's romanticism:

> Rabbit is the *son-sun* with all of the metaphysical connotations of the pun, and the female characters are the satellites in orbit around him: Janice; Ruth; his mother; Lucy Eccles; Mim, his sister; and even old Mrs. Smith his employer, and Becky, his fated baby. A good part of Rabbit's frustration is that he seeks fulfillment of an ideal nearly as impossible to realize as his vague religious search: he wants to find in one woman the security of the mother and the excitement of the lover. (41)

I would state it a bit differently. Rabbit, I think, is looking for someone who is a woman but not a human being (this is why the "mermaids" of West Virginia so appeal to him). He wants, in other words, a relationship with a woman that will allow him to slip through the net of imperfect, oppressive human society. He wants a woman who is all space, all hole—and that is not entirely an obscene joke.

Having missed his chance with the mermaids and returned to Mt. Judge, Rabbit tries to achieve his transcendent ideal through a relationship with the biblically named Ruth, who at first seems exactly to embody the paradox he seeks. Voluptuous to the point of bulkiness, and a former prostitute to boot, she is thoroughly a fleshly woman; yet she does not entangle him with archeological layers of shared history, as his wife Janice does, so she is, symbolically at least, no one, an airy vacuum in which he can be free.

Ruth is introduced into the novel with language and imagery evoking the idea (ideal?) of nothingness. Having spent a night without Janice, Rabbit feels as if he is floating in space, like a balloon; and Tothero—his child-hero basketball coach, who is about to introduce him to Ruth—is the wind: "He feels freedom like oxygen everywhere around him; Tothero is an eddy of air, and the building he is in, the streets of the town, are mere stairways and alleyways in space. So perfect, so consistent is the freedom into which the clutter of the world has been vaporized by the simple trigger of his decision, that all ways seem equally good" (51). At the Chinese restaurant where Rabbit meets Ruth, Tothero seems to turn into a balloon ("his face is lopsided like a tired balloon" [67]), and then even the restaurant becomes one—fragile, insubstantial, helium-filled. Rabbit realizes that the young Chinese waiter, who has been speaking with a thick accent, has just been play-acting, and the whole restaurant seems to float away, carried along by the punchline of a joke that the waiter is telling the cashier: "—and then this other cat says, 'But man, mine was *helium!*' " (71).

And so, the world "vaporized," Rabbit goes with Ruth to her apartment, and he finally begins a relationship with a woman who, paradoxically, embodies nothingness. She says she has no job ("Nothing," she answers when he asks what she does [62]), and she has no beliefs either ("No. It seems obvious just the other way. All the time," she says when he asks her if God's existence seems self-evident [87]). Before having sex with her, Rabbit notices a rose window glowing in a church near her apartment, and it seems like "a hole punched in reality"; similarly, Ruth's eyes are like "gaps" cut out of the world's substantive clutter (78). Her body, too, is nothing, no thing, a shadow ("Her belly is a pond of shadow deepening to a black eclipsed by the inner swell of the thighs" [79]). He insists that it be encumbered with nothing—no ring, no birth control device—and that it be absolutely clean. Indeed, this relationship with Ruth, despite its adulterousness, exactly fits Rabbit's definition of "clean": "Clean, clean: it came to him what clean was. It was *nothing* touching you that was not yourself" (134, my italics).

His devotion to what he perceives as Ruth's nothingness—her lack of thing-ness, her cleanness—shows that Rabbit's sexual restlessness is motivated by romantic idealism, a rebellion against the clutter of the day-to-day, rather than simply by hormones. When he revisits his own apartment, the dialectic is presented quite explicitly. The apartment is cluttered with substance, stuff: "Though the apartment is empty, it is yet so full of Janice he begins to tremble; the sight of that easy chair turned to face the television attacks his knees. Nelson's broken toys on the floor derange his head; all the things inside his skull, the gray matter, the bones of his ears, the apparatus of his eyes, seem clutter clogging the tube of his self; his sinuses choke with a sneeze or tears, he doesn't know. The living room has the feel of dust" (93–94). Ruth, on the contrary, is the blankness that is freedom: "Yesterday morning the sky was ribbed with thin-stretched dawn clouds, and he was exhausted, heading into the center of the net, where alone there seemed a chance of rest. Now the noon of another day has burned away the clouds, and the sky . . . is blank and cold, and he feels nothing ahead of him, Ruth's blue-eyed nothing, the nothing she told him she did, the nothing she believes in. Your heart lifts forever through that blank sky" (93). Ruth, like the vista from the parking lot of the mermaids' diner, is "Blue beyond blue under blue" (96).

But, of course, Ruth is after all a human being rather than a nothingness, and Rabbit—like such other romantics as Alain-Fournier's Meaulnes, Hardy's Jocelyn (in *The Well-Beloved*), and, of course, Fowles's Clegg—increasingly finds her particular humanity incompatible with his ideal. Already in the middle of the novel, Rabbit begins to find a substantial other person looking back at him through Ruth's eyes, and he is disturbed: "She looks at him now, squarely with eyes bloodshot from being in the water. She shades them with her hand. These aren't the eyes he met that night by the parking meters, flat pale discs like a doll might have. The blue of her irises has deepened inward and darkened with a richness that, singing the truth to his instincts, disturbs him" (136). It is entirely in keeping, therefore, with his romantic idealism that he remain unsatisfied, that he repeat the quest for the great nothing, that he run. "Ah: runs. Runs."

So, despite his creator's reputation for suburban realism, Rabbit Angstrom embodies a romantic pattern which neatly matches the one sketched out by the professed existential-romantic novelist John Fowles; he rebels against the oppressiveness of the ordinary world in favor of pure immediacy, a secret place, a Well-Beloved—a nothingness that is freedom. However, another aspect of the romanticism of Fowles's Clegg is his surprising linguistic lyricism. And the lush language with which Updike presents the thoughts of the similarly uneducated, lower-middle-class Rabbit is a great deal more lyrical.

Among other things, *Rabbit, Run* is a stylistic tour de force (we have already seen how the novel uses present tense in a stylistically flashy way). Updike conveys Rabbit's consciousness with an almost Joycean luxuriousness; just as Joyce has to do with Leopold Bloom, Updike must convince us that this ordinary, literate but not literary man has such a luxurious consciousness. He does this, as Joyce does, by making the contents of his character's mind quite unexceptional—they are simply tidbits of American culture—while nonetheless conveying them with a linguistic vividness that makes the character's perception of them seem downright epiphanic. Thus, much as Fowles's Miranda would have despised it, the litany of pop songs and radio ads that we overhear through Rabbit's consciousness during his drive south, with news of the Dalai Lama folded in as a kind of leitmotif, has a hypnotic quality that is truly poetic. And such lyricism—technically the third-person narrator's, but implicitly Rabbit's—is something else that Rabbit the Romantic shares with Clegg the Romantic.

His rebellion against the clutter of the dull adult world and his quest instead for pure immediacy, for a secret place, and for a Well-Beloved, as well as the very lyricism of his stream of consciousness, place Rabbit squarely in the romantic tradition. And his underlying quest for a freedom founded on nothingness places him in a post-existentialist, even postmodernist, branch of this romantic camp that, of contemporary writers of fiction, is perhaps most prominently occupied by John Fowles.

Rabbit the Destroyer

Rabbit, then, is a romantic idealist, even a kind of hero. And for many critics, this is the last word on *Rabbit, Run.* David Galloway considers Rabbit a Camusian saint. Similarly, Joyce Markle considers him a "star player," a spiritually uplifting mystic; she compares him to Jesus Christ (47, 52). He is trying, Markle claims, to transcend the mediocre physical world, looking for "a level of meaning above the human plane" (60); and he fails not because of any inherent flaw but because the hostile world of Updike's skeptical, even nihilistic novel cannot abide mystics.

But it should already be clear—perhaps even clearer than in my discussion of the romantic dimension of Clegg (who ultimately is a nastier character)—that I do not consider Rabbit a thoroughly noble idealist. Almost as much as Clegg's, Rabbit's appealing romanticism is counterbalanced by a devotion to death and deadness, a kind of necrophilia; Rabbit's Camusian "metaphysical rebellion" is as much that of Sade as that of Prometheus. The clash between romanticism and necrophilia in *The Collector* reflects, in a starkly schematic way, the key Fowlesian dialectic of idealism and mechanical materialism; in *Rabbit, Run,* a similar clash establishes an Updikean dialectic that Joseph Waldmeir calls a conflict between transcendentalism and pragmatism, but that is perhaps more simply equated with the often-discussed "yes, but" quality of Updike's fiction. (Correcting a misunderstanding of the "yes, but" principle, Updike told a *Paris Review* interviewer, "No, I meant my *work* says, 'Yes, but.' Yes, in *Rabbit, Run,* to our inner urgent whispers, but—the social fabric collapses murderously" [Plimpton 439–40].) Joyce Markle lauds Rabbit for his transcendent, "upward-oriented . . . concept of life" and declaims the "horizontal, social orientation" of characters like the Episcopal priest Jack Eccles (47). But the Christian Updike claims to have been branded, in his youth, "with a Cross . . . an obdurate insistence that at the core of the core there is a right-angled clash . . ." ("Dogwood Tree" 181). This Cross, this right-angled clash, points in two directions:

vertically *and horizontally*. And however admirable Rabbit's idealism—his vertical-directedness—may be, his relations with the
social, horizontal world are frequently deadly.

"That's what you have, Harry: life," Rabbit is told by the elderly
Mrs. Smith, for whom he has worked as a gardener during his
truancy from marriage and family. "It's a strange gift and I don't
know how we're supposed to use it but I know it's the only gift we
get and it's a good one" (207). Mrs. Smith sounds oracular here, and
critics who canonize Rabbit often call attention to this little
speech, as if it is the hidden key that clinches their point. The
speech, however, is not hidden at all—it virtually pummels the
reader, and the context of the speech drenches it in irony. First of
all, Mrs. Smith, immediately previously, has not seemed like a very
good oracle: while delivering her proclamation, she has been
utterly unconscious of her surroundings (little Nelson has been
spitting out the candy she gave him into daddy Rabbit's hand).
More importantly, within two weeks, this man whom she has been
praising for his gift of life will have indirectly caused the death of
his baby daughter Becky. Indeed, Ruth sounds just as oracular as
Mrs. Smith when she tells Rabbit, at the end of the novel, "You're
Mr. Death himself. You're not just nothing, you're worse than
nothing. You're a rat, you don't stink, you're not enough to stink"
(279). Rabbit is not only a dreamer, he is also a destroyer: he
injures women—including Ruth, Lucy Eccles, and, of course,
Janice—by reducing them to objects; his selfishness leads to the
literal death of Becky; and his devotion to holes, to nothingness,
metaphorically annihilates the world itself.

It is true that Rabbit's sexual voracity is not simply the result of
overactive hormones, that Rabbit is an idealist. But as Peter
Conradi has said in his analysis of *The Collector,* sexual idealism is
not as sweetly romantic as it is cracked up to be: "The puritan and
destructive power of sexual idealism confused with gentility and
male power is a commonplace symptom within the culture of the
West—one within which women have long felt cruelly imprisoned
and from which they increasingly urgently seek escape. Fowles
addresses himself to it in all his books" (37). Updike also reveals
the dark, necrophiliac side of sexual idealism. We have already
seen how Rabbit is attracted precisely to Ruth's seeming nothingness—her "blue-eyed nothing, the nothing she told him she did,
the nothing she believes in." There is something rather mystical
about such a concept; Ruth is for Rabbit a kind of *via negativa.* But
there is also something antihuman and deadly.

A human being is not a *via negativa,* and Rabbit must force Ruth
to act like one; beneath the idealism, then, there is—as with Clegg

and Miranda—a sadistic power game going on here, a struggle by the man to reduce the woman to an object. From a feminist perspective, at least, this surely explains why he demands that she be clean and unencumbered with a diaphragm when he has sex with her: he wants nothing to touch her but himself. As early as their first night together he reveals his possessiveness, his desire to "collect" Ruth: "Ruth tenses at his threat to bite, and her hands shove at his shoulders, but he clings there, his teeth bared in a silent exclamation, crying out against her smothering throat that it is not her body he wants, not the machine, but her, her" (77).

"I made you," he tells her later (103), and later still we are told that her body hardens him "all over with the chill clench of ownership" (133). Like Miranda, however, Ruth reveals that she is not some butterfly to be collected; in a rare departure from Rabbit's point of view, Updike switches for a few pages to Ruth's stream of consciousness, highlighting our sense that she is neither an object for Rabbit to possess nor a nothingness within which his freedom can roam (136–40). Rabbit himself increasingly senses this fact; his idealism, like that of other romantics, remains unsatisfied, and he repeats his quest. First, however, he reifies her in a brutal, sadistic way.

Camus says of Sade that he uses "the sexual instinct" as "the blind force that demands the total subjection of human beings, even at the price of their destruction" (38). Rabbit's treatment of Ruth in the infamous fellatio scene is perhaps not so apocalyptically devastating, but it is qualitatively similar.

Superficially, the fact that Rabbit and Ruth—and implicitly Updike—make such a fuss about oral sex has dated the novel a bit; that fellatio is an act which dare not speak its name now seems a bit quaint:

> She asks, "Are you sure we're talking about the same thing?"
> "What do you think we're talking about?" He's too fastidious to mouth the words.
> She says.
> "Right," he says.
> "In cold blood. You just want it." (173)

But that last statement of Ruth's is not quaint. Regardless of the particular act, it is the coldbloodedness of Rabbit in this scene that makes it truly shocking. The point is not that Rabbit and Ruth perform an act of oral sex; the point is that Rabbit, for all intents and purposes, rapes Ruth, bullies her into engaging in sex against her will in order to dominate her, to reduce her to his property. In Camus's words, he demands her "total subjection":

> "... I need to see you on your knees."
> "Well just that—"
> "No. Not just that."
> ... "If I did it what would it prove?"
> "It'd prove you're mine." (174)

And when Jack Eccles telephones Rabbit right after this grisly interaction, the voice he hears is clearly not that of the romantic dreamer he has come to love; it is Rabbit the Destroyer:

> "Hello." A man's voice, but not Harry's. It is more sluggish and brutal than that of his friend.
> "Is Harry Angstrom there?" Sunglasses mock his sunk heart; this is not the number.
> "Who's this?"
> "My name is Jack Eccles."
> "Oh. Hi."
> "Is that you, Harry? It didn't sound like you. Were you asleep?"
> "In a way." (176–77)

This scene contains the most flamboyant example of Rabbit's brutal reification of women, but it is hardly the only example. Rabbit treats Jack Eccles's wife Lucy, for instance, with a leaden, witless machismo that ought to make even his most dedicated supporters wince:

> "Angstrom. Of course. Aren't you the one who dis-appeared? The Springers' son-in-law?"
> "Right," he replies smartly and, in the mindless fol-low-through, a kind of flower of coordination, she hav-ing on the drop of his answer turned with prim dismissal away from him, slaps! her sassy ass. Not hard; a cupping hit, rebuke and fond pat both, well-placed on the pocket. (112)

A flirtation between Rabbit and Lucy Eccles begins here that will surface periodically throughout the book. And the flirtation ends with a scene in which, before coolly rejecting her possible sexual favors, he luxuriates in the feeling of power over her: "He knows only this: underneath everything, under their minds and their situations, he possesses, like an inherited lien on a distant piece of land, a dominance over her, and that in her grain, in the lie of her hair and nerves and fine veins, she is prepared for this dominance" (222).

This final interaction with Lucy leads up to the book's other notoriously shocking episode, the drowning of baby Becky. And, as with the fellatio scene, the superficial shock value of this section of the book has faded with time, while the underlying chilly brutality of Rabbit has emerged more starkly. At the very beginning of the episode, he is feeling "jazzed" by Lucy Eccles (whether or not she really wanted him to sleep with her is of no consequence to Rabbit in this solipsistic mood—he is absorbed in his own power), and he returns to his apartment "clever and cold with lust" (224). And now the problem with home is not that it is crowded with the dull trappings of middle-class suburbia; it is simply that Janice, having just given birth to Becky, does not feel up to sex. "Why can't you try to imagine how I *feel?*" she asks him; "I've just had a baby." But Rabbit answers, with calm selfishness, "I can. I can but I don't want to, it's not the thing, the thing is how *I* feel. And I feel like getting out" (230). Which he does, again, leaving Janice to become depressed and drunk and to drown the baby. It is this, among too many other things, that drives Ruth to call him "Mr. Death."

Similar considerations cause George Hunt, one of the wisest of all Updike critics, to call Rabbit a "Nothing-man." Hunt does not use this term flatteringly, as some existentialists (Fowles, perhaps) might. From Hunt's philosophically Christian position, creation—being—is good, and evil is precisely that which lacks this is-ness; a Nothing-man, therefore, is an evil man, an anti-saint: "Just as the opposite of goodness is Nothingness, so too the opposite of a good man is a Nothing-man" (46). And although Hunt is a good deal more sympathetic toward Rabbit than a number of critics are, he sees this destructive quality in the background of virtually all of Rabbit's actions: "The two major fascinations of Rabbit—basketball and sex—are always intermixed in his mind with the imagery of Nothingness, emptiness, darkness, holes, and the like. Even his positive instincts reflect the grip of the powers of Nothingness" (47). Therefore, Rabbit's devotion to nothingness (previously discussed as an example of his heroic "romanticism"), although it may be partially or wholly motivated by a desire to transcend the ordinary, has a dark, annihilating dimension. Like Clegg's, Rabbit's passion sounds substantially, if not tonally, like that of Camus's metaphysically rebellious Sade: "His inordinate thirst for a form of life he could never attain was assuaged in the successive frenzies of a dream of universal destruction" (36–37).

I have argued, however, that even the most distasteful element of Clegg's characterization—his destructive possessiveness—has a

somewhat positive existential significance within the Fowlesian
schema: Clegg's attachment to dead things mirrors Sade's (and
Fowles's) absolutely uncompromising rebellion against nature and
God. And some critics, notably canonizer Galloway, try even more
staunchly to claim that Rabbit's destructive actions are really
positive. For Galloway, Rabbit only seems destructive to those
characters who lack his transcendent vision. If Rabbit's behavior
appears necrophiliac, the problem is perspectival; from the standpoint of the dull everyday world, life looks like death:

> Updike portrays Rabbit as a contemporary saint who
> cannot resist the search for truth, even when the search
> ironically converts him into an ominous figure of death.
> The reader is constantly reminded that Rabbit has a gift
> to give man. . . . Strangled beneath the net of traditional
> Christian Humanism, Eccles, Janice, Ruth, and Rabbit's
> parents cannot recognize this gift. In fact, the love and
> integrity which Rabbit offers is so antithetical to their
> world that it appears poisonous. (32)

But it is one thing to say, as I said when discussing Clegg, that
destructiveness can represent a violent and uncompromising rejection of God, and quite another to say that it is an embodiment of
"love and integrity." In the final section of this chapter, I will
propose a resolution of the antithesis set up by *Rabbit, Run,* a
resolution that is as different from that of *The Collector* as Kierkegaard is from Camus, and as Updike is from Fowles. For now,
however, I simply maintain that the ambiguities within Rabbit's
positive/negative characterization stand; they are a manifestation
of the "yes, but." Updike himself describes the "insolvable prob-
lems" of *Rabbit, Run* in this way:

> There is no reconciliation between the inner, intimate
> appetites and the external consolations of life. You want
> to live forever, you want to have endless wealth, you
> have an endless avarice for conquests, crave endless
> freedom really. And yet, despite the aggressive desires,
> something within us expects no menace. But there is no
> way to reconcile these individual wants to the very real
> need of any society to set strict limits and to confine its
> members. *Rabbit, Run,* which is a book much on my
> mind lately, I wrote just to say that there is no solution.
> It is a novel about the bouncing, the oscillating back and
> forth between these two kinds of urgencies until, even-

tually, one just gets tired and wears out and dies, and
that's the end of the problem. (Gado 92)

I think that Updike has exaggerated, here, the negative, fatalistic
tone of his novel. But he has very eloquently summed up the way
the tension between Rabbit's desire to transcend the "stuff" of his
world and his need to attend to such stuff is an essential tension in
the book. To call Rabbit Angstrom either a saint or a monster is to
miss this point.

Rabbit the Theist

" 'God' is not," says John Fowles in *The Aristos;* "but its not-
being is universally present, and universally affects" (23). Despite
his atheism, then, Fowles is really a kind of mystic. He considers
the very nonexistence of a supreme being to provide an always-
present absence that allows individual human beings not only to
be free but to experience freedom's potentiality: "The ubiquitous
absence of 'God' in ordinary life is this sense of non-existing, of
mystery, of incalculable potentiality; this eternal doubt that hovers
between the thing in itself and our perception of it; this dimension
in and by which all other dimensions exist. The white paper that
contains a drawing; the space that contains a building; the silence
that contains a sonata; the passage of time that prevents a sensation
or object continuing for ever; all these are 'God' " (27). In many
ways, Rabbit's idealism—in both its constructive and destructive
forms—is a Fowlesian kind of negative mysticism. Insofar as he is a
"Nothing-man," in search of those holes, gaps, spaces of nothingness that allow him to experience his own free self and nothing
else, he is in quest of this God that is not.

But if Rabbit's idealism is dialectical, containing both a heroic
and a sadistic dimension, his religious attitudes are even more
definitely so. Rabbit is not just looking for the hole in the world
through which his private self can escape; he makes it quite clear
that the God he is in search of is not nothing but something, some
Thing, a being with actuality as well as transcendence. Rabbit is
looking beyond the crowded stuff of his suburban world not (or
not always) to annihilate that world but precisely to find this
something. He says to Jack Eccles: " 'Well I don't know about all this
theology, but I'll tell you, I *do* feel, I guess, that somewhere behind
all this'—he gestures outward at the scenery; they are passing the
housing development this side of the golf course, half-wood half-
brick one-and-a-half stories in little flat bulldozed yards holding

tricycles and spindly three-year-old trees, the un-grandest land-scape in the world—'there's something that wants me to find it' " (120).

Updike's preference for the thought of German Protestant theo-logian Karl Barth is well-known. Updike himself has described Barth as "the most prominent, prolific, and (it seems to me) persuasive of twentieth-century theologians" ("Faith" 273). And Rabbit's theology, if it can be called that, is similarly Barthian. His devotion to the forces of death and nothingness is at least partially offset (redeemed?) by a Christian/Barthian devotion to Being, to a God who most decidedly *is*. And it is this notion of a substantial something beyond the self that, beneath all the similarities, ulti-mately distinguishes *Rabbit, Run* from *The Collector,* and John Updike from John Fowles. So let us look at the way Barth's theology of substantiality is presented in *Rabbit, Run,* and in the next section of this chapter, we will see how this theology generates— as a theology of absence does, in a different way, for Fowles—a narrative founded on repetition.

" 'God,' " says Fowles, careful to place the word in quotation marks "to except it from its common meanings," "is a situation. Not a power, or a being, or an influence" (*Aristos* 22). It is precisely such a reduction of God to a human concept that Karl Barth fights vigorously. God, for Barth, cannot be defined in mythical, psycho-logical, or historical terms, and God is certainly not just a "situa-tion." God is "wholly other"—this is the key Barthian term for describing God's ontological independence from human experi-ence (quite a different thing) of the divine.

This stress on the radical difference between God and humans may sometimes lead Barth (along with Updike) toward apophatic theology, the *via negativa,* which would ironically place him in Fowles's camp after all. Ultimately, though, God is not only tran-scendent for Barth, but is also particular. God's being, although it cannot be tied down to humanly defined concepts, has substance, even personality. When Paul is dazzled by his religious vision, he is dazzled, Barth asserts, not by a mystical obliteration of being but by an actual and distinct being: "This man evidently sees and hears *something* which is above everything, which is absolutely beyond the range of my observation and the measure of my thought" (62– 63, my italics). And this something, though it is beyond human observation and thought, nonetheless has content—a story, which is contained very specifically in the Bible. Barth's "evangelical" theology is founded on the particular biblical revelation of God's thoughts, words, and actions:

It is not the right human thoughts about God which
form the content of the Bible, but the right divine
thoughts about men. The Bible tells us not how we
should talk with God but what he says to us; not how we
find the way to him, but how he has sought and found
the way to us; not the right relation in which we must
place ourselves to him, but the covenant which he has
made with all who are Abraham's spiritual children and
which he has sealed once and for all in Jesus Christ. It is
this which is within the Bible. The word of God is within the Bible. (43)

The point of this claim, I think, is not that we should read the Bible
in a doggedly fundamentalist way, but simply that God is a being
with a specific, substantive story; God is not a "situation." "God,"
says Barth, in one of his most striking aphorisms, "is *God*" (48).

Humanity's relations with this infinitely transcendent ("wholly
other") and yet minutely particular being must necessarily be
paradoxical, a dialectical tension between a No and a Yes. Barth's
work is marked by a firm, even strident, no to the human and
merely social world. Barth asserts that "it is because *God himself*
and *God alone* lends our life its possibility that it becomes so
impossible for us to live. It is because *God* says Yes to us that the No
of existence here is so fundamental and unescapable" (169). A
human being must reject the here-and-now because it is radically
unsatisfying: "He does not cry for solutions but for salvation; not
for something human, but for God, for God as his Saviour from
humanity. . . . The answer pointed to in his life's relationships, the
subject implied by his life's predicates, the meaning hinted at in his
life's runes, the end suggested by the abortive beginnings which
together constitute his life's endeavor—the reality, in a word, lies
beyond the sea of his experience, always beyond" (190–91).

But the No by itself, Barth says, can lead no one to God. This
negative religious way, the "way of self-criticism," can affirm what
humanity is not, but not what God is: "The only part of our
assertion of which we are *certain,* the only part we can *prove,* is
that man is negatived, negated" (204). A Yes is needed, an affirmation about what this particular being, God, is like. And for Barth,
whatever the value of dogmas and orthodoxy may be, this Yes is
most clearly stated simply by the Apostles' Creed, "with all its
hardness" (201). This is not to say that the creed thoroughly
contains God; such an idea would deny God's transcendent otherness. A dialectician to the end, Barth claims that God is the "living

center" on which both the Yes and the No are founded; neither movement alone can be a way to God: "Our task is to interpret the Yes [by] . . . the No and the No by the Yes without delaying more than a moment in either a fixed Yes *or* a fixed No; to speak of the glory of God in creation, for example, only to pass immediately to emphasizing God's complete concealment from us in that creation (as in Romans 8); to speak of death and the transitory quality of this life only to remember the majesty of the wholly other life which meets us at the moment of death" (207).

Two other important elements of Barth's theology require explanation prior to a discussion of the way in which *Rabbit, Run* incarnates many of its principles. First, as the above statement suggests, death is a crucially important part of the Barthian No. Death is the boundary that shows human beings, in a radical, absolute way, the incompleteness of the earthly world; "Would God be God," Barth wonders, "if he met us any other way?" (168). And finally, it is notable that Barth adds an additional dialectical step to his theological schema, especially later in his career: he softens the fierce No that he has directed at the earthly and "merely" human, and he more thoroughly espouses kataphatic theology, the *via affirmativa*. Through the Incarnation, the concrete, particular, transcendent God also became a concrete, particular, human God; so the human world itself—even its most ordinary elements and stories—ultimately can be affirmed rather than rejected.

To say that Rabbit says the Barthian "No" loudly and clearly is too obvious to merit much discussion. His tendency to run away from all his social constrictions, his search for the cosmic hole in the oppressive doughnut of life—this is Rabbit's negative religious quest. But to circumvent complaints that I am misrepresenting Barth, that he would never have countenanced such irresponsible neglect of family as Rabbit demonstrates, I must quote a particularly relevant description of Barth's No movement. In a 1919 address on "The Christian's Place in Society," Barth says:

> However we may be justified in wagging our heads over modern youth's fantastic drive for freedom, it is certain that our final attitude cannot be surprise and opposition; the youth movement of the present time in all its phases is directed against *authority for its own sake*, and whoever desires to be an educator today must . . . stand in principle upon the side of our young people. However dangerous to the things we hold most sacred the present plainly observable dissolution of the family may be,

we cannot, for all our astonishment and opposition, ignore the point that in the last analysis this is an attack
upon the *family for its own sake*; and the family has
been in truth not a holy thing but the voracious idol of
the erstwhile middle classes. (292)

Change "modern youth" and "our young people" to "Rabbit," and
"the youth movement of the present time" to "Rabbit's running,"
and Barth's words seem a perfect analysis of Rabbit's rebellion.

But showing that Rabbit says no is the easy part; indeed, George
Hunt calls Rabbit a "Nothing-man" in precisely Barthian terms: for
Hunt, Rabbit makes the negative movement without the dialectically necessary positive one. And although I think Hunt is more
correct than a canonizer like David Galloway would admit, I
nonetheless see some evidence of the primary Barthian Yes—an
affirmation of a substantial God—in Rabbit's quest. (The next
section of this chapter will be a discussion of the even more
striking way in which the character and his novel embody the
secondary Barthian Yes, the affirmation of the day-to-day world.)

I began this section with a statement that Rabbit makes to the
priest Jack Eccles—"there's something that wants me to find it"—
which by itself indicates that Rabbit is negating the ordinary world in
search, ultimately, of a substantive Other rather than mere nothingness. There are other indications of this as well. Throughout his
lengthy discussions with Eccles, Rabbit mixes the nihilistic, solipsistic assertions of a Nothing-man ("All I know is what's inside *me*. That's
all I have" [102]) with frequent statements about his intuitions of a
transcendent God. And it is clear that despite his skepticism—or,
indeed, because of it—Eccles reveres these intuitions:

"Harry," he [Jack] asks, sweetly yet boldly, "why have
you left her [Janice]? You're obviously deeply involved
with her."
"I *told* ja. There was this thing that wasn't there."
"What thing? Have you ever seen it? Are you sure it
exists?" . . .
"I tell you, I know what it is."
"What is it? What *is* it? Is it hard or soft? Harry. Is it
blue? Is it red? Does it have polka dots?"
It hits Rabbit depressingly that he [Jack] really wants to
be told. Underneath all this I-know-more-about-it-than-you
heresies-of-the-early-Church business he really wants to be
told about it, wants to be told that it is there, that he's not
lying to all those people every Sunday. (125)

Eccles is not the only person with whom Rabbit shares his intimations of immortality (or of an immortal Other). With Ruth—who is for Rabbit to a large degree an embodiment precisely of the nothing rather than the something—Rabbit also experiences, and talks about, this transcendent God. I have already noted how Rabbit's very first sexual encounter with Ruth evokes images of nothingness—a nearby church's rose window seems like "a hole punched in reality" (78). But we should also note that this hole itself is dialectical: it is a No, annihilating reality, but it also leads to a Yes, a light beyond. The entire passage reads, "There is only the church across the way, gray, grave, confident. Lights behind its rose window are left burning, and this circle of red and purple and gold seems in the city night a hole punched in reality *to show the abstract brilliance burning underneath*. He feels gratitude to the builders of this ornament, and lowers the shade on it guiltily" (78, my italics). So as Rabbit begins his nothingness-bound, and ultimately brutal, relationship with Ruth, he is at least partially aware of another way of saying no—a way of punching through the ordinary in order to reveal something, rather than nothing, beyond. He proceeds to talk about God with her—"Well now if God doesn't exist, why does anything?" (87)—with a conviction that she finds more than a little exasperating.

Later, having walked with Ruth up Mt. Judge to the "Pinnacle Hotel" (the religious suggestions of this trek and its destination are obvious), Rabbit has one of his most vivid intuitions of God's being. This experience is linked, in a quintessentially Barthian way, with the notion of death:

> His day has been bothered by God: Ruth mocking, Eccles blinking—why did they teach you such things if no one believed them? It seems plain, standing here, that if there is this floor there is a ceiling, that the true space in which we live is upward space. Someone is dying. In this great stretch of brick someone is dying. The idea comes from nowhere: simple percentages. . . . He moves his eyes to find the spot; perhaps he can see the cancer-blackened soul of an old man mount through the blue like a monkey on a string. He strains his ears to hear the pang of release as this ruddy illusion at his feet gives up this reality. (108)

This trek up the mountain is only a rehearsal for Rabbit's even more overwhelming death-related epiphany at the book's sublime/ghastly finale—at his daughter Becky's funeral, and afterwards when he runs up Mt. Judge again, "Uphill exultantly" (272). Critic

Edward Vargo sees this as Rabbit's great moment of grace: "The Grace comes to Rabbit; he feels a harmony and unity of purpose in all of existence at this moment." For Vargo, this is the moment when Rabbit unequivocally — if only temporarily — achieves a transcendent Barthian No-that-is-a-Yes: "At last he has found the hole through which to move toward the beyond. Death has become for him a matter of joy in new life rather than a cause of fear and mourning" (75).

Vargo judges this climactic scene to be unambiguously epiphanic; even Rabbit's cruel graveside proclamation about Janice ("*She's* the one [who killed Becky]'") is, for Vargo, merely Rabbit's "instinctive reaction to his realization that she [Janice] is still earthbound, unwilling to cast her guilt on Christ, an impediment that blocks his communion with the transcendent" (76). Vargo's reading of Updike is almost Manichaean in its insistence that the world of matter — represented here by Janice — is a "trap" (69) to be transcended and that Rabbit's ultimate failure really to escape this trap is unfortunate. As I will explain shortly, I find Updike's theology of substantiality — epitomized by his affirmation of Kierkegaardian repetition — much more "earthbound" than Vargo takes it to be, and I find Rabbit's behavior at the graveside, therefore, partially cruel and irresponsible. Nonetheless, some sort of epiphany does occur here. The novel reveals here, as it does frequently, that the Grail which Rabbit is pursuing is not entirely equatable with a Sartrean nothingness.

As the narrator of *Rabbit, Run* puts it, Rabbit's "feeling that there is an unseen world is instinctive, and more of his actions than anyone suspects constitute transactions with it" (217). Rabbit is hardly Paul or John of the Cross, but he does seem to have some kind of faith in, or at least a hope for faith in, a something beyond himself. His desire for a hole in which his sole self can be absolutely free, which is the source of his Sade-like desire to annihilate his surroundings, is in a dialectical tension with an alternate desire. And Karl Barth calls such painful hope an introduction to his entire theological scheme: "According to the eighth chapter of Romans, there is more hope when one sighs *Veni Creator Spiritus,* than when he exults as if the spirit were already his. You have been introduced to 'my theology' if you have heard this sigh" (134).

In his balance of romanticism and a kind of sadistic necrophilia, Rabbit is an uncanny mirror image of the very unsavory Fowlesian "hero" Frederick Clegg. And his novel, or novel sequence, itself mirrors the Fowles novel in its structural dependence on a device that, in J. Hillis Miller's terms, can make narrative an annihilatingly

deconstructive activity: repetition. But insofar as he hears the
"sigh" described by Barth, Rabbit hears a sound that could never
penetrate the fictional universe of John Fowles. It is this sigh that
transforms Rabbit's repetition into something quite different from
Clegg's.

Repetition

We have seen how the two movements in *The Collector—*
Clegg's romantic-heroic quest for the ideally, even spiritually,
beautiful and his destructive drive to reduce all to dead matter—
issue in two equal and opposite narrative repetitions: the ideally
beautiful always fades and dies, so the quester must continually
seek another embodiment of beauty; and life always springs up
around dead matter, so the killer must destroy again. These two
kinds of repetition define the structures of, respectively, the
romance and the thriller, the two literary genres that Fowles plays
with in his novel. Both forms can be diagrammed as circles,
whirling around an absent center. When superimposed upon each
other, as they are in *The Collector,* the circles themselves are, in a
sense, annihilated, canceled out, leaving neither substantial center
nor substantial circumference. So Fowles has, with this novel,
devised a repetitive narrative structure which assures that his
central character's impulses toward both creativity and destructiveness will generate a third, and most important, Fowlesian term:
nothingness/freedom. In J. Hillis Miller's terms, this is a pure form
of Nietzschean repetition.

It should be clear by now that, in *Rabbit, Run,* Updike sets up a
rather similar conflict between his central character's creative and
destructive impulses. And each of these impulses is constituted,
narratively, by similar kinds of repetition: Rabbit seeks a secret
place and a Well-Beloved but, finding something less, he must start
the quest again; Rabbit tries to reduce people and things to his
objects but, finding them incorrigibly resilient, he must try again
and again. However, the third term of this Updikean process,
sketched out in *Rabbit, Run* almost as purely as Fowles's schema is
sketched in *The Collector,* is not nothing but something, a reality
beyond self as actual and particular as the Barthian/Christian God.
The center of the circle, then, is not an absence but a presence; the
circle itself, the narrative action that constitutes the novel, is not
obliterated into a mystical/existential nothingness but is instead
affirmed into actuality, being-ness. And Updike accomplishes this,
narratively, by making use of a form of repetition that is essentially
Kierkegaardian: it is founded on a Christian belief in presence

rather than absence, but it nonetheless contains all of the unpredictability and surprise of the kind of repetition that J. Hillis
Miller calls "Nietzschean."

Miller considers a theory of repetition that is founded on what
he calls "Christian affirmation" (16) to be fundamentally Platonic,
not Nietzschean. A Platonic repetition, for Miller, presumes a pre-
modernist world of substantive things rather than the deconstructionist world constituted by mere plays of difference: Miller's
Platonic repetition is an exact image of an ontologically solid
model. And this concept of repetition, Miller claims, is the source
of a rather naive mimetic literary theory:

> "Platonic" repetition is grounded in a solid archetypal
> model which is untouched by the effects of repetition.
> All the other examples are copies of this model. The as-
> sumption of such a world gives rise to the notion of a
> metaphoric expression based on genuine participative
> similarity or even on identity, as when Gerard Manley
> Hopkins says he becomes Christ, an "afterChrist,"
> through the operation of grace. A similar presupposi-
> tion, as Deleuze recognizes, underlies concepts of imita-
> tion in literature. The validity of the mimetic copy is
> established by its truth of correspondence to what it
> copies. This is, so it seems, the reigning presupposition
> of realistic fiction. (6)

Although Miller acknowledges that this theistic/mimetic form of
repetition does sometimes coexist with the radical, anticonven-
tional Nietzschean variety, he thinks that any worldview founded
on a belief in a solid, objective reality—and especially, I take it, on
a belief in a God—is essentially governed by this naive, reductive
idea of repetition-as-imitation.

Kierkegaard's concept of repetition, however, is thoroughly
Christian without being in the least naive or simplistic and without
leading to a view of art as simply, predictably imitative. Kierkegaard introduces a concept of repetition which perhaps allows
postmodernist ambiguity to be theological rather than radically
skeptical—not to reveal nothingness but rather to bring "the
hidden spark or spirit back into the open," as J. Hillis Miller
himself, in the MLA Address quoted in my introduction, suggests
that deconstruction can do. It is this kind of repetition, described
primarily in Kierkegaard's *Repetition* and secondarily in *Fear and
Trembling,* that governs the world inhabited by Rabbit Angstrom.

Repetition, one of the most consciously literary of Kierkegaard's works, is actually a kind of novel. The pseudonymous

author (a stand-in for Kierkegaard or a thoroughly fictional narrator?) Constantin Constantius tells the story of an acquaintance of his, a young man involved in an impossible romantic relationship. The young man is in love—or he *was* in love. His very consciousness of his love for a young woman distances him from her and from the immediacy of his feelings about her; even when he is with her, his reflection places her, in a sense, in the past (the relevance to *Rabbit,* with its present-tense immediacy, should be apparent). The young man, therefore, feels that to marry this young woman would be an act of cruelty; he *did* love her, but he *does not.* Consequently, his only ethical choices are either to end the relationship himself by telling the woman the truth or to induce *her* to end it by pretending to be involved with another woman.

The young man's plight leads Constantius to reflect on the distance between the ideal and the real in terms that are similar to those of the idealism-pragmatism dichotomy discussed by Joseph Waldmeir in relation to Updike. And Constantius thinks about two key romantic devices for bridging this gap: hope and recollection. Feeling alienated from the present, "hope" looks forward to fulfillment in some Utopian future, while "recollection"—something Wordsworth, of course, cherished—looks backward to a lost innocence. Unfortunately, both are unsatisfying; both leave the person in the present separated from his or her heart's desire—indeed, separated from the world altogether.

Constantius thinks, however, that there is another movement that the self can make, although neither he nor the young man is able to make it (indeed, Constantius feels that it entails a kind of miracle): repetition. Repetition bridges the gap between self and world by truly giving back to the person the world that he or she lost on achieving conscious adulthood. Repetition allows continuity between a person's past, present, and future selves; precisely because it gives back—repeats—the past, it allows all these selves to be the same self rather than a collection of fragments. Repetition, therefore, is satisfying in a way that the romanticisms never are:

> Repetition's love is in truth the only happy love. Like recollection's love, it does not have the restlessness of hope, the uneasy adventurousness of discovery, but neither does it have the sadness of recollection—it has the blissful security of the moment. Hope is a new garment, stiff and starched and lustrous, but it has never been tried on, and therefore one does not know how becoming it will be or how it will fit. Recollection is a dis-

carded garment that does not fit, however beautiful it is, for one has outgrown it. Repetition is an indestructible garment that fits closely and tenderly, neither binds nor sags. Hope is a lovely maiden who slips away between one's fingers; recollection is a beautiful old woman with whom one is never satisfied at the moment; repetition is a beloved wife of whom one never wearies, for one becomes weary only of what is new. (131–32)

Constantius's use of marriage as a metaphor for repetition is not accidental here. Marriage—the necessary/impossible commitment of self to other not just in the present but in the future, which implies a concurrent belief in the continuity of an integral self into the future—is, for Constantius (and, probably, for Kierkegaard), the key to the young man's particular case, and to anyone's ability to achieve repetition. If Kierkegaard's young man made the movement of repetition he would marry this young woman, and by a kind of magic—"by virtue of the absurd" (185), or by faith—the woman and his love for her would be recollected into the future, so to speak; the ideal would be incarnated, actualized. Kierkegaard's brand of repetition, in other words, is a way of talking about, and of bringing into human experience, the Christian paradox: the God-become-human, essence-become-existent, ideal-become-pragmatic. Repetition is the miracle, the surprising gift from God, that would have allowed Thomas Hardy's Jocelyn Pierston, after losing his ideal Well-Beloved, to receive her back in the flesh, and to marry her and live with her into a ripe old age.

Two of Kierkegaard's most striking Biblical analyses illustrate this complicated notion of repetition. The first is probably his most famous, his analysis of the story of Abraham in *Fear and Trembling;* the second is the analysis of the Book of Job in *Repetition.*

The pseudonymous author of *Fear and Trembling,* Johannes de Silentio, uses Abraham as an illustration of the awesome incomprehensibility of real faith; faith, Johannes asserts, is not the automatic movement that people in a "Christian" culture take it to be. Abraham is called the Father of Faith for choosing to commit an act that from any human, ethical perspective is an atrocity: killing his son Isaac. But his belief that, in committing this human atrocity, he is obeying a higher authority (the command of Yahweh) does not in itself make Abraham a "knight of faith." The willingness to sacrifice the finite in favor of the infinite (in Barthian terms, absolutely to say No to the world) is, for Johannes, not faith but "infinite resignation"; this giving up of the ordinary for the ideal is a grand, even heroic movement, but it is infinitely less grand than faith. Abraham, the "knight of faith," is able precisely to repeat the ordinary itself. He does not merely believe that in giving up the thing in the world he loves best, his son, he is serving God; rather, he believes "the preposterous" (20), that he will receive Isaac again, not in some heavenly afterlife but in this life—"that is, by virtue of the absurd, by virtue of the fact that for God all things are possible" (46).

Kierkegaardian faith, in other words (and repetition is really the same movement), is founded in the world of the ordinary: after being negated by the transcendent, the ordinary is returned by an infinitely, absurdly gracious God. And the knight of faith himself is seemingly the most ordinary of mortals: "The instant I first lay eyes on him, I set him apart at once; I jump back, clap my hands, and say half aloud, 'Good Lord, is this the man, is this really the one—he looks like a tax collector!' . . . He belongs entirely to the world; no bourgeois philistine could belong to it more" (38–39). (Constantius/Kierkegaard could almost be describing Rabbit Angstrom here.) It is only such faith as that of Abraham, founded in a repetition of the earthly, that is able "absolutely to express the sublime in the pedestrian" (41).

And, like Abraham's, Job's God is also a God of infinite surprise within the finite. The young man in *Repetition,* deeply in despair over his impossible love, turns to Job for inspiration. The latter section of the book is dominated by the young man's reflections on Job, and, as Louis Mackey puts it, Job's story is "a different discourse altogether" that erupts into Kierkegaard's text: "The language of Job breaks through the bounds of immanence and forces a word from beyond" ("Once More" 99). The word is that "there is a repetition, after all" (Kierkegaard 212).

Job, having had everything dear to him taken away by God, has been subjected to a divine ordeal at least as terrible as Abraham's was. And by the very act of complaining to God, Job, too, exhibits a kind of absurd faith: "Job continues to take the position that he is in the right. . . . Furthermore, Job maintains his position in such a way that in him are manifest the love and trust that are confident that God can surely explain everything if one can only speak with him" (208). In his deepest agony, Job does receive an answer—the thunderstorm, the voice of God's transcendence, which blasts away Job's pain and ushers in the surprise, the miracle, the repetition:

> The storms have spent their fury—the thunderstorm is over—Job has been censured before the face of humankind—the Lord and Job have come to an understanding,

they are reconciled, "the confidence of the Lord dwells again in the tents of Job as in former days"—men have come to understand Job. *Now* they come to him and eat bread with him and are sorry for him and console him; his brothers and sisters, each one of them, give him a farthing and a gold ring—Job is blessed and has received everything *double.* —This is called a *repetition.* (212)

It is called a repetition because, although it comes through an encounter with the transcendent, the gift bestowed on Job is itself not transcendent but earthly: the ordinary human abundance that he has had before. Job, like Abraham, receives grace through and in the day-to-day.

Although both Abraham and Job receive repetitions, they do not earn them by their piety. Indeed, although their stories both end similarly with a miraculous return of the worldly, they themselves exhibit very different attitudes about their ordeals: Abraham accepts his quietly—though not without "anxiety" (28)—while Job complains vociferously. But as Barth says, the Bible is not about human beings' actions toward God but about God's actions toward human beings. What both of these stories show is that the force that controls the universe gives fortuitous, surprising gifts—repetitions. Louis Mackey very eloquently describes this God of fortuitous surprises by discussing the ultimate (and literally most down-to-earth) repetition—God's return to the human world, after the Fall, not as an awesome spirit but as a baby in a manger:

> The historical incarnation, the Christ who is also Jesus, is, like the characters and situations in farce, a fortuitous concretion. . . . Although the concretion is fortuitous (how can it be otherwise when the category to be incarnated is the Absolutely Other?), yet it *is the* concretion of the Absolutely Other and therefore the Absolutely Other itself. . . . [T]he gratuitousness of the incarnation of the Word in the man Jesus, like the second birth of every new Christian, is no accident. Although it is an absolute surprise. ("Once More" 111)

This Christian repetition, it should already be clear, is not only a surprise; it is a *redemptive* surprise. Mackey claims that the Abraham story is, for Kierkegaard, primarily a figure for that absurdity—divine forgiveness—which allows sinning human beings to possess again the world that they have tossed away (*Poet* 225). This dimension of repetition is explicitly presented within the parable of the merman in *Fear and Trembling*. The merman is a monstrous Kierkegaardian aesthete, a seducer, who attacks the perfectly innocent Agnes. Agnes defeats the merman with her very innocence; she looks at him with "absolute faith . . . and with this look she entrusts her whole destiny to him in absolute confidence" (94). The merman "breaks down"; he is unable to continue his cruel seduction of Agnes because he "cannot withstand the power of innocence" (94). But he cannot love Agnes either, because he is a monster. The only ethical thing he can do is perform an act of infinite resignation—leaving Agnes to God, he will withdraw into a monastery.

There is, however, another possibility. The merman can be saved by the miraculous, a repetition. He is enabled to "grasp the actual again," not "under his own power" but "by virtue of the absurd" (99); the person, says pseudonymous author Johannes de Silentio, "who has made the monastic movement has only one movement left, the movement of the absurd" (101). Practically speaking, this absurd movement allows the unmarriageable monster to marry Agnes after all; he is reunited with the world of actuality that his monstrous nature has cut him off from. Theologically, it means that he has been redeemed from his monstrosity; he has been forgiven.

Whether Kierkegaard himself believed in repetition, in all of its thoroughly worldly implications, is questionable: like the young man in *Repetition,* and unlike the merman, he never married his Well-Beloved, Regine Olsen. But in his peculiar description of repetition—something that is an inevitable part of any narrative, factual or fictive—he found the quintessential literary structure for capturing a Christian incarnational/redemptive worldview. It is this worldview—founded on providential, surprising, substantive repetitions rather than on repetitions of an absence (like those of *The Collector*)—that informs the universe in which Rabbit runs.

The theologian John S. Dunne crystallizes this redemptively repetitious worldview in a fable that he calls "the Parable of the Mountain," a prototype of Rabbit's own tale:

> Man, let us say, is climbing a mountain. At the top of the mountain, he thinks, is God. Down in the valley are the cares and concerns of human life, all the troubles of love and war. By climbing the mountain and reaching the top man hopes to escape from all these miseries. God, on the other hand, is coming down the mountain, let us say, his desire being to plunge himself into the very things that man wishes to escape. Man's desire is to be God, God's is to be man. God and man pass one another going

in opposite directions. When man reaches the top of the
mountain he is going to find nothing. God is not there.
... [M]an learns that climbing was a mistake and that
what he seeks is to be found only by going down the
mountain. (14)

Rabbit, like this "man," is always walking (or running) up a kind of
mountain. Indeed, in a discussion of Rabbit's mysticism, Suzanne
Uphaus reminds us that in two crucial scenes—with Ruth early in
the book, and after Becky's funeral at the end—Rabbit makes
explicitly religious pilgrimages by going up Mt. Judge (Uphaus
29). As we have seen, Rabbit's quests seem destructive as often as
they seem heroic, but nonetheless they have, at times, underpin-
nings of a search for God. In each case, however, Rabbit's attempt
to climb this mountain of transcendence is thwarted; the day-to-
day always turns up again like a bad penny, and he slides back down
into the "valley" of the "cares and concerns of human life." And
these retreats down the mountain lead Uphaus—like Vargo—to
conclude that Rabbit's story is one of futility: "Rabbit finds the
loneliness of the mountaintop too frightening, and so he flees"
(30). But if Dunne's model fits Updike's narrative, and I think it
does, then Rabbit's regressions back into the valley of ordinary
human cares are good. These repetitions turn out to be his real
experiences of what Pascal, in a passage that Updike used for his
novel's epigraph, calls "The motions of Grace." These returns to
the valley, these grace-filled repetitions, are worth examining.

We have already seen some of the ways in which Rabbit's story is
structured around a series of repetitions. Rabbit Angstrom, loaded
with angst, is continually driven to repeat a number of the patterns
that have constituted his life. The novel's opening pages have him
romantically repeating his youth by rediscovering basketball,
something that made him a high-school star: "That his touch still
lives in his hands elates him. He feels liberated from long gloom"
(11). And all his other quests—for a secret place, for a perfect
woman, for nothingness—are repetitions of this successful teen-
age quest to find a hole in a net. And all of them drive him to repeat
and repeat the single act that defines Rabbit: "he runs. Ah: runs.
Runs."

But these repetitions, it will be argued, hardly are evidence of
divine providence. They seem, if anything, to be manifestations of
the Freudian repetition *compulsion,* evidence of a human being's
instinct to slip back into inorganic materiality. Freud describes the
compulsion this way: "In what way is the instinctive connected
with the compulsion to repetition? ... *An instinct would be a*

tendency innate in living organic matter impelling it towards the reinstatement of an earlier condition, one which it had to abandon under the influence of external disturbing forces—a kind of organic elasticity, or, to put it another way, the manifestation of inertia in organic life" (158). This sounds like the kind of repetition that Fowles, with his commitment to a materialistic determinism, plays with in *The Collector;* the fact that similar repetitions occur in *Rabbit* is another indication of Updike's kinship with Fowles, but it hardly seems to represent the "motions of Grace."

There are other repetitions in the novel, however, that do not seem compulsive because they seem not to come from within Rabbit—at least not from within his personal reservoir of unconscious cravings—but from beyond him. These are the repetitions that take him by surprise and that move his narrative forward. The paradigm of these providential repetitions is the episode that, for many critics, precisely typifies the book's futility: Rabbit's aborted journey south at the beginning of the novel.

We have already seen how this journey is structurally a kind of romantic quest for the "secret place." But we have also seen that, in terms of content, the description of the journey is filled with exactly the kind of bourgeois thingness that an *aristos* like Miranda Gray would despise. And finally we have seen that the lyrical way in which Updike captures this mundane content in prose demonstrates his downright Joycean skill as a stylist. What harmonizes all these apparently contradictory dimensions of the episode is precisely the idea of Kierkegaardian repetition.

The quest is of course prompted by Rabbit's Camusian rebellion against—or Barthian "No" to—his very ordinary surroundings. But Rabbit's night-long drive shows that his world will not be denied so easily. It follows him on the radio (the songs he hears are the same he has heard countless times on stations in Mt. Judge, and they uncannily happen to deal with troubled love, running away, growing up); it seems to follow him outside his car window ("The land refuses to change. The more he drives the more the region resembles the country outside Mt. Judge" [37]); and it even seems to draw him back, like a "wizard" ("The trip home is easier. Though he has no map and hardly any gas, an all-night Mobilgas appears near Hagerstown as if a wizard waved a wand and green signs begin to point to the Pennsylvania Turnpike" [40]). It is true that this is what leads some critics, as well as Rabbit himself, to consider the journey futile; Joseph Waldmeir, who roots for Rabbit's quests for transcendence, complains that in this early episode "the vulgarity of [Rabbit's] existence travels with him on the car radio and assaults him at the drive-in restaurant" (19). But I think that this continual return—repetition—of the ordinary, of that which Rabbit is trying to escape, is ultimately a positive thing. The prose, for one thing, is lyrical, transforming "vulgarity" into something sublime. The drive-in restaurant, furthermore, is a kind of vision, the mundane apotheosized as gift, and no less than the Dalai Lama wanders through the news reports on the radio. This is the Updikean poetry of the familiar (not unlike what Dickens called, in the preface to *Bleak House,* "the romantic side of familiar things"). And even if Rabbit himself does not realize it yet—and perhaps he never will entirely—this lyricism indicates something that a reader who stays with Rabbit for the entire novel series *will* eventually realize: grace, in the world of these novels, is a return of and to the ordinary. It is repetition.

So this quest for a secret place, which becomes just a circular automobile drive, is a paradigm of the novel's repetitions. Besides a secret place, however, Rabbit is also in quest of a transcendently perfect woman, a Well-Beloved, and this quest also generates repetition.

At first Ruth fills this Well-Beloved role, simply because she is no one: she possesses, as far as Rabbit is concerned, no content, no past history. But of course, this nothingness is only a temporary phenomenon. In another particularly fine section of writing already referred to (*Rabbit, Run* 136–40), Updike departs from Rabbit's point of view and enters Ruth's for several pages, revealing that Ruth is distinctly someone; and almost immediately afterwards, Rabbit's relationship with Ruth thickens, takes on some of the moral complicatedness (even boredom) of marriage. Of course, Rabbit rebels against this mundane familiarity—it is this more than anything else that prompts him to demand oral sex with Ruth. But ultimately the rediscovery of marital ordinariness operates as a kind of Kierkegaardian gift: a repetition, by virtue of the absurd, of his marriage to Janice.

More than Updike himself, I imagine, knew when he wrote it, *Rabbit, Run*—in light of its sequels—is a novel about marriage as repetition. Nothing in the novel is so saturated with repetition, both Freudian and Kierkegaardian, as Rabbit's relationship with his wife Janice. In obvious ways, this dull wife is just a TV rerun of the real Janice, one Rabbit remembers nostalgically as the boyhood sweetheart with whom he once engaged in romantically furtive sex: "Just a girl. Nerves like new thread. Skin smelled like fresh cotton. Her girl friend at work had an apartment in Brewer they used. Pipe-frame bed, silver medallions in the wallpaper . . ." (18). Rabbit's relationship with this woman, in other words, partially fits in with his compulsion to return to the simplicity of his basketball-star past, the compulsion that Freud calls a "manifestation of inertia in organic life." But whatever her limitations as an adult, and however imperfect this marriage is, Rabbit's continual returns to Janice, both mental and physical, seem fundamentally to exemplify that absurd repetition of the ordinary that Kierkegaard sees as the form of redemption itself.

The novel's Kierkegaardian repetition is embodied within the paradigmatic initial episode depicting Rabbit's drive south. And it is Janice herself who becomes this episode's center. During the attempted escape to that extraordinary secret place Rabbit continually receives gifts from the world of the ordinary—and thoughts about Janice are the first and last of these unasked-for gifts. These thoughts concern Janice's unpredictability (her very dopiness gives her a substantive otherness that Ruth at first lacks):

> He taps his pocket and fear hits him. He doesn't have the [car] key. Everything depends, the whole pure idea, on which way Janice was sloppy. Either she forgot to give him the key when he went out or she never bothered to take it out of the ignition. He tries to imagine which is more likely and can't. He doesn't know her that well. He never knows what the hell she'll do. She doesn't know herself. Dumb. (26)

Then there are thoughts about her ordinary cooking—

> His mind nervously shifts away from the involuntary vision of Janice's meal sizzling in the pan, chops probably, the grease-tinted water bubbling disconsolately, the unfrozen peas steaming away their vitamins. (28)

and about her panic—

> Suddenly Janice shivers in memory. . . . Poor Janice would probably have the wind up now, on the phone to her mother, somebody, wondering why her supper was getting cold. So dumb. Forgive me. (28)

> He wonders where his son slept, what Janice has done, where his parents and her parents hunted. . . . He feels the faded night he left behind in this place as a net of telephone calls and hasty trips, trails of tears and strings of words, white worried threads shuttled through the night and now faded but still existent. . . . (43)

Finally, he drifts off to sleep in his car with thoughts of Janice's body:

> There were good things: Janice so shy about showing
> her body even in the first weeks of wedding yet one
> night coming into the bathroom expecting nothing he
> found the mirror clouded with steam and Janice just out
> of the shower standing there doped and pleased with a
> little blue towel lazily and unashamed her bottom bright
> pink with hot water the way a woman was of two halves
> bending over and turning and laughing at his expression
> whatever it was and putting her arms up to kiss him, a
> blush of steam on her body and the back of her soft
> neck slippery. (43)

After all his searching, these are his secret place and his Well-
Beloved: a bathroom and Janice, his wife.

Yes, Janice is the dull net that Rabbit the Camusian rebel is
trying either to escape from (like Meaulnes) or to destroy (like
Sade). But she is also the gift—the ordinary, to which Rabbit has
said No—that he receives again (and again and again) by virtue of
the Kierkegaardian absurd. A few more examples of Janice's repetitions in *Rabbit, Run,* as well as a glimpse ahead to the Rabbit
sequels, will sufficiently suggest the bases of my contention that
Rabbit's story is essentially not about an existential rebellion of
nothing-self from substantive being but about an absurd marriage
of substantive self to substantive other.

Janice first "returns" to Rabbit via a telephone call from Jack
Eccles. Immediately after Rabbit's sadistic attempt to prove his
dominance over the world by forcing fellatio on Ruth, the world
reasserts its supremacy: Janice, Eccles tells Rabbit, has just given
birth to a girl. Rabbit's guilt-filled reunion with Janice is accompanied by his very specific realization that the substantial world,
which he thought he had rebelliously annihilated, is actually
becoming even more substantial; it is "thickening":

> Harry asks [the doctor], "Can I see her?"
> "Who?"
> Who? That "her" is a forked word now startles
> him. The world is thickening. "My my wife." (187)

Indeed, the birth of his daughter gives substance to all the people
of his life that Rabbit has tried to make nothingnesses—including
not only Janice but also Ruth. Lying in bed waiting for Janice to
return from the hospital, Rabbit experiences a very human, though
far from blissful, repetition:

> Like an unsteered boat, he keeps scraping against the
> same rocks: his mother's ugly behavior, his father's gaze

> of desertion, Ruth's silence the last time he saw her, his
> mother's oppressive not saying a word, what ails her? . . .
> No. He doesn't want to think about that. . . . Though he's
> lying there alone he feels crowded, all these people
> troubling about him not so much their faces or words as
> their mute dense presences, pushing in the dark like
> crags under water and under everything. (213–14)

The mere existence of a wife and baby has made the world of
people return with the ontological solidity of rocks—"mute dense
presences." Again, the day-to-day is repeating and, although Rabbit
does not yet see it this way, its continued ability to find him despite
his No is evidence of grace.

Of course, he runs from Janice again, but again she is returned to
him by another human absolute—not birth this time but that
Barthian absolute, death, the death of baby Becky (for which
Rabbit is partially responsible). Again Janice functions as a repetition of the ordinary precisely at the moments when Rabbit thinks
he has climbed his transcendent mountain. On the morning of the
funeral, for instance, Rabbit awakens after having had a grandly
mystical dream about founding a new religion. But what he sees on
awakening does not look like the face of God as he would have
imagined it: "He opens his eyes. Janice stands by the bed in a brown
skirt and a pink sleeveless blouse. There is a drab thickness of fat
under her chin he has never noticed before" (260).

And Janice most clearly serves this function (repeating the
mundane) at the funeral itself, when her physical ordinariness
blocks Rabbit's typically otherworldly vision: "The sky greets him.
A strange strength sinks down into him. It is as if he has been
crawling in a cave and now at last beyond the dark recession of
crowding rocks he has seen a patch of light; he turns, and Janice's
face, dumb with grief, blocks the light" (271). Rabbit, of course,
considers Janice to be a wretched distraction from his mystical
intuition, but he is mistaken. Actually, Janice prompts Rabbit to
anchor his intuition in the world of real human responsibility,
precisely by driving him to do something grotesquely irresponsible that is nonetheless founded on an attempt to perform the very
act that constitutes the Kierkegaardian/Christian repetition: the
act of forgiveness.

> "Don't look at *me,*" he says. "I didn't kill her."
> They misunderstand. He just wants this straight. He
> explains to the heads [of the people at the graveside],
> "You all keep acting as if *I* did it. I wasn't anywhere near.
> *She's* the one." He turns to her, and her face, slack as if

slapped, seems hopelessly removed from him. "Hey it's O.K.," he tells her. "You didn't mean to." (271)

This is hardly an ideal act of forgiveness, of course, and it does not make everything "O.K." Indeed, the failure of the act drives Rabbit to run again up Mt. Judge on one of those pilgrimages that Suzanne Uphaus writes of. And the novel will end after a few more inconclusive pages with Rabbit running yet again. He remains unable to accept the gifts of the ordinary that continually come his way — gifts that only a foolish sentimentalist would see as unequivocally positive, but that in the aggregate are absurdly providential. And despite Rabbit's resistance, the very structure of the novel — from that first paradigmatic drive south until this final attempt to escape from Janice's "dumb" face — reveals that the gifts are unceasing. The impingement and re-impingement of the ordinary are what spur all the actions of the book, driving Rabbit to run and yet giving him a life story which has narrative substance.

These gifts also add to Rabbit's story a dimension of surprise. Like *The Collector*, *Rabbit, Run* is an open-ended novel: it ends on the verge of a repetition of the action it began with ("he runs"). It can be read, therefore, as a kind of antinovel, a book that overturns the narrative conventions of beginning, middle, and end, a book that leaves its protagonist in the void of suspended animation ("Ah: runs") that Fowles himself will play with even more strikingly at the end of *The Magus*. But there is an important difference between this final repetition and that of the kind of antinovel which espouses radical meaninglessness. Rabbit's repetitions are Kierkegaardian rather than Nietzschean; although they are not mimetic copies of a prior model, they are founded on presence rather than absence — they are spurred by the substantial (even ordinary) world, which returns with the surprise of a providential gift. Therefore, while *The Collector* leaves us hanging structurally (having canceled out both of his narrative genres, the romance and the thriller, Fowles leaves us dangling in mid-air), we are left in no real narrative uncertainty: Clegg is on the verge of mechanically repeating his previous action, and the only imaginable sequel to his story is *The Collector* itself, word for word, all over again. But Rabbit leaves us with genuine narrative uncertainty; his story truly leaves us with a sense of ambiguous, open-ended mystery. Rabbit will receive the "real" again, no doubt, but there is no telling in exactly what form. Rabbit has a substantial, continuous self; like Abraham, Job, and the merman, Rabbit has a story that can be "recollected forward" (Kierkegaard 131).

Indeed Updike has, approximately once every decade since he wrote *Rabbit, Run,* engaged in the repetitious (in Kierkegaard's sense) task of recollecting Rabbit's story forward, and the book's first two sequels elegantly demonstrate that Rabbit's story is an embodiment of Kierkegaardian repetition. *Rabbit Redux* is the story of the return and loss and return of Janice. In this novel, Rabbit slips even more deeply than in the original into the darkest part of his guilty, private, alienated self; a kind of literary repetition of the "Circe" chapter of Joyce's *Ulysses,* the book is almost a surreal nightmare. But like Leopold Bloom's, Rabbit's story ends with a quiet repetition of marriage with his ordinary but increasingly appealing wife; the novel ends by echoing, albeit a bit more tentatively, that great final Molly Bloomian affirmation: "He slides down an inch on the cool sheets and fits his microcosmic self limp into the curved crevice between the polleny offered nestling orbs of her ass; he would stiffen but his hand having let her breasts go comes upon the familiar dip of her waist, ribs to hip bone, where no bones are, soft as flight, fat's inward curve, slack, his babies from her belly. He finds this inward curve and slips along it, sleeps. He. She. Sleeps. O.K.?" (*Redux* 352).

The repetition of *Rabbit Is Rich* is perhaps even more striking, and it is certainly more Job-like. After nearly five hundred pages of battles with his now-adolescent son Nelson, Rabbit gets a surprising gift from Nelson himself (and/or from God): Nelson's baby daughter is a repetition—different and yet the same, substantial, real, as ordinary and as miraculous as human life itself—of baby Becky:

> Oblong cocooned little visitor, the baby shows her profile blindly in the shuddering flashes of color jerking from the Sony, the tiny stitchless seam of the closed eyelid aslant, lips bubbled forward beneath the whorled nose as if in delicate disdain, she knows she's good. You can feel in the curve of the cranium she's feminine, that shows from the first day. Through all this she has pushed to be here, in his lap, his hands, a real presence hardly weighing anything but alive. Fortune's hostage, heart's desire, a grandaughter. His. Another nail in his coffin. His. (437)

I can only speculate about the ways in which the repetitions will continue in the fourth novel of the series, *Rabbit at Rest;*the book is not yet published as I write this analysis. In an interview discussing the new book, which is set in the late 1980s, Updike called it "a depressed book about a depressed man written by a depressed man" (in Roger Miller E6), so the novel apparently will not be an unambiguously optimistic portrayal of providential repetition—but then, neither are the other Rabbit books. Nonetheless, Updike said that *Rabbit at Rest* ends with a device which mimics the theatre's long revered celebration of repetition, the curtain call: "As I wrote this book I did it thinking that this was the end, and every character comes 'round and takes a little bow" (Roger Miller E6). And Updike even admitted that this novelistic curtain call, which would seem to indicate closure, the final repetition, may in fact leave room for future surprises, future repetitions, yet another sequel; talking about a rabbit that had appeared as a kind of gift and taken up residence in his yard, Updike remarked: "I worry about whether Rabbit in some other guise is coming back to demand that sequel" (Roger Miller E6).

Like *The Collector,* then, *Rabbit, Run* is an early and rather clear sketch of its author's vision. And structurally the books are uncannily similar. Although Updike's primary genre is, and will continue to be, social realism, while Fowles's genre here is the thriller, both novels are informed by a romantic existentialism, an interest in the kind of rebellion against the ordinary that Camus discusses in *The Rebel.* Like Frederick Clegg's, Rabbit Angstrom's rebelliousness is both gloriously idealistic and dreadfully destructive—an uneasy marriage of Alain-Fournier and Sade. Like the Fowles novel, furthermore, *Rabbit, Run* never resolves the tension between individual rebellion and the mundane external world. The book is open-ended; the repetition of the conflict is indefinite.

However, the difference between Updikean and Fowlesian repetition reflects a very significant difference between the two writers and their contemporary rethinkings of existentialism. Quite literally, there is nothing behind Fowles's repetitions (except, perhaps, the absolutely free will of the artist himself); they are the product of chance, of hazard, and therefore they are signs of the radical aloneness, and thus the radical freedom, of the human self in the universe. Nothingness also lurks as a dark possibility in Rabbit's story (and throughout Updike's fiction), but there is some Thing, the "wholly other" Christian God of Karl Barth's theology, behind Updike's repetitions here. Updike seems to be tentatively asserting the ontological solidity of Being—a substantial is-ness that defines the human self, giving it substance rather than nothingness, and that also transcends the human self.

This substantiality is infinitely surprising; it never has the predictability of J. Hillis Miller's Platonic repetitions. Updike's novels, then, for all their reputed realism, will continue to have a great deal of the Nietzschean volatility of Fowles's own increasingly deconstructionist writing; the parallels between these two novelists and their careers continue to be startling. But while Fowles's works fundamentally present a world of absence, a *via negativa,* the Updike *via,* although often uncertain, is finally quite *affirmativa.*

4

Biographical Excursion

As different as Fowles's and Updike's life stories are from one another (Updike is American, Fowles English; Updike is a Christian, Fowles an atheist; Updike is urban/suburban, Fowles rural), each records a similar experience as a life-changing one: a move away from his suburban childhood home to the country. And they have used uncannily similar metaphors for describing their respective youths: both of them have written autobiographical pieces that are built around memories of trees. Fowles's *The Tree* is a short philosophical book that records his attitude about nature, but a large part of it focuses on the difference between the trees of his childhood home and the trees in a forest. Similarly, Updike's "The Dogwood Tree: A Boyhood" is generally a chatty remembrance of things past, but it is sparked by thoughts about a dogwood tree that grew in the yard of his parental home. In this chapter I discuss these writers' lives and attitudes, especially as they are presented in these pieces, and I compare their uses of this key romantic, organicist image—the tree. My comparison will reveal that, like their fictions, the persons of these writers are mirror images: they are polar opposites, with opposing world views, and yet they confront each other with remarkably similar features. The comparison will primarily show, however, that the writers' respective uses of this tree image—and of their boyhood stories in general—indicate Fowles's preference for liberating nothingness, a *via negativa,* and Updike's for that *via affirmativa,* a highway through earthly things.

John Fowles and Trees

In his book *The Tree,* Fowles describes himself (not surprisingly, considering the themes he presents in *The Collector*) as a rebel. His rebellion is couched in terms of his relationship with trees: some trees represent that which he rebels against, and some represent that which his rebellious quest is aiming for.

What Fowles is rebelling against is suburbia and things suburban, and while certain suburban trees become the clearest metaphors for this detested realm, the person who philosophically stands for what Fowles resists is his father. Fowles has often called his art an Oedipal activity, and writing about secret places and romantic quests does seem strikingly opposite from the life of his commonsensical, businesslike, logical father, at least as Fowles describes him in *The Tree.*

Born in 1926, John Fowles grew up in a semi-detached house in Leigh-On-Sea, Essex, which he calls "a 1920s suburb at the mouth of the Thames, some forty miles from London" (3). And Fowles says that his father Robert was a conventional devotee of city and suburbs, and that he himself always differed from his father in this respect:

> In most outward ways he [Robert Fowles] was conventional and acutely careful not to offend the mores of the two worlds he lived in, suburbia and business London. . . . [E]very day when I was small my father, like most of his male neighbors, went off in suit and bowler to London: an hour by train there, an hour back. I very early decided that London was synonymous with physical exhaustion and nervous anxiety, and the one thing I would never be was a commuter. . . . (8–9)

His father's businesslike suburbanism extended to most areas of his life, Fowles claims. He was "intensely cautious" about money ("a trait," Fowles says, "he neither inherited from his own father nor passed on to me" [10]), and even in non-monetary matters, he had an "obsession with yield" (12). He was also an intensely logical man; though his deep affection for German philosophy was a bit anomalous, his skill as a near-professional logician was very much in keeping with the rest of his rationalistic personality: "Philosophical arguments with him," Fowles asserts, "could grow painfully like cross-examination, far more forensic than Socratic." And, again voicing his rebellion, Fowles adds, "and I have shunned the logical ever since" (17–18).

The image that Fowles uses to sum up his father is a garden. Robert Fowles was a great lover of trees; his attachment to trees, however, was thoroughly suburban—not, to his son's taste, sufficiently naturalistic: "The back garden was tiny, less than a tenth of an acre, but my father had crammed one end and a side-fence with grid-iron espaliers and cordons. Even the minute lawn had five orchard apple trees, kept manageable only by constant debranching and pruning" (3). These trees, Fowles opines, were likely "the most closely pruned, cosseted and prayed for in the whole of England" (4); allowing a tree to "grow as it liked" would, for Robert Fowles, be "a blasphemous breaking of his own eleventh commandment: Thou shalt prune all trees" (20).

The family lost this perfectly manicured garden for a while; from 1940 until 1945, the "hazards of the Second World War" (7) drove the Fowleses to a small village in Devonshire. This escape from the city and suburbs to the green countryside was John Fowles's great liberation, and all his fiction is, in a sense, a celebrative repetition of the experience. But for Robert Fowles—at least according to his son—the country was too bare. It broke apart those rigorous structures that gave his life, and garden, order:

> I sense that the memory of suburbia must have represented to my father . . . something like the famous old fellowship of the trenches, the consoling feeling of everyone being in the same boat; all genteelly in the same reduced financial circumstances, with the same vague hopes, abiding by the same discreetly agreed codes. Things were far too transparent in Devon, too close to unfair value-systems that were in turn too close to nature. . . . [H]e regarded even the shortest walks, the simplest picnics away from houses and roads as incipiently dangerous, so many steps towards total anarchy. (15–16)

When the war ended, therefore, Robert Fowles brought his family (of which at least one member was very displeased) back to Essex and to his safe, pruned, carefully controlled garden: "It was not financial caution or love of suburbia in itself, it was not anything but his trees and the sanctuary they offered . . . in no sense, in that minute garden, a physical sanctuary, but a kind of poetic one, however banal the surroundings: a place he could control" (18–19). John Fowles would become a novelist who celebrates the existential act of throwing oneself into the void, the universe ruled over by "hazard." But his father, he claims, had the opposite way of reconciling himself with hazard: "He had himself been severely pruned by history and family circumstance, and this [carefully pruned garden] was his answer, his reconciliation with fate—his Platonic ideal of the strictly controlled and safe, his Garden of Eden" (19).

His father and his father's trees become for Fowles, throughout this reflective little book, an image of many of the things that he rebels against (and yet we will see, paradoxically, he also in some ways accepts them—but that is leaping ahead). His father's garden, for instance, reminds him of that of Carl Linnaeus, whom he calls "the great warehouse clerk and indexer of nature" (24). And Linnaeus's cataloguing of species is, for Fowles, a type of that greater human tendency to analyze, isolate, collect reality instead of simply allowing it to be. It is a tendency to reduce the essentially unknowable Being-in-itself to an object, and to place the wild, immediate *now* in the past tense. Nature, from such a perspective, is "an immense green cloak for Satan" (68).

If his father's garden, along with London and its suburbs in general, is the world that Fowles rejects, the Devonshire country-side—which he visited and then was taken away from—was his own Garden of Eden:

> Despite the external horrors and deprivations of the time, they were for me fertile and green-golden years. I learnt nature for the first time in a true countryside among true countrymen, and from then on I was irre-deemably lost as a townsman. I have had to spend long years in cities since then, but never willingly, always in daily exile. I even preferred the antiquated class-system of village life, with its gentry and its 'peasants' and infi-nite grades between, to the uniformity of street after suburban street of same houses, same fears, same pre-tensions. (14–15)

Fowles's Eden, unlike his father's, is not pruned at all. "My own 'orchards,'" Fowles says, "were, from the moments I first saw them, the forgotten and increasingly deserted copses and woods of the West of England, and later, of France" (20). Indeed, Fowles now lives in a "big eighteenth-century rococo house" (Huffaker 15) that is bordered by a garden which is Edenic in a very Fowlesian way, and which Fowles's father found shockingly indecorous: "I think I truly horrified him [Robert Fowles] only once in my life, which was when, soon after coming into possession, I first took him around my present exceedingly unkempt, unmanaged and unmanageable garden. . . . He thought it madness to take on such a 'jungle', and did not believe me when I said I saw no need to take it on, only to leave it largely alone, in effect to my co-tenants, its wild birds and beasts, its plants and insects" (22).

Fowles claims that this wild garden is not an image of disorder, but of an order that is natural rather than mechanical. But it is not an order that he can describe in any definitive way; as an atheist, he believes that the natural order lacks any sort of controlling logos, and that it is therefore futile (and even destructive) to try to analyze it and its benevolent effects: "What I gain most from nature is beyond words. To try to capture it verbally immediately places me in the same boat as the namers and would-be owners of nature: that is, it exiles me from what I most need to learn. . . . To enter upon such a description is like trying to capture the uncapturable" (32–33). As it always tends to be, Fowles's mysticism here is a kind of *via negativa*—founded on mystery and silence rather than on any definable content.

Nonetheless, it is not without an image: if the trees Fowles rejects are presided over by his father, the trees he loves are themselves the home of a new, imaginative father—the "green man," who is a part of nature rather than an isolated, analytical consciousness:

> One of the oldest and most diffused bodies of myth and folklore has accreted round the idea of the man in the trees. In all his manifestations, as dryad, as stag-headed Herne, as outlaw, he possesses the characteristic of elusiveness, a power of 'melting' into the trees, and I am certain the attraction of the myth is so profound and universal because it is constantly 'played' inside every individual consciousness.
>
> This notion of the green man—or green woman, as W. H. Hudson made her—seen as emblem of the close connection between the actuality of present consciousness (not least in its habitual flight into a mental greenwood) and what seems to me lost by science in man's attitude to nature—that is, the 'wild' side of his own, his inner feeling as opposed to the outer, fact-bound, conforming face imposed by fashion—helped me question my old pseudo-scientist self. (38)

This unnamed and unnaming one is Fowles's new father, and he lurks in virtually all of Fowles's fiction.

But so far, Fowles sounds like a fairly conventional romantic nature-worshipper, one who is spending his literary adulthood trying artistically to recapture the Devonshire experience of his youth. And although this is to a large degree the case, it misses sight of the Fowles who is—as I asserted in my discussion of *The Collector*—a rigorous, atheistic, twentieth-century mechanist. The romantic "green man" is not Fowles's only father; the fiercely logical tree-pruner retains significant psychological power. The passage I have just quoted from *The Tree,* for instance, is immediately qualified by a warning against romantic anti-intellectualism. Having disparaged his own earlier scientific propensity to name (and collect), he now asserts that such analysis is to a certain degree necessary and valuable: "In the 1950s I grew interested in the Zen theories of 'seeing' and of aesthetics: of learning to look beyond things-in-themselves. I stopped bothering to identify species new to me, I concentrated more and more on the familiar, daily nature around me, where I then lived. But living without names is impossible, if not downright idiocy, in a writer; and living without explanation or speculation as to causality, little better—for Western man, at least" (38–39). Having said that naming (or categorizing or collecting) alienates an individual perceiver from the world perceived, Fowles now asserts that such activity is inevitable for thinking beings.

And then he adds another rather chilling, unsentimental twist to his discussion of people and trees. Unlike that prototypal romantic, Wordsworth, Fowles sees the natural world not as a "presence" (remember Wordsworth's joyful resolution in "Tintern Abbey": "And I have felt / A presence that disturbs me with the joy / Of elevated thoughts") but as an absence: "There is a kind of coldness, I would rather say a stillness, an empty space, at the heart of our forced co-existence with all the other species of the planet. Richard Jefferies coined a word for it: the ultra-humanity of all that is not man . . . not with us or against us, but outside and beyond us, truly alien" (40). Fowles does soften this stark position, suggesting that if we realize nature's "unconscious alienation from us," we can cease to be alienated from nature by our own knowledge, greed, and vanity; but nonetheless, his claim that nature is present-but-absent remains clear.

His final, lyrical discussion of trees generates precisely such an image of impenetrability, of absence. Fowles describes a visit to a "secret wood, perhaps the strangest in all Britain" (81); it is called "Wistman's Wood," a name likely derived "from the old Devonshire dialect word *wisht,* which means melancholy and uncanny, wraith-like" (83). And if absence can, as Sartre asserts, be experienced, that is what Fowles experiences here. Everything in the wood is alien, mysterious, secret; even an "invisible" hedgesparrow seems to sing out, "My wood, my wood, it never shall be yours" (86). The lesson that Fowles learns in Wistman's Wood, insofar as it can be articulated at all, is that absence, a faceless otherness without mediation, *is,* and that it is good: "We still have this to learn: the inalienable otherness of each, human and non-human, which may seem the prison of each, but is at heart, in the deepest of those countless million metaphorical trees for which we cannot see the wood, both the justification and the redemption" (90–91).

Fowles frequently describes his life as a chosen exile: by living in the countryside, far from literary London, he exiles himself from mainstream English culture and also from the more trendy Joycean exile on the European continent. And his autobiographical musing about trees eventually celebrates two larger philosophical gaps or exiles that delineate a kind of Camusian rebellion similar to that presented in *The Collector* (and throughout the Fowles corpus). The first exile is the rather obvious one: Fowles has exiled himself from urban and suburban culture by moving to out-of-the-way Lyme Regis. The second we have just discussed: Fowles eschews the traditional romantic notion that there is an emotional, spiritual connection between the self and its surroundings (either natural or human). Rather, he believes that mechanistic science, not some Coleridgean religion or mysticism, is the best tool we have for describing the world (as in his mechanical discussion of human thought in *The Aristos*); and he accepts the consequences of this fact—alienation.

Indeed, this double exile/alienation is precisely what, for Fowles, endows the self with a unique value. Alternately rejecting both science and Zen, *The Tree* ends up glorifying a new "man in the trees" in a new secret place: the individual self itself, which Fowles calls "the unique experiencer, the 'green man' hidden in the leaves of his or her unique and once-only being" (43). Fowles asserts that this is what art celebrates; this is what differentiates it from science (and, I assume, from religion): "What is irreplaceable in any object of art is never, in the final analysis, its technique or craft, but the personality of the artist, the expression of his or her unique and individual feeling" (42). Obviously this is a long-standing romantic position; the important point, however, is not that Fowles is not a romantic but rather that his romanticism—despite his espoused naturalism—is more like Shelley's or Blake's apocalyptic, rebellious romanticism of absence than like Wordsworth's or Coleridge's romanticism of connection and presence.

My examination of Fowles's autobiographical statement ends with three concerns Fowles mentions in *The Tree* that seem to flow directly from this double exile, dramatizing his striking similarity to and contrast with John Updike.

The first of these concerns is probably the least important, but it deserves mention both because it is a warning to Fowles's critics not to look for thoroughgoing theoretical systems in his works and also because it differentiates Fowles from the methodical Updike: Fowles claims that he does not plan his fiction and that he is generally not a very disciplined person. He claims to "have method in nothing, and powers of concentration, of patience in acquiring true specialized knowledge, that would disgrace a child" (57). He turns his haphazard treks through mysterious forests into a metaphor for his own experience of composing, and he suggests that this manner of writing is of a piece with his Devonshire exile, his desire to be not-quite-there (in the London suburbs):

> I do not plan my fiction any more than I normally plan woodland walks; I follow the path that seems most promising at any given point, not some itinerary decided before entry. . . . It is the peculiar nature of my adolescent explorings of the Devon countryside (peculiar because I had not been brought up in a rural atmosphere, could not take the countryside for granted, indeed it came to me with something of the unreality, the not-quite-thereness of a fiction) that made me what I am—and in many other ways besides writing. (55–6)

The second of these three areas of concern is an issue that, as previously noted, he deals with again and again in his writings: religion. Once again Fowles demonstrates that his avowed atheism has a paradoxically religious slant; he asserts that his love of trees, his "feeling towards woods," contains a "religious element." And he goes on to describe in a downright druidical way the sacred aura of forests:

> [Woods'] mysterious atmospheres, their silences, the parallels—especially in beechwoods—with columned naves that Baudelaire seized on in his famous line about a temple of living pillars, all these must recall the manmade holy place. . . . Even the smallest woods have their secrets and secret places, their unmarked precincts, and I am certain all sacred buildings, from the greatest cathedral to the smallest chapel, and in all religions, derive from the natural aura of certain woodland or forest settings. (58)

It should be noted how genuinely, experientially religious Fowles's attitude is here; Fowles has a profound, even liturgical, sense of religious mystery. But (again to differentiate him from the other religious writer we are considering, John Updike) Fowles's is entirely a *natural* religion; a Karl Barthian transcendent God, for Fowles, is precisely what cannot exist. Fowles's "other" is wholly immanent in nature, and is also so hidden—so absent—that it almost cannot be talked about: "In [woods] we stand among older, larger and infinitely other beings, remoter from us than the most bizarre other non-human forms of life: blind, immobile, speechless (or speaking only Baudelaire's *confuses paroles*), waiting . . . altogether very like the only form a universal god could conceivably take" (58–59). And yet, Fowles's religious view is like that of the

Barthian Updike in one way: it is erotic. Woods, Fowles says, "are in any case highly sensuous things" (59).

Perhaps the most important result of what I have called Fowles's "double exile," his exile from both suburbs and forests, is his powerful sense of individual freedom. Even as a boy, Fowles claims, he loved walking through woods because the paths were multiple—seemingly infinite—rather than determined, paved. Indeed, he considers his grown-up activity of fiction-writing to be a re-creation of that experience of freedom:

> This is the main reason I see trees, the wood, as the best analogue of prose fiction. All novels are also, in some way, exercises in attaining freedom—even when, at an extreme, they deny the possibility of its existence. Some such process of retreat from the normal world—however much the theme and surface is to be of the normal world—is inherent in any act of artistic creation, let alone that specific kind of writing that deals in imaginary situations and characters. (75)

And exile from the suburbs, from the "normal world," is not the only movement that the self must make; again, Fowles does not allow for a simple, romantic union of self and nature any more than he endorses a union of self and society. The final experience of freedom is an experience of absence, of the self—Sartre's Being-for-itself, which is nothingness—alone: "A part of that retreat must always be into a 'wild', or ordinarily repressed and socially hidden, self: into a place always a complexity beyond daily reality, never fully comprehensible or explicable, always more potential than realized; yet where no one will ever penetrate as far as we have. It is our passage, our mystery alone" (75–76).

John Updike and a Tree

On the surface, Updike's "The Dogwood Tree," written in 1960, is an inversion of everything proposed in Fowles's *The Tree*. Where Fowles rejects his suburban home and ordinary father, Updike remembers both fondly. Indeed, while Fowles's beloved trees are those growing wild in woods—the antitheses of his father's carefully pruned Essex specimens—Updike's essay is built around his loving memory of a single tree planted by his family in the side yard of his suburban childhood home: "When I was born, my parents and my mother's parents planted a dogwood tree in the side yard of the large white house in which we lived throughout my boyhood.

This tree, I learned quite early, was exactly my age, was, in a sense, me. . . . The tree was my shadow, and had it died, had it ceased to occupy, each year with increasing volume and brilliance, its place in the side yard, I would have felt that a blessing like the blessing of light had been withdrawn from my life" (151). Updike's essay, then, reveals an imagination textured profoundly differently from Fowles's; his living tree is tamed, suburban, planted by humans, rather than wild and secret. So, as we would expect, the aesthetic and philosophical views that Updike voices in this meditative piece—and further develops in his more recent book-length memoir *Self-Consciousness*—are quite different from Fowles's. And yet the piece also reveals that Updike resembles Fowles in a number of ways: like his English contemporary, Updike has an existential/romantic interest in the mystery of the human self and—though in a dissimilar manner—a religious interest in the mystery of God.

Born in 1932, Updike is Fowles's junior by six years (though this precocious American published his first novel four years before *The Collector*). Updike's upbringing, though, was certainly as suburban as Fowles's. He was born in Shillington, Pennsylvania, just outside Reading, and his memories are a litany of suburban objects. In the section of his essay titled "History" (itself indicating a more external, fact-based orientation than Fowles's in *The Tree*), Updike ruminates about "The vacant lot beside our home . . . The houses along the street . . . The high-school grounds . . . The softball field . . . the school and its boilerhouse . . . the poor farm fields . . . A little gravel alley . . . an untidy sequence of back buildings (chicken houses, barns out of plumb, a gunshop, a small lumber mill, a shack where a blind man lived . . .)" (153–54).

And Updike's thoughts about Shillington's middle-class suburbanism are not in the least tinged with an ironic distaste, as Fowles's descriptions of suburbia always are. Indeed, Updike describes with real romantic lyricism an "enchanted grotto" in Shillington, but it is no hidden, wooded retreat; it is a garage, "whose cement floors had been waxed to the lustre of ebony by oil drippings and in whose greasy-black depths a silver drinking fountain spurted the coldest water in the world, silver water so cold it made your front teeth throb" (154). In *Self-Consciousness*, Updike adds a religious resonance to such suburban lyricism; after describing the magazines, coloring books, and candy at a hometown variety store, he announces that "In Henry's Variety Store life's full promise and extent were indicated: a single omnipresent manufacturer-God seemed to be showing us a fraction of His face, His plenty. . . . Department stores, with their escalators and clouds of perfume and ranks of nylon lingerie, were like Heaven itself" (11).

Updike is also kinder than Fowles to urban (as opposed to suburban) environs. His rather autobiographical narrator in *The Centaur* considers New York a Promised Land; and Updike himself, in "The Dogwood Tree," describes the city of Reading with a kind of awe:

> To me Reading is the master of cities, the one at the cen-
> ter that all others echo. How rich it smelled! Kresge's
> swimming in milk chocolate and violet-scented toilet
> water, Grant's barricaded with coconut cookies, the vast
> velveted movie theatres dusted with popcorn and a cold
> whiff of leather, the bakeshops exhaling hearty brown
> drafts of molasses and damp dough and crisp grease and
> hot sugar, the beauty parlors with their gingerly stink of
> singeing, the bookstores glistening with fresh paper and
> bubbles of hardened glue, the shoe-repair nooks black-
> ened by Kiwi Wax and aromatic shavings, the public lav-
> atory with its emphatic veil of soap, the hushed, brick-
> red side streets spiced with grit and the moist seeds of
> maples and ginkgos, the goblin stench of the trolley car
> that made each return to Shillington a race with nau-
> sea—Reading's smells were most of what my boyhood
> knew of the Great World that was suspended, at a small
> but sufficient distance, beyond my world. (162)

Like the lengthy lists of middle-class banalities in the Rabbit books, this description of Reading—filled with images that are decidedly without glamor—has a cumulatively romantic effect. Reading, therefore, has for Updike the same dialectical significance that the country has for Fowles in *The Tree* (and throughout his fiction): it is the place "beyond my world." Nonetheless, Updike's romantic *domaine* (to use one of Fowles's favorite words) is loaded with content, with stuff (ordinary stuff at that); it has, therefore, a different tone—indeed, a different metaphysic—than Fowles's.

But despite his fascination with Reading, the very middle-class, suburban Shillington was the young Updike's home, and Updike asserts that he was anything but a rebel against it ("I was not," he says, "a very daring boy" [156]—a statement that would seem to bar him from the league of metaphysical rebels). Indeed, he claims that his parents always considered Shillington merely a temporary home, but that he himself "belonged to the town" (155).

He also, he asserts, was quite happy to belong to his father. Wesley Updike was a teacher at Shillington's public high school, and his position was one of the things that gave his son a feeling of belonging, that established John Updike's powerful sense of place:

"My father's job paid him poorly but me well; it gave me a sense of, not prestige, but *place*. As a school-teacher's son, I was assigned a role; people knew me. When I walked down the street to school, the houses called, 'Chonny.' I had a place to be" (166). Updike's special place is not a nowhere; it is not a secret Eden that is always absent. Rather, it is very distinctly somewhere—Shillington, Pennsylvania—a town loaded with particular and mundane things. And likewise his father is not an absence, neither a victim of Oedipal annihilation nor an imaginary "green man." He is a presence, a living face, no less ontologically solid and particular for being mysterious and awe-inspiring:

> All the years I was at the elementary school the high school loomed large in my mind. . . . It was there that my father performed his mysteries every day. . . . At the end of each summer, usually on Labor Day Monday, he and I went into his classroom, Room 201, and unpacked the books and arranged the tablets and the pencils on the desks of his homeroom pupils. Sharpening forty pencils was a chore, sharing it with him a solemn pleasure. To this day I look up at my father through the cedar smell of pencil shavings. To see his key open the front portals of oak, to share alone with him for an hour the pirate hoard of uncracked books and golden pencils, to switch off the lights and leave the room and walk down the darkly lustrous perspective of the corridor and perhaps halt for a few words by an open door that revealed another teacher, like a sorcerer in his sanctum, inscribing forms beside a huge polished globe of the Earth— such territories of wonder boyhood alone can acquire. (169–70)

Such a memory of his father will be, in more ways than one, the seed of Updike's novel of education, *The Centaur,* and it is interesting to note how Updike's language ("like a sorcerer in his sanctum") evokes the world of Fowles's novel of education, *The Magus.* But it is also noteworthy that Updike's primary sorcerer is no mysterious illusionist on a faraway Greek island; he is merely a high-school teacher—and Updike's own father.

A psychoanalytic theorist would perhaps suggest that this difference between the two writers' attitudes about their fathers— one rebels Oedipally and creates an absent darkness in his father's place, while the other would "look up at" his father amid mundane but very solid surroundings—explains the religious differences between Fowles and Updike. Fowles's god, like his father, is *not,* while Updike's God is transcendent, wholly other and wholly substantive. But I reject this psychoanalytic position, as appealing as it is, because its causality is too pat. Atheism and rebellion against a father are parts of a Fowlesian pattern (a pattern founded on absence), as Christianity and reverence for a father are parts of an Updikean one (founded on some kind of presence). I am examining these patterns from as many perspectives as possible; I do not think that any one psychological key explains them.

In any case, the Updikean pattern does not include a romantic love of forests. In fact, if Updike mentions any youthful rebellion in "The Dogwood Tree," it is a rebellion against the very thing that Fowles claims to have always craved: walks in the woods. Updike describes his intense distaste for the "peace and solace"—the mysterious Fowlesian hush—of the woods: "I disliked these walks. . . . In the woods I would hurl myself against dead branches for the pleasure of feeling them shatter and of disturbing whatever peace and solace my parents were managing to gather. . . . I was a small-town child. Cracked pavements and packed dirt were my ground" (158). It is not surprising that the end of Updike's idyll is the event that marked the beginning of Fowles's: Updike's family, like Fowles's, moved away from the suburbs, to the country. Leaving the tame, cultivated dogwood tree for a home doubtless surrounded by the wild trees that Fowles prefers, the young Updike felt that he was deserting his very self: "Against the broad blank part [of the Shillington house] where I used to bat a tennis ball for hours at a time, the silhouette of the dogwood tree stood confused with the shapes of the other bushes in our side yard, but taller. I turned away before it would have disappeared from sight; and so it is that my shadow has always remained in one place" (187).

And although he never again lived in Shillington—from the family farm ten miles outside the town, Updike proceeded to Harvard, then Oxford, then New York, and finally a series of increasingly wealthy Boston suburbs—he never was what Fowles calls a "countryman" again. As a still-frequent contributor to *The New Yorker* (Frederick Crews has somewhat sarcastically called him a "genially urbane *New Yorker* essayist" [14]), Updike has hardly exiled himself from the urban/suburban literary scene. Nor has he exiled himself from the social scene. In the 1960s, he said that he was very active in the Ipswich, Massachusetts, community: "I'm on the Congregational church building committee," he told a *Paris Review* interviewer, "and the Democratic town committee, and while the *Couples* fuss was in progress . . . I was writing a pageant for our Seventeenth-century Day" (Plimpton 431). And in 1989's *Self-Consciousness,* he paints a detailed portrait of himself as someone still deeply involved in ordinary New England society. Indeed, he links his active Christianity with his need to rub elbows with fellow townspeople: "Of churchgoing, it might be added that it is among other things a social exercise, what small towns have where they lack concert halls and opera houses. . . . Church in a small town is one of the places 'where the people are,' and the only cultural institution dealing in two-thousand-year-old rites and six thousand years of history" (250–51).

Updike's love of suburbia and dislike of the country is obviously a direct inversion of John Fowles's attitudes, and the fact that both state their preferences in essays built around trees is a handy coincidence. But Updike's suburbanism is more than an interesting biographical tidbit; as much as Fowles's naturalism, Updike's devotion to the day-to-day ordinariness of town life is integrally connected with his philosophy and aesthetic. If Fowles's is a poetic of the nothing-that-allows-freedom, Updike is a poet of the thing; as much as Keats did, Updike attempts to encounter an ontologically solid something. In another meditative piece called "The Sea's Green Sameness," he describes his attempt to encounter even in the seemingly formless ocean an immediate, substantial presence:

> If you lie down, put your head in the sand, and close one
> eye, the sea loses one dimension and becomes a wall.
> The black rim of the perfectly smooth top seems as
> close to me as the pale, acidulous bottom. . . . I . . . feel—
> and feel, as it were, from the outside, as if I were being
> beckoned—that if I were to run quickly to it, and press
> my naked chest against its vibrating perpendicular sur-
> face, and strain my body against it from my head to my
> toes, I should feel upon the beating of my heart the an-
> swer of another heart beating. ("Sameness" 163)

And this rather eccentric thought experiment leads Updike to state his Keatsian aesthetic goal: "All I expect is that once into my blindly spun web of words the thing itself will break: make an entry and an account of itself" ("Sameness" 164).

And yet "The Sea's Green Sameness" also reveals a way that Updike's goal matches Fowles's. Although Updike seems more interested than Fowles in capturing thingness, and certainly more willing to believe in a substantive God, Updike's respect for the mystery of an object—a mystery that eludes scientific analysis— sounds romantic and Fowlesian. He contrasts human knowledge of the sea with knowledge of scientific facts about it—"Its chemistry, its weight, its depth, its age, its creatures so disturbingly suggestive of our own mortality" ("Sameness" 163)—and, like Fowles, prefers the vitality of the former.

But, of course, Updike's ideas about mystery differ from Fowles's, and so do his attitudes about key concerns that he and Fowles very decidedly share: work habits, sex, religion, and the self. I ended my discussion of Fowles's autobiographical piece by noting these concerns, and I do the same here with my discussion of "The Dogwood Tree."

Updike has repeatedly talked about his work habits, and he considers them as methodical and businesslike as Fowles considers his own haphazard. In "The Dogwood Tree" Updike describes his boyhood conception of an artist as "someone who lived in a small town like Shillington, and who, equipped with pencils and paper, practiced his solitary trade as methodically as the dentist practiced his." Then he adds, "And indeed, that is how it is at present with me" (185). In *Self-Consciousness,* Updike describes the activities of his profession in a bluntly pragmatic way—"its dispersal and multiplication of the self through publication, its daily excretion of yet more words, the eventual reifying of these words into books"—and says that his work is a "practical consolation" (228). It is, in other words, quite important to Updike that writing be a homey, unethereal activity. He does acknowledge, in "The Dogwood Tree," that his boyhood self flirted with a love for grand blankness, sublime nothingness: "He loved blank paper and obedience to this love led me to a difficult artistic attempt. I reasoned thus: just as the paper is the basis for the marks upon it, might not events be contingent upon a never expressed (because featureless) ground? Is the true marvel of Sunday skaters the pattern of their pirouettes or the fact that they are silently upheld?" (185). But unlike Fowles, who writes novels about the stripping away of the conventional to expose the nothing beneath, Updike claims that—despite the growing preponderance of the fiercely extraordinary in the contemporary world—life's profound mystery is best revealed precisely by an artistic transcription of the ordinary, of "middleness": "To transcribe middleness with all its grits, bumps, and anonymities, in its fullness of satisfaction and mystery: is it possible or, in view of the suffering that violently colors the periphery and that at all moments threatens to move into the center, worth doing? Possibly not; but the horse-chestnut trees, the telephone poles, the porches, the green hedges recede to a calm point that in my subjective geography is still the center of the world" ("Dogwood Tree" 186). For Updike, then, a writer is no magus; he or she is an ordinary human being, who does ordinary, methodical work—like a dentist.

Ordinariness may be the key to all Updikean mysteries. Updike, like Fowles, is notoriously interested in sex, and in "The Dogwood Tree" he describes sex as one of "the Three Great Secret Things"; but where Fowlesian eroticism is shadowy and wooded, Updike's sexual imagery in this essay is as earthy (quite literally) and even vulgar as it could be: "The major sexual experience of my boyhood was a section of a newsreel showing some women wrestling in a pit of mud. The mud covered their bathing suits so they seemed naked. . . . Thenceforth my imaginings about girls moved through mud" (180). All of us who talk piously about the religious overtones of Updike's erotic writing should occasionally remind ourselves that it all began with a boy watching female mud wrestling.

But Updike's interest in religion is quite serious, and he says some revealing things about his religious concerns both in this autobiographical essay and in *Self-Consciousness*. Despite his claim, in "The Dogwood Tree," that religion is one of the "Secret Things," laden with mystery, and that the Lutheran Church in which he was brought up "seemed positively to dislike" him, Updike considers the Christian religion to contain, at core, an "oddly lucid thing." His God is not an absence ("blind, immobile, speechless," as Fowles puts it [*Tree* 58]) but an incarnate presence: "If the first article of the Creed stands, the rest follows as water flows downhill. That God, at a remote place and time, took upon Himself the form of a Syrian carpenter and walked the earth willfully healing and abusing and affirming and grieving, appeared to me quite in the character of the Author of the grass" ("Dogwood Tree" 182). This is a God of the suburbs, not of the hushed woods.

If Updike radically differs from John Fowles here (indeed, the entire difference between the two writers can be summed up as a theological one—the difference between a universe in which God is and one in which God is not), he nonetheless agrees with Fowles that the self is the supreme mystery. After his rather domestic description of God, Updike describes the self as anything but a "lucid thing": "The mystery that more puzzled me as a child was the incarnation of my ego—that omnivorous and somehow preexistent 'I'—in a speck so specifically situated amid the billions of history. Why was I I? The arbitrariness of it astounded me; in comparison, nothing was too marvellous" (182).

Updike, though, does not define this self as something that is absolutely alone, in a cosmic vacuum which is freedom; even as a boy, he claims, he precisely situated himself:

There was the movie house, and the playground, and the
schools, and the grocery stores, and our yard, and my
friends, and the horse-chestnut trees. My geography
went like this: in the center of the world lay our neigh-
borhood of Shillington. Around it there was greater Shillington, and around that, Berks County. Around Berks
County there was the State of Pennsylvania, the best, the
least eccentric, state in the Union. Around Pennsylvania,
there was the United States, with a greater weight of
people on the right and a greater weight of land on the
left. (163)

And the final chapter of *Self-Consciousness,* which considers the
mystery of the self and of its possible immortality, ends with a
sentence that gracefully links the transcendent with the mun-
danely particular: "The self's responsibility ... is to achieve rap-
port if not rapture with the giant, cosmic other: to appreciate, let's
say, the walk back from the mailbox" (257).

It is, I think, largely because he sees the human self as thoroughly situated (living next to that dogwood tree; walking back from
that mailbox) rather than separate that Updike considers an active,
gift-giving God to be a boon to the self rather than a limitation on
the self's freedom. Although his characters are often troubled,
lonely, divorcing, despairing, John Updike is not a prophet of exile.

John Fowles considers the workaday busyness of the suburbs to
be deadening—to the self and, by analogy, to trees. In a poem
called (appropriately, considering the subject of this chapter) "A
Tree in the Suburbs," he describes this spiritual torpor:

I see them in their orange hosts,
Frail phalanx of the nearly dead.
They hang there in the window's eye
Like very ancient votive dolls
Whose meanings learned men dispute.
Trite yet tragic seem their falls—
That slip, that twirl, that touch
And swirl—and then oblivion,
The sodden grass. Meanwhile indoors
We find we have no contacts left,
No rites, no gods, no open lines.
And every winter things get worse. (*Poems* 85)

But for Updike, that very domestic dogwood tree, surrounded as it was by people, houses, and mundane activities, grew "with increasing volume and brilliance" in a kind of Augustinian City (or Suburb) of God. The religious Updike aims his poetic lashes not at the suburbs but at the "easy Humanism" (perhaps he would include the position espoused by Fowles in *The Aristos*) that reduces God to a characterless "Demi-urge" that is easily frozen out of existence:

> . . . throughout phenomena
> Flashes the sword of Universal Law;
> Elegant formulations sever Chance
> From Cause, and clumsy Matter learns to dance. . . .
> The Demi-urge expands up to a rim
> Where calculable cold collapses Him. ("Midpoint" 39)

Then he proceeds to praise the ordinary itself in terms that are satirical but also truly generous:

> Adulthood has its comforts: these entail
> Sermons and sex and receipt of the mail,
> Elimination's homely paean, dreams'
> Mad gaiety, avoidance of extremes,
> The friendship of children, the trust of banks,
> Thoracic pangs, a stiffness in the shanks,
> Foretastes of death, the aftertaste of sin,
> In winter, Whiskey, and in summer, Gin. ("Midpoint" 43)

So in their lives as much as in their fictions, Fowles and Updike have circled around the same issues: the suburbs, the country, discipline, freedom, God, the self. And trees. And although in many ways the positions they have arrived at—like the fictional structures they have chosen to develop—are wholly different, the shared issues reflect shared intellectual orientations. For one thing, both continue to be existentialists in this skeptical postmodernist age that has often dismissed the moral concerns of existentialism; they are neither metaphysicians on the one hand (for both, existence precedes essence) nor behaviorists on the other (they do not—like Robbe-Grillet, for instance—see existence as reducible to external, material phenomena). Of course, they favor different existentialists; Fowles has acknowledged an interest in Camus and Sartre, while Updike is a notorious Kierkegaardian. But in their works and in their autobiographical statements, both examine—one in shadowy wooded places loaded with absence, one in the busy, barely treed suburbs—the mystery of the self and its search for meaning.

5

Self and Other in Two *Bildungsromane:* *The Centaur* and *The Magus*

Infinity and the Other: Updike's *The Centaur*

The Rabbit books contain some of Updike's theological ideas: his ideas about God and about human beings' uneasy relationship with God. God, in these books, is the Barthian "Wholly Other" — utterly beyond us — and yet humans paradoxically encounter this Other through surprising, providential repetitions within the temporal world.

The Centaur also looks at the human encounter with the Wholly Other, but its terms are phenomenological rather than overtly theological. Unlike the Rabbit books, this novel is not directly about religion at all; it is about a boy and his father. Nonetheless, within this human framework it looks at the dynamics of a self-other relationship that is clearly analogous to Rabbit's relationship with that something that wants him to find it. Indeed, the *Bildungsroman* form, of which this is at least a partial example, always has this phenomenological structure: the novel of education is always about a young person's orientation within the world of otherness — the world of the not-self.

But in many — perhaps most — *Bildungsromane,* this world of otherness is of subordinate interest; the real emphasis is on the development of the self of the protagonist. This narrative form, in other words, is focused on the self; it is precisely about the self's consciousness of its own story as important. And Updike's novelistic characters — such as, for example, the *Bildungsroman* protagonist of *The Centaur,* Peter Caldwell — surely have the self-consciousness to dominate this kind of novel. With his lyrically meditative prose, Updike makes his characters busily, fluidly self-reflective entities.

For all their fluidity, however, Updike's characters also tend to have a solidity, a kind of ontological substance. This substantiality is based not only on their ability to encounter themselves in acts of what might be called "meta-consciousness," but also, more importantly, on their ability to face an other, a something beyond the boundaries of self—either the Barthian Other sought by Rabbit, or another human being, or simply a concrete, temporal object. In other words, Updike's metaphysic of selfhood is dualistic, other-directed, based on a dualistic epistemology (which postulates the existence of a real Known separate from the Knower), rather than monistically self-oriented. That is why it is almost inevitable that Updike's nearest approximation to a *Bildungsroman* is a book primarily about not the self but the other.

This respect for an other, radically different and separate from the self while nonetheless substantially present and visible, is the ethical side of the Christian theological orientation we find in the Rabbit books. For Updike, the other has real, substantive importance, and the ethical encounter with the other, which points metaphorically toward the Other, the Christian God, grants substantive value to the self. (The relativistic view put forward by many postmodernists—which is close to the vision that Fowles puts forward in his own *Bildungsroman, The Magus*—would reject this substantive dualism, asserting instead that "self" and "other" are mere words, signifiers signifying signifiers in a center-less web of relative difference.) And if Updike is theologically allied with Karl Barth, he is philosophically and ethically allied with Emmanuel Levinas, the renegade phenomenologist who attacks both Heidegger and Husserl for failing sufficiently to consider the infinite otherness of the other.

Levinas's problem with Heidegger's philosophy of Being and Husserl's transcendental idealism (and he is also troubled by Hegel's philosophy of Mind or Spirit) is that these schemas are enclosed totalities—self-sufficient systems that purport to contain and explain all reality. Heidegger's Being contains *everything;* and if there is a real reality outside Husserl's conscious intentionality, Husserl would ask us to "bracket" it as unimportant. The intent of Levinas's great work, *Totality and Infinity,* is to break open these totalities by introducing the notion of "infinity," of an Other infinitely different and separate from the "same," the enclosed, the self.

Levinas predicates his theory of "alterity" on a claim that the history of metaphysical thought is a quest for something other, a quest that cannot be satisfied by anything that is contained or can be contained within the self (Rabbit Angstrom, in other words, was engaged in this grand metaphysical quest without even knowing it):

The term of this movement, the elsewhere or the other, is called *other* in an eminent sense. No journey, no change of climate or of scenery could satisfy the desire bent toward it. The other metaphysically desired is not "other" like the bread I eat, the land in which I dwell, the landscape I contemplate, like, sometimes, myself for myself, this "I," that "other." I can "feed" on these realities and to a very great extent satisfy myself, as though I had simply been lacking them. Their *alterity* is thereby reabsorbed into my own identity as a thinker or a possessor. The metaphysical desire tends toward *something else entirely,* toward the *absolutely other.* (33)

This "*absolutely other*" becomes, for Levinas, a kind of messianic revelation of the Jewish deity (as Updike's human other points toward the God of Christianity), but his theory is phenomenological and experiential rather than theological; Levinas espouses a belief in a God that exists through human relationships rather than in the "personal God" (88) of "positive religions" (77). This is why Levinas's schema, more than Barth's, is valuable for studying the design of a *Bildungsroman* that is not explicitly religious but that nonetheless is founded not on the self but on the other.

I will say much more about Levinas's Other as I discuss *The Centaur.* For now I will present only a few key attributes of this Other, which will also emerge as crucial elements of Updike's book.

Levinas's Other, for one thing, is in no way dependent on the self for either its existence or its revelation; the form of this Known is in no way an a priori cognitive structure of a Kantian Knower. Indeed, for Levinas it is the Other that calls the self into real existence, real involvement with the world; it is the Other that transforms a solipsistic dreamer into a *cogito.* Levinas takes very seriously Decartes's claim that the *cogito* is founded on God: "This awakening comes from the Other. Before the *cogito,* existence dreams itself, as though it remained foreign to itself. . . . The knowing of the *cogito* thus refers to a relation with the Master — with the idea of infinity or of the Perfect. . . . The *cogito* in Descartes rests on the other who is God and has put the idea of infinity in the soul, who had taught it, and has not, like the Platonic master, simply aroused the reminiscence of former visions" (86). And the Other not only awakens the self; the Other remains above the self. The self must look up at the transcendent Other: "The dimension of *height* in which the Other is placed is as it were the primary curvature of being from which the privilege of the Other results, the gradient [denivellement] of transcendence" (86–87).

The primacy and transcendence of the Other makes the self-other relation inherently ethical. To know the Other—which for Levinas is always an ethical *teacher*—is to know that the powers of the self are limited, that the self does not control the totality; the self "shalt not kill" the Other: "The Other, whose exceptional presence is inscribed in the ethical impossibility of killing him in which I stand, marks the end of powers. If I can no longer have power over him it is because he overflows every *idea* I can have of him" (87). For Levinas, the Other is a limitation on the freedom of the self; and the welcoming of the Other, therefore, is precisely conscience: "If we call a situation where my freedom is called in question conscience, association or the welcoming of the Other is conscience" (100). Levinas is no Sartrean existentialist, and John Fowles—whose *Bildungsroman,* as we will see, is a large glorification of the self's freedom—would perhaps be appalled by Levinas's criticism of freedom: "My freedom," Levinas says, "does not have the last word; I am not alone" (101). That *The Centaur* also affirms this proposition is what separates Updike from Fowles, and Updike's *Bildungsroman* from Fowles's.

The Other is also profoundly paradoxical. The Other is a presence (a "face," as we will see), but it is a presence that is always infinitely distant: an absence. So for all its ethical impact on the self, the Other is absent from the world of the self; it is not grasped by the self as any kind of object of cognition: "The relation with the face is not an object-cognition. The transcendence of the face is at the same time its absence from this world into which it enters, the exiling [depaysement] of a being, his condition of being stranger, destitute, or proletarian" (75).

I should mention, before beginning my specific Levinasian analysis of *The Centaur,* that Updike's connection with Levinas's ideas divorces Updike from the godfather of deconstruction, Jacques Derrida, whose essay "Violence and Metaphysics"—a refutation of Levinas—will serve as my model for analyzing Fowles's *The Magus.* His philosophy of absence leads Derrida to accept the *absent* qualities of Levinas's "infinity," but to reject its presence, its visibility; in the end, then, Derrida cannot countenance a self and other that truly face each other across an infinite gap, so he replaces this absolute, paradoxical encounter with the concept of relative difference within the totality. For Levinas, Derrida's step eliminates the possibility of philosophical discourse altogether, turning all language into self-enclosed babbling—"an unintermitting psychoanalysis or philology or sociology, in which the appearance of a discourse vanishes in the Whole" (88). We will examine Derrida's argument in much more detail later in the chapter, but it is worth noting that, for all his revolutionary deconstructionism, it is Derrida who cannot accept a philosophy that is "unforeseeable in formal logic" (Levinas 276), that challenges the law of noncontradiction by asserting that something can be both present and absent.

Levinas's schema, therefore, is quite radical, and its radicalism is shared by *The Centaur;* Updike is not the neatly realistic writer that many consider him. His *Bildungsroman* is in some ways an overturning of the *Bildungsroman* form—a kind of deconstruction of the form (though in Levinasian rather than Derridean terms). This book is the first of his novels in which Updike adopted the most classically self-oriented (and even, frequently, textually self-reflexive) artistic posture: the book is overtly a portrait of an—if not the—artist, and it has often been treated as a straightforward example of that subtype of *Bildungsroman* called the *"Künstlerroman."* Generally, the *Künstlerroman* is the most monistic of narrative types: an "artist novel," more even than the ordinary novel of education, is usually a record of one consuming creative ego taking all the things of its life and turning them into a personal myth. Such works tend to be artistic renderings of the process that Levinas calls "Nourishment, . . . the transmutation of the other into the same [i.e., the self]." For such a self, Levinas says, "to live is a sort of transitive verb, and the contents of life are its direct object" (111). Even within the traditionally totalizing, ego-enclosed form of the *Künstlerroman,* however, Updike manages to open up a dualistic universe, a universe in which the self encounters and addresses, but does not consume, the other (non-self, another human being) and, at least analogically, the Other (the absolutely transcendent, the Judeo-Christian God). In Levinas's terms, *The Centaur* invokes—without, of course, entirely containing—not totality but infinity.

It is hard to imagine anyone wondering who the protagonist is in a typical *Künstlerroman.* Critics may find David Copperfield a bit more bland and colorless than some of the characters he associates with, but no one would challenge his central position in Dickens's novel; likewise Stephen Dedalus is inarguably the hero of Joyce's *Portrait,* as is Marcel of Proust's *Remembrance of Things Past.*

Superficially, at least, *The Centaur* seems to be safely in this tradition. Peter Caldwell, the narrator of several chapters of Updike's book, has much in common with David, Stephen, and Marcel: like all of them, Peter is in many ways his author's admitted autobiographical portrait (see Plimpton 432–33); and like David and Marcel, Peter himself, as a grown-up artist, tells a story about his youth.

Some critics have indeed asserted that *The Centaur* emanates from Peter's consciousness in the most thoroughgoing way. Edward Vargo, for example, sees the entire book as a record of the adult Peter's own ritualistic reenactment, while in bed with his lover, of three days with his father during his adolescence. Even the chapters that are not explicitly narrated by Peter are, according to Vargo, explainable as "the dreams that come to Peter between his periods of narration, or the meanderings of Peter's semi-conscious mind" (84). James Mellard goes one step further; while expressing admiration for Vargo's reading, he denies that Peter's act has the "public and ceremonial" qualities of a ritual. For Mellard, rather, the novel is an utterly private piece of lyricizing, and Peter alone is both author and audience: "As Peter realizes, an 'external' audience 'doesn't matter,' for the lyrical expression, whatever form it takes, is mainly personal and private. The poet is his own audience" (113). Even at its most Proustian, Proust's *Remembrance* could never seem more onanistic than that.

There are, however, opponents to such readings. While granting, for example, that it is possible to read "the whole novel as Peter's recollection" (70), Robert Detweiler maintains that the novel's technical point of view is not consistently Peter's; rather, the book is structurally a kind of Cubist "*Gestalt* of simultaneous perspectives": "When one asks what the formal point of view of *The Centaur* is, one discovers that it has none. It is mainly Peter's story; but Peter is, at the same time, a teenager and an adult; he reminisces lucidly but also recollects from the subconscious; he speaks in the first-person singular confessional and also with his father inhabits a scenic point of view" (67). George Hunt even more significantly questions whether the novel's perspective is wholly concurrent with Peter's. Hunt maintains that the book as a whole absolutely upends artist-Peter's own "Promethean" narrative aspirations; he says that Peter's "contentious impulse as an abstract expressionist testifies to his desire to break the bonds of finitude and deny the limits of space and time and, by doing so, 'know more than our fathers.' The brilliance of the novel's ultimate structure, however, is meant to remind us that Peter's Promethean task is impossible" (57).

Even Joyce's *Portrait,* though, can be said to undermine its central character's proclaimed aspirations; an underlying structural irony, issuing from what Wayne Booth calls the "implied author," does not in itself dislodge a *Künstlerroman*'s protagonist from his or her focal position (for Booth's discussion of Joyce's *Portrait,* see Booth 323–36). The more telling question, in this case, is whether Peter is the central character at all: despite his occasional appearances as narrator and Updike's own autobiographical links with him, Peter often remains in the shadow of his father, George Caldwell. Indeed, the most conventional, commonsensical readings of the novel have always treated George as central (he is explicitly "the Centaur"), and at least one critic, Joyce Markle, has brushed aside the notion that this is Peter's *Künstlerroman* at all. The world view of the book, Markle asserts, is religious rather than aesthetic, George's rather than Peter's:

> The sense that the world is enriched with mystery and invisible meaning makes it clear, I think, that this is certainly Caldwell's story, and not Peter's. The employment of an external frame in which a thirty-five-year-old Peter recalls parts (or all?) of the story tempts some critics to consider the book as a species of *kunstlerroman.* But Peter's artistic tendencies antedate the period of the narrative [so the book is *not* a portrait of his development as an artist]. ... (69)

But all these readings err by assuming that the book belongs *either* to George *or* to Peter. Critics who claim that the novel is George's tend to be looking at it in fairly traditional, thematic terms: for such readers, George and his semimythologized grapplings with temporality and death point to objective ideas outside the book—truths (religious, perhaps, or existential) about the human condition. Those, on the other hand, who concentrate on Peter-as-narrator tend to prefer a more avant-garde, metafictional reading; Updike's text, according to such critics, is best read as a self-referential record of the process of subjectively systematizing phenomena. Both sorts of readings are trapped in a subject-object orientation; they differ only in their choice whether to turn outward toward an object or to look self-reflexively at the subject. My contention, though, is that Updike has created a fictional world in which the logical totality of subject and object has been replaced by the volatile infinity of self and other. Peter is the *Künstlerroman* hero, the self, and yet his subjectivity does not contain George, a novelistic embodiment of otherness. George is infinitely distant from Peter and unknowable by him; as father, nonetheless, George calls Peter into existence, and as teacher he faces and ethically speaks to him. *The Centaur,* therefore, is a very paradoxical book: an antinovelistic text that is substantive and ethical, and a traditionally solid novel that is as volatile as nitro-glycerin.

For Levinas, the solipsistic ego becomes a conscious, speaking self only when it is confronted by non-self, another person, an Other. The ethically challenging emergence of the Other, there-fore, marks the birth of a human world in which thought and language can exist. The Other arises before the self, Levinas says, as teacher before pupil; considering teaching to be exactly what the Other does when he (Levinas specifically speaks of the Other as masculine) reveals himself to (faces) the self, and hence consti-tutes language and thought, Levinas writes that "the first teaching of the teacher is his very presence as teacher from which represen-tation comes" (100). And the opening pages of *The Centaur* do, in a rather flamboyant way, present the birth of a human world precise-ly as the emergence of a teacher, George Caldwell.

The novel's first paragraphs depict a metaphorical birth, and centaur/teacher George is, paradoxically, both deliverer and deliv-ered. The event begins with George's own consciousness of pain, his awakening birth pang ("Caldwell turned and as he turned his ankle received an arrow"), which is linked with his simultaneous consciousness of the birth of the universe ("His eyes were forced upward to the blackboard, where he had chalked the number 5,000,000,000, the probable age in years of the universe" [9]). This is followed by the comically symbolic birth itself. With blood streaming from his injured ankle, George flees from the classroom in which he has been teaching science and enters a kind of birth canal: "The dim walls of the ochre hall wavered; the classroom doors, inset with square numbered panes of frosted glass, seemed experimental panels immersed in an activated liquid" (9). The organic imagery describing the hallway multiplies. George the Centaur's "head and torso" (this is not a breech birth) are drawn toward the "faint and watery blur" of light shining through the doors at the end of the hall; the atmosphere is "viscid," and the light hangs "like water in oil" (10). And then George pushes through, into the outside world, into existence, into the novel: "In a tumult of pain, . . . he threw himself down the short flight of steps to the concrete landing. . . . Caldwell gripped the brass bar and, his mouth thin with determination beneath his pinched and frightened eyes, he pushed into the open" (10). And in case the reader has not noticed that this is all a birth metaphor, Updike, near the end of his description, supplies a last amusing clue: in the vestibule between the concrete steps and the outer door (a kind of vaginal proto-corridor), a student has inscribed a single inevitable word, "Fuck."

This opening sequence is not just an Updikean tour de force. The narrator, here, is insisting, perhaps excessively, that George is an individual, independent existent, and that his emergence calls the world itself into existence. Indeed, a few pages later, after garage-mechanic Hummel has removed the arrow from George's ankle, we find this passage: "Before entering [the school building, George] gasped fresh air and stared sharply upward, as if in answer to a shout. Beyond the edge of the orange wall the adamantine blue zenith pronounced its unceasing monosyllable: I" (20). The presence of George, the Other, allows the universe to reveal itself, to speak.

It seems to me impossible, in the face of this vivid establishment of his ontological status, to claim that George Caldwell exists in the novel only within the lyrical reverie of his son Peter, a character who has not yet even been introduced into the book. It also seems erroneous, therefore, to assume that George's metamorphoses into Chiron, the centaur, are merely Peter's fanciful mythologizings of a past reality. Critics who read *The Centaur* as an unambiguous *Künstlerroman* appear to be able to account totally for the book's strange shifts between realism and fantasy—"When Peter remembers his father in mythical terms," Suzanne Uphaus asserts, "he pictures him as the centaur Chiron" (32)—but such psychologizings ignore George's carefully depicted autonomy. A more defensible explanation of the book's mythic elements, which does not relegate George Caldwell to his son's musings, is the rather conventional one that points out Updike's thematic, conceptual use of Greek myth. The mythologizing, it is argued, is Updike's way of emphasizing the Karl Barthian theme presented in the novel's epigraph: "Heaven is the creation inconceivable to man, earth the creation conceivable to him. He himself is the creature on the boundary between heaven and earth." (George Hunt, a Jesuit priest, has done a particularly good job of explaining this statement by Barth [Hunt 63–66].)

But neither the psychological nor the thematic interpretation of the novel's mythic dimension can wholly account for the reader's disquieting experience of George-teacher/George-centaur. We must look elsewhere for a satisfactory explanation of the mythologizing Updike does here. And without rejecting the insightful hypothesis espoused by Joyce Markle and others—that the novel's mythic strain imbues the book with a religious depth, a dimension of "mystery and invisible meaning" (I am, in fact, simply examining this religious dimension from a phenomenological rather than explicitly theological perspective)—I suggest that the fluid shifts between reality and myth are an important part of Updike's depiction of George Caldwell as a character who is truly, in the Levinasian sense, other. George, in other words, is a something—or someone—and not a mere nothingness created in the freedom of Peter Caldwell's mind.

For Levinas, when an image congeals into a single, "plastic" form, it no longer can be a true expression of the Other in all its infinitely uncontainable alterity; an entity, when frozen into a single form, becomes "adequate" to the same, enclosed within the imagination of the observing self (66). So the true Other is not a form but a continually changing "face," a face that, in its revelation of its own endless mystery, unforms each of its temporary forms. Only such a face can really teach, can really engage in discourse— a dialogue between two (a self and a real other) rather than a monologue within one: "The face is a living presence; it is expression. The life of expression consists in undoing the form in which the existent, exposed as a theme, is thereby dissimulated. The face speaks. The manifestation of the face is already discourse. He who manifests himself comes, according to Plato's expression, to his own assistance. He at each instant undoes the form he presents" (Levinas 66). The Ovidian metamorphoses of the first chapter of *The Centaur* establish George Caldwell as a character who continually undoes the form he presents.

We have seen that the novel's opening pages explicitly depict George's birth into the book, his emergence as an ontologically solid character. But it is, strangely, a fluid solidity that is established. He is a real, credible teacher—but a teacher who is being shot with an arrow, just as (according to the introductory statement by Josephine Peabody) Chiron the Centaur was. The text, therefore, immediately presents this ordinary science teacher as "The Centaur."

George's pain is then described in distinctly animal rather than human terms: "The pain extended a feeler into his head and unfolded its wet wings along the walls of his thorax, so that he felt, in his sudden scarlet blindness, to be himself a large bird waking from sleep" (9). In this early sentence, we may still be willing to read the animal imagery in metaphorical terms, but Updike's prose nonetheless has already cloaked itself in Ovidian mystery.

Then things really become strange. Although we learn that George is an ordinary man from Passaic, we are told shortly afterwards that he "tried to keep [his wounded] leg from touching the floor, but the jagged clatter of the *three remaining hooves* sounded so loud he was afraid one of the doors would snap open and another teacher emerge to bar his way" (10, my italics). By the time he has left the school building (after his "birth"), he is established in all his equine glory: "Caldwell's strange silhouette took on dignity; his shoulders—a little narrow for so large a creature—straightened, and he moved, if not at a prance, yet with such pressured stoic grace that the limp was enrolled in his stride" (11). When he arrives at Hummel's garage to have the arrow removed, however, he again seems quite human: "He put his injured foot up on a severed fender and lifted his trouser leg" (13). He remains human for a while; several pages later, though, after he has returned to the school, he passes an idyllic interlude in an Olympian garden, no longer as George the centaur/teacher, but explicitly as Chiron himself. Then he is suddenly George again, returning to his class to teach a lesson.

So far the novel—and especially its hero—has been constituted by a series of transformations, of forms repeatedly unforming themselves. Updike has chosen not to keep the two levels of his story, the mythic and the naturalistic, separate—as Joyce, for example, chose to do in *Ulysses*. George, as a result, seems from the beginning to be much more an elusive figure, an absent presence, than Joyce's Leopold Bloom; Bloom—until the "Circe" chapter, at least—is always distinctly himself, while George (to paraphrase Iago) is not what he is. And yet he *is*. For all his infinite distance from us, he faces us; and we are prepared, in this initial chapter, to enter a novel in which we will learn from him about infinite mysteries as surely as those students who care to listen to his science lessons—filled with incomprehensibly huge, essentially infinite numbers (the age of the universe; the weight of the sun; our solar system's distance from, and the pun is hardly accidental, Alpha Centauri)—learn about them.

George Caldwell, therefore, is an *absent* presence, but also distinctly an absent *presence:* a teacher who reveals the new and the surprising, who genuinely speaks. Levinas, in fact, connects teaching not only with the supremely important appearance of the Other, but also with the genesis of speech itself (and we have already seen that, in a sense, George's presence makes the universe speak): "The calling in question of the I, coextensive with the manifestation of the Other in the face, we call language. The height from which language comes we designate with the term teaching" (171). So teaching is the original act, the act that creates a world of autonomous entities as opposed to a self-enclosed dream; the divine, creative words "Let there be light" are, for Levinas, the act of teaching: "Teaching signifies the whole infinity of exteriority. And the whole infinity of exteriority is not first produced, to then teach: teaching is its very production" (171).

This has been a long way of saying that, in *The Centaur,* George

Caldwell *is,* and that what he is is a teacher. But those small statements have large implications in the novel. If Updike's notion of the teacher, and of the teacher's supremely constitutive function, is similar to Levinas's (and the opening chapter indicates that it is), then it is clear that the presence of George—an uncannily protean yet solid character, who happens to teach for a living—at the threshold of a novel recording another character's lyrical reminiscence is deeply significant. George's paradoxically absent presence, as well as his vocation as teacher, guarantees that his son/student Peter, who will become a sort of qualified *Künstlerroman* narrator, both is and is not a radically isolated self. Peter is alone, but he faces a true, even if in a sense absent, other. Indeed, the opening words of the second chapter, the beginning of Peter's first-person narrative, are "MY FATHER."

Peter's invocation of his father creates a bridge from the first chapter into the second; once we have crossed the bridge, however, we feel (initially, at least) that we have entered a world that is different in substantial, even ontological, ways. If George's chapter impresses us with its otherness—George thrusts himself into autonomous existence, teaches infinite mysteries, and unforms his forms before we can absorb them into our consciousness—Peter's narrative seems to be a conventional depiction of an internally sufficient, lyricizing self. Far from being unabsorbable by a consciousness, Peter *is* consciousness. He is lying in bed, utterly inactive, talking to a sleeping lover (and therefore, essentially talking only to himself) about his adolescence. He is in a self-enclosed reverie of silence, dreams, atheism: "I wake now often to silence, beside you, with a pang of fear, after dreams that leave a sour wash of atheism in my stomach" (40).

Atheism, as it turns out, is precisely the metaphor that Levinas uses to describe the situation of the self, the ego, the "same" (as distinct from the Other): "One can call atheism this separation so complete that the separated being maintains itself in existence all by itself, without participating in the Being from which it is separated.... One lives outside of God, at home with oneself; one is an I, an egoism" (58). Although Peter finds atheism to be sour, Levinas does not judge it so harshly. Atheism for him is simply the natural state of a self that is a self and nothing else. To be an independent psyche is, for Levinas, to be atheistic: "The soul, the dimension of the psychic, being an accomplishment of separation, is naturally atheistic" (58). But the atheistic self is called, according to Levinas, to an ethical relationship with the Other—called to be a pupil and a son or daughter. This second chapter not only establishes Peter in his selfhood, his atheism, but it also eventually depicts the call of an other, his father, across a seemingly infinite distance; this call is a "rupture" that constitutes Peter as a talking self rather than a deaf, dumb particle of undifferentiated being, "outside all communication and all refusal to communicate—without ears, like a hungry stomach" (Levinas 134).

While the first chapter was fluid, each form unforming itself, the second begins with images of iciness. In the older Peter's reminiscence about his own past, the boy Peter—an image of the Levinasian same as opposed to the Other—is at home in a frozen, static world; even telephone wires, usually instruments of active conversation, seem encased in ice: "I turned my head, as sleep's heaviness lifted from it, and looked through the window. . . . Everything looked frozen; the two strands of telephone wire looked locked into place in the sky's blue ice" (41). Peter, awakened and reawakened for school by his impatient mother, continually slips back into private, autoerotic dreams in which there is no other ("there was no sense of *faces*" [43, my italics]) but only self. Even after he leaps out of bed, he protects himself from his surroundings: "Careful to keep my skin from touching anything hard, . . . I set about dressing" (44). And he immediately begins almost to revel in a physical affliction, psoriasis, an allergy to nearly everything that exists apart from his own body ("I generated it," he claims, "out of myself"). Although he will not touch external objects, he takes a kind of masturbatory pleasure in touching these scabs: "For the innermost secret, the final turn of my shame was that the texture of my psoriasis . . . privately pleased me. The delight of feeling a large flake yield and part from the body under the insistence of a fingernail must be experienced to be forgiven" (45–46). Peter Caldwell has been born into *The Centaur* with as much vivid autonomy as his father George has been granted; the two characters, however, seem to exist in narrative worlds that are radically, metaphysically incompatible.

From the beginning of the reminiscence, though, Peter is being prodded into an awareness of his father. In his bedroom, he has been overhearing bits of a conversation between his parents from which he infers that his father is ill. And when he goes down to breakfast, he is even more vigorously bombarded by his father's active unpredictability, a kind of Levinasian infinity that cannot be safely comprehended within Peter's totalizing imagination. Budding-artist Peter enters the kitchen and begins contemplating a picture he once painted of the old family home; the picture's ability to freeze time, to keep forms from unforming, reminds him why he is drawn to art: "I relived the very swipe of my palette knife, one second of my life that in a remarkable way had held firm. It was this firmness, I think, this potential fixing of a few passing seconds, that attracted me, at the age of five, to art" (51). But George ruptures Peter's time-freezing reverie, deconstructing his carefully constructed self-protection: "Gobble your coffee, kid. Time and tide for no man wait."

Hustle and bustle and a cliché ("Time and tide . . .") are juxtaposed here with Peter's dreamy aestheticism. And George, the unformer of forms, is not satisfied with his deconstructive cliché; he proceeds elaborately to deconstruct the deconstruction:

> "I've been hearing that time and tide line all my life, and I don't know what it means. What does it mean? You ask anybody, and the bastards won't tell you. But they won't be honest. They won't admit they don't know. . . .
>
> "I was a minister's son. I was brought up to believe, and I still believe it, that God made man as the last best thing in His Creation. If that's the case, who are this time and tide that are so almighty superior to us?" (52)

Poor Peter, who has been trying to eat his cereal and keep his world static and aesthetic, finds that even simple truisms metamorphose at the hands of his endlessly curious father: "My father's anxious curiosity," he says, "had quite drained the saying's simple sense away." And then he describes his father—infinitely distant, ineluctably present—in words that could almost have been taken directly from *Totality and Infinity:* "His face, compounded of shiny lumps and sallow slack folds, to me seemed both tender and brutal, wise and unseeing; it was still dignified by the great distance that in the beginning had lifted it halfway to the sky" (53).

Throughout the rest of the chapter, the tension persists between Peter's static aestheticism and George's unpredictability. As Peter and his father drive together to Olinger High School, passing rural townships that make Peter "sweat with claustrophobia" (60), the boy silently meditates on the perfect paintings of his hero, Jan Vermeer. He remembers that, during his single visit to New York, he was unable to visit the Frick and the Metropolitan, where he could have entered the sacramental presence of Vermeer's "heavenly and cool" (63) paintings, "a Real Presence so ultimate I would not be surprised to die in the encounter" (68). He missed this experience, he says, because "my father's blundering blocked it. We never entered the museums; I never saw the paintings. Instead I saw the inside of my father's sister's hotel room" (68). He also waited, seething, while his father stopped on New York streets to talk to strangers, who "resisted entanglement in his earnest, circular questioning" (68). And now, on the way to school, George again inflicts a stranger on his son; he picks up a hitchhiking hobo. Peter's attempts aesthetically to freeze the world are thawed by yet another unassimilable face: "The hitchhiker's face, unfrozen, was terrible—a puddle; it . . . moved toward me with a smear of a smile and an emanation of muddy emotion. I flinched and rigidly cringed" (69). This changing, imperfect, foreign world—so disruptive to the crystalline certainty of his internal, atheistic self—fills Peter with anger: "That my existence at one extremity should be tangent to Vermeer and at the other to the hitchhiker seemed an intolerable strain" (67).

Peter resents his father for forcing all this substantial otherness on him. By the end of the chapter, however, Peter's whiney resentment has metamorphosed into a more touching human sadness based on a thawing of the childish myth of self-creation and self-perpetuation. Peter at last acknowledges that he is a son, and he begins to realize something which science-instructor George has been teaching his students for years—that a multi-generational species is predicated on the fact that individual members of the species die: "My father provided; he gathered things to himself and let them fall upon the world; my clothes, my food, my luxurious hopes had fallen to me from him, and for the first time his death seemed, even at its immense stellar remove of impossibility, a grave and dreadful threat" (73).

Infinity's "infinition," according to Levinas, "is produced in the improbable feat whereby a separated being fixed in its identity, the same, the I, nonetheless contains in itself what it can neither contain nor receive solely by virtue of its own identity. Subjectivity realizes these impossible exigencies—the astonishing feat of containing more than it is possible to contain" (26–27). I have been showing in my discussion of Peter Caldwell that Updike has used a *Künstlerroman* convention to do something more startling than most critics who read *The Centaur* as a *Künstlerroman* seem to have noticed. Even Peter's first-person narrative, taken in isolation, is more than a bit of private, subjective lyricizing. Rather, it is a record of subjectivity broken open by an ability to contain more than it is possible to contain. The vehicle of this infinite revelation—the disrupter of the self-contained certainties—is George, Peter's father and teacher, who, in relation to Peter (and therefore, in a sense, to the world of the novel) is distinctly other.

The book as a whole, with its multiple narrators and complex mythic layers (we have looked only at the two initial chapters, but Peter's straightforward first-person narration will frequently be shoved aside throughout the rest of the novel), goes even beyond the individual characters in this deconstruction of *Künstlerroman* conventions. Although I think that it remains valid to look at *The Centaur* as Updike's "Portrait of the Artist as a Young Man," a meditation on the origins of Updikean art using an admittedly autobiographical character, it should be clear by now what an unusual *Künstlerroman* this is. It is dualistic rather than monistic: George Caldwell, an elusively absent presence, shares the spotlight with his son Peter, and Updike's story of an artist's reminiscence becomes more a narrative of a teacher and his pupil. Updike seems, again, to be espousing an aesthetic that is founded on a Levinasian ethic (which, as I have noted, complements Updike's Barthian theological stance): "The transitivity of teaching," Levinas says, "and not the interiority of reminiscence, manifests being; the locus of truth is society" (101). So the vision of the artist presented secondarily through Peter Caldwell and primarily through the novel as a whole is one that springs not from a notion of radical self-reflexiveness, but rather from a belief in the relationship between a self and a real other; in other words, the art in this artist novel is not founded on the nothingness of Sartrean consciousness/freedom, but on a real, autonomous something.

I have said that *The Centaur* is a deconstruction of the *Künstlerroman* form, and I have described George Caldwell, the novel's "other," as a teacher who unforms forms, who deconstructs. And as I have noted, the deep Levinasian critique of enclosed totalities that underlies this novel is quite radical, an affront to logic—downright deconstructive. It is important to reiterate, however, that this Levinasian deconstruction is rather different from the Derridean sort. A Levinasian unformer of forms, the kind I see in this novel, is not just a Derridean absence but is an absent *presence*. It is a presence, furthermore, that is never contained within the "same," the self, as an object is contained within the subject in a philosophy of conscious intentionality. Such a paradox—that an infinitely distant, deconstructive nonself can nonetheless face and address the self—has elements of the miraculous, of the providential, of a sort of Eucharistic intersection of the temporal and the infinite. And Updike's novel (which, after all, carries the epigraph from Karl Barth that calls a human being "the creature on the boundary between heaven and earth") contains a number of strikingly religious moments of revelation, moments which heighten our awareness of the divine Other that has loomed above Updike's human otherness. I end my discussion of *The Centaur* by describing two such moments, which epitomize the aims of the entire novel and underline its difference from the Fowlesian novel it in many ways resembles, *The Magus*.

The first of these moments is almost explicitly Eucharistic, sparked by a coughdrop that Peter, during his strained ride with his father and the hitchhiker, remembers to have eaten in New York. While visiting the dreamlike city that houses paintings by Vermeer, Peter discovered—"right in the throat of Paradise, on a counter in Grand Central Station"—a box of coughdrops manufactured in Alton, Pennsylvania, a town only a few miles from his home: "The two cities of my life, the imaginary and the actual, were superimposed; I had never dreamed that Alton could touch New York. I put a coughdrop into my mouth to complete this delicious confusion and concentric penetration; my teeth sweetened and at the level of my eyes, a hollow mile beneath the ceiling that on an aqua sky displayed the constellations with sallow electric stars, my father's yellow-knuckled hands wrung together nervously through my delay" (67–68). Peter's atheistic dreamworld (New York, the lights of Grand Central Station) and the external world that he prefers to ignore (Alton, his father's hands) are rationally irreconcilable. But they are joined, for a while, by a kind of sacrament, a symbol that carries healing grace; the symbolic coughdrops temporarily bridge the infinite gulf between son and father:

> In a temple of pale marble I forgave him and wanted to thank him for conceiving me to be born in a county that could insert its candy into the throat of Paradise. We took the subway to Pennsylvania Station and caught a train and sat side by side as easy as twins all the way home, and even now, two years later, whenever in our daily journey we went up or down Coughdrop Hill [the site of the mansion owned by the Alton coughdrop magnate], there was for me an undercurrent of New York and the constellations that seemed to let us soar, free together of the local earth. (68–69)

The second revelation I wish to mention is described much later in the book, at the end of chapter 7; it is, I think, the symbolic climax of the novel, the melting of Peter's frozen egoism by his father. It occurs after George's car has gotten stuck in the snow (it is stuck, significantly, at the bottom of Coughdrop Hill). Father and son are forced to walk, in a blizzard, three miles to town. Predictably, Peter deals with the icy, miserable experience by allowing his

consciousness to contract to a self-contained point, a near-noth-
ingness:

> There is an excising simplicity in it. First, all thoughts of
> past and future are eliminated, and then any extension
> via the senses of yourself into the created world. Then,
> as further conservation, the extremities of the body are
> disposed of—the feet, the legs, the fingers. If the dis-
> comfort persists, if a nagging memory of some more de-
> sirable condition lingers, then the tip of the nose, the
> chin, and the scalp itself are removed from considera-
> tion, not entirely anesthetized but deported, as it were,
> to a realm foreign to the very limited concerns of the ir-
> reducible locus, remarkably compact and aloof, which
> alone remains of the once farflung and ambitious king-
> dom of the self. (197–98)

Peter has attained the Sartrean pinprick of consciousness, the
essence of Levinasian atheism; add an explicit notion of freedom,
and we would have the sort of freeze-frame ending that Fowles
gives *The Magus.*

And then something happens: "The sensations seem to arrive
from a great distance outside himself when his father, now walking
beside him and using his body as a shield against the wind for his
son, pulls down upon Peter's freezing head the knitted wool cap he
has taken from his own head" (198). This image of teacher/father
George putting his cap on the head of a freezing Peter embodies
Updike's solution both to an aesthetic problem (how to open up
the monism of the *Künstlerroman* form) and an ethical one (how
to bridge the gap between human beings without denying their
autonomy). The solution—a revelation of the possibility of com-
passion (the ability to "suffer with"), which breaks through self-
enclosed monism without dissolving entities' differences, their
individual substantiality—is a traditional one, as old, at least, as the
Christian story of God's Incarnation. But, like that ancient story, it
remains infinitely surprising and miraculous.

Play of Difference in *The Magus*

Like *The Centaur, The Magus* is a novel about teachers, a bad
one (Nicholas, the protagonist, teaches at a prestigious Greek
boarding school—and not very well, it seems) and a good one
(Conchis, the title character, is referred to as "the greatest teacher
in the world" [487]). In fact, as much as Updike's book, this is a
Bildungsroman, a story of the protagonist's own education (al-

though it is probably not quite a *Künstlerroman,* since the protagonist decides that he is not an artist); his interactions with
Conchis push Nicholas to a new view of himself and of the world.
So *The Magus,* like *The Centaur,* seems to be a meditation on the
theme presented by Levinas—the need for the self, the same, to be
confronted by an other.

There are all sorts of other interesting similarities between the
novels—both, for instance, use classical myths as primary structur-
ing devices, which give the books a mysterious, even otherworldly
flavor, and both were even published at about the same time—that
make a comparison of them almost irresistible. Fowles's education
novel, however, is founded on some premises that differ profoundly from Updike's, premises that starkly highlight the differences between the writers. As we have seen, for Updike (as for
Levinas) the act of teaching is precisely a revelation of the Other, of
the Other's face—a revelation that so transcends what the self
could experience on its own that it ultimately points toward the
selfhood of the absolutely transcendent Other, God. But for Fowles,
the teaching—which takes place in what is called "the godgame"—
has no face to reveal. It is entirely negative; as the oracular Lily de
Seitas tells Nicholas, it is called a godgame "because there is no
God, and it is not a game" (637). There is no substantive Other to
be revealed here, and certainly no God. Robert Huffaker points out
that Lily de Seitas's name actually means "self" (62), and for all its
emphasis on teachers and students, the book's action really occurs
within the boundaries of the "same," of the self.

Although it would be too easy just to call Fowles a thoroughgoing Derridean deconstructionist (and it would also be erroneous,
since such pigeonholing would not sufficiently note his connections to romanticism, naturalism, and existentialism), *The Magus*
can be fruitfully examined as a gloss on Jacques Derrida's critical
discussion of Levinasian otherness called "Violence and Metaphysics: An Essay on the Thought of Emmanuel Levinas." Fowles, I
suggest, veers from the artistic vision of *The Centaur* in the same
way that Derrida veers from the philosophical vision of *Totality
and Infinity.* So my discussion of *The Magus* will begin with an
examination of Derrida's answer to Levinas; then I will look at the
novel itself, showing how it, like *The Centaur,* is structured around
an encounter between a single self (a young man in need of
education) and an other (a teacher or "magus"), but that the goal in
this case is not the revelation of substantive other, self, and world
but rather the opening up of a space, a nothingness.

Radical as Derrida's deconstruction of language systems may be,
it is interesting that his criticism of Levinas is that *he* is too radical.

Levinas's Other is profoundly paradoxical, and Derrida describes the paradox as one that shakes all language and Western philosophy at its foundations:

> It can be said only of the other that its phenomenon is a certain nonphenomenon, its presence (*is*) a certain absence. Not pure and simple absence, for there logic could make its claim, but a *certain* absence. Such a formulation shows clearly that within this experience of the other the logic of noncontradiction, that is, everything which Levinas designates as "formal logic," is contested in its root. This root would be not only the root of our language, but the root of all western philosophy. ... (91)

Derrida goes on to explain that the philosophy of alterity has made Levinas distrustful of both classical ontology and modern phenemonology because both tend to neutralize the Other—either by making the Other a part of Being (which can be grasped by reason, and therefore brought into the realm of the self) or by making it a phenomenon (an object of the self's consciousness). For Levinas, Derrida says, only the idea of metaphysical otherness "can free the other from the light of Being or from the phenomenon which 'takes away from Being its resistance' " (96). Levinas's theory is based on the assertion that something—some*one*—breaks through experience from an infinite distance, and it is not reducible to anything but itself. But Derrida, in this essay, states his preference for both ontology and phenomenology, which accommodate the idea of otherness instead of allowing it radically to contest the "Greek source" (81) of philosophy; indeed, Derrida's entire piece is ostensibly a defense of the Greek logos.

Derrida is also defending the metaphor; indeed, for him the inclusion of all reality within Heideggerian Being or Husserlian phenomenality, and all language within the logos, guarantees that there is no external, Archimedean reference point that allows us to go beyond the metaphorical. And this is why the Levinasian Other is so subversive: it cannot be contained within any philosophical system, and its revelation, the face, cannot be reduced to a metaphor. "The face is presence," Derrida says (and this, as we will see, troubles him). "The face is not a metaphor, not a figure" (101). The concept of the face, Derrida complains, implies that there is a substantial something behind linguistic signs, an external ground beneath language: "To express oneself," Derrida says, is for Levinas "to be *behind* the sign" (101). And such a grounding outside language is, of course, anathema to Derridean deconstruction.

Language, Derrida asserts, cannot talk about anything as transcendent as the Levinasian Other, which is not just outside the self's inside but is infinitely beyond the spatial altogether. That does not mean that language must bask in the "egoity" of the same. It can talk about exteriority, but only negatively; instead of invoking some positive presence beyond space—which Derrida calls "unthinkable-impossible-unutterable" (114)—language uses metaphors that point beyond themselves by their own self-negation, but that nonetheless stay within the same and its spatial realm:

> Space being the wound and finitude of birth (of *the*
> birth) without which one could not even open language, one would not even have a true or false exeriority to speak of. Therefore, one can, by using them,
> *use up* tradition's words, rub them like a rusty and devalued old coin; one can say that true exteriority is non-exteriority without being interiority, and one can write by crossing out, by crossing out what already has been crossed out: for crossing out writes, still draws in space.
> (112)

Derrida, in other words, is willing to talk about the other only as an absence, not as an absence/presence. His otherness, therefore, is not a call to go beyond the same, but merely a call to negate the language of the same—to show language's inability to mediate anything like Levinasian presence: "To say that the infinite exteriority of the other *is not* spatial, is *non*-exteriority and *non*-interiority, to be unable to designate it otherwise than negatively—is this not to acknowledge that the infinite (also designated negatively in its current positivity: in-finite) cannot be stated?" (113).

Levinas would agree with Derrida's final clause (he does acknowledge that the Other is not finally assimilable; that is precisely what makes it other), but he would add that the Other does at least have a *face* which allows it to be addressed, conversed with. The face is, for Levinas, precisely what draws language beyond a self-contained system of metaphors that build and then dismantle themselves. Derrida dismisses Levinas's notion of the face, saying that a face is bodily and therefore incompatible with the infinite (115); again, Derrida is refusing to violate logic, the law of noncontradiction, while Levinas has argued that the experience of the absent/present Other absolutely subverts logic. For Derrida, the face is exactly what Levinas says it cannot be—a metaphor: "The expression 'human face' is no longer, at bottom, as foreign to metaphor as Levinas seems to wish. . . . The Other resembles God.

. . .' Is this not the original metaphor?" (143). Indeed, it is the metaphor of metaphors, since Derrida's "God" is not a positive presence (it is hardly the substantial "Wholly Other" of either Levinas or Barth) but is simply the very "Difference" that generates metaphor:

> Metaphysical transcendence cannot be at once transcendence toward the other as Death and transcendence towards the other as God. Unless God means Death, which after all has never been *excluded* by the entirety of the classical philosophy within which we understand God both as Life and as the Truth of Infinity, of positive Presence. But what does this *exclusion* mean if not the exclusion of every particular *determination?* And that God is *nothing* (determined), is not life, because he is *everything?* and therefore is at once All and Nothing, Life and Death. Which means that God is or appears, *is named,* within the difference between All and Nothing, Life and Death. Within difference, and at bottom as Difference itself. (115–16)

John Fowles, who calls God "Not entity or non-entity, but the situation in which there can be both entity and non-entity" (*Aristos* 22), would doubtless find this situational rather than substantive notion of God quite amenable.

And because violence (even Sade-ism) is so much a part of the fabric of Fowles's fiction, it is worth noting that for Derrida human discourse, since it is limited to a play of difference without an absolute referent, is inherently violent.

Derrida accepts Levinas's assertion that anything existing only in the realm of the same, without encountering a transcendent other, is violent; by itself the same is mere self, ego, which has a totalizing (even totalitarian) drive forcibly to assimilate all into itself. For Levinas, though, the Other ethically calls the same out of this state of total domination. This is why for Levinas real discourse, which is conversation between same and Other, reveals a halt to violence. But since Derrida considers Levinas's Other to be unthinkable-impossible-unutterable, he claims that all discourse is violent. Its telos may be peaceful, but that telos—a fullness and presence, something like Levinas's Other—is infinitely deferred because it is outside the same (the only human realm) altogether:

> If . . . all discourse essentially retains within it space and
> the Same—does that not mean that discourse is origi-
> nally violent? And that the philosophical logos, the only
> one in which peace may be declared, is inhabited by
> war? . . . Nonviolence would be the telos, and not the es-
> sence of discourse. Perhaps it will be said that some-
> thing like discourse has its essence in its telos, and the
> presence of its present in its future. This certainly is so,
> but on the condition that its future and its telos be non-
> discourse: peace as a *certain* silence, a certain beyond of
> speech, a certain possibility, a certain silent horizon of
> speech. (116–17)

Peace, in other words, is for Derrida outside the logos; it is
always not-yet, a presence that is absent (the opposite, therefore,
of Levinas's Other, which is an absence that is present). So it is
obviously outside discourse; since this peace is nothing, no thing
within the system of the logos, the best discourse can do is point to
it by negation. In other words, we are back to those self-negating
metaphors. Derrida considers genuinely philosophical discourse
to be discourse that is violent (as it must be) but that uses the
violence against itself, pointing itself away from the regressive,
"finite" silence before speech ("primitive and prelogical silence,"
which is "an absolute violence" [130]) and toward the peaceful
silence beyond speech: "Peace, like silence, is the strange vocation
of language called outside itself by itself. But since *finite* silence is
also the medium of violence, language can only indefinitely tend
toward justice by acknowledging and practicing the violence
within it. Violence against violence" (130). The discourse itself
always stays in between these two silences. It can never penetrate
to a real Other; at best it "can only *do itself violence,* can only
negate itself in order to affirm itself, make war upon the war which
institutes it" (130).

Levinas, as we have seen, also talks about forms that unform or
dismantle themselves, but he is specifically referring to the forms
of the Other, which refuse to be concretized and assimilated by the
same. For Derrida, however, this self-dismantling property belongs
to discourse itself, which takes place within the realm of the same;
it is not, in other words, a matter of an other transcending a totality,
but of a totality canceling itself. (The significance of this idea to
Fowles's work should already be apparent. We have already observed the way Fowles's Clegg cancels himself out, and the deconstructive godgame in *The Magus* will even more directly embody
this Derridean notion of discourse.)

So Derrida's answer to Levinas is that there is no Other that addresses the self with authority; indeed, Derrida's "same," his battlefield of difference, does not really allow for an integral self either. What we are left with in the Derridean schema is not entities that address each other with authority but rather a "dialogue" that is opened "interminably" (133). Derrida brushes aside Levinas's notion of positive otherness as "empiricism," "the *dream* of a purely *hetero-logical* thought at its source" (151); it is divorced altogether from true philosophy, which for Derrida must maintain the interminable dialogue within the same. "We say the *dream*," he adds, "because it must vanish *at daybreak*, as soon as language awakens" (151).

Derrida sums up the difference between Levinas's views and his own by asserting that Levinas is Hebrew while he himself is Greek. Levinas's "Judaism," he says, is grounded in the "face," a phemonological way of conceptualizing the One Who Is; for Derrida, that is, Levinas's wholly other really is Karl Barth's Wholly Other. And it is this Hebrew emphasis on the face, I think, that leads Levinas to concentrate on the theme of "unveiling," which Derrida finds "risky" ("Is it not risky . . . to speak of the thinking of Being as of a thought dominated by the theme of unveiling . . . ?" [144]). Derrida says that his own "Greek" view, on the other hand, is grounded in a faceless Being that, apart from particular existents, is "nothing; nonhistory; nonoccurrence; nonphenomenality" (147). Derrida's founding principle, far from showing its face, is always concealed: "It follows that Being, since it is always, in fact, determined as an existent and is nothing outside the existent, is always dissimulated. . . . Being not existing before the Existent—and this is why it *is History*—it begins by hiding itself beneath its determination" (144). At the risk of oversimplification, then, I would suggest that Derrida is describing Levinas as a prophet of revelation (which Derrida considers sadly illusory) and himself as a philosopher of concealment.

It should already be clear how much Fowles's ideas resonate with Derrida's reply to Levinas; certainly Fowles's interest in the secret place, the *domaine perdu,* makes him much more a poet of concealment than of revelation, and his grounding reality—far from being a God with a face—is faceless hazard. And I am about to show how *The Magus* can fruitfully be looked at as a *Bildungsro-man* that, far from presenting a substantial self that is ethically called into being by a substantial other, is a kind of meditation on Derridean metaphor: everything in the book is a play of difference, with silence (nothing) beneath it. But I should say at the start that there is a difference between Fowles's vision here and that pre-sented by Derrida in the essay on Levinas. His lingering fidelity to existentialism leads Fowles to espouse a more precise belief than Derrida (with his thoroughly relativized notion of self) does in the Sartrean idea that the underlying nothingness is freedom, consciousness, the Being-for-Itself. Paradoxically, as we will see, this belief in nothingness as existential freedom gives *The Magus* a goal that is more definite than Derrida's play of questions, but that is also more distinctly *nothing.*

Even this concept, however, is not utterly foreign to Derrida. I will end my discussion of the reigning deconstructionist by noting the imagery he uses to describe the "creative imagination," which has a definite kinship with the Sartrean *pour-soi* (the imagination is, according to Derrida, "the essential nothing on whose basis everything can appear and be produced within language"):

> To grasp the operation of creative imagination at the greatest possible proximity to it, one must turn oneself toward the invisible interior of poetic freedom. One must be separated from oneself in order to be reunited with the blind origin of the work in its darkness. This experience of conversion, which founds the literary act (writing or reading), is such that the very words "separation" and "exile," which always designate the interiority of a breaking-off with the world and a making of one's way within it, cannot directly manifest the experience; they can only indicate it through a metaphor. ("Force" 8)

Derrida uses some key Fowlesian language in this description of the self in its own nothingness/consciousness: "invisible interior," "freedom," "separation," "exile."

And the story of *The Magus* is summed up here, too. Fowles's *Bildungsroman* presents a character who undergoes an "experience of conversion," but this one is remarkably literary: Nicholas Urfe is forced to exile himself from the world by reading (in a sense) a work of fiction. It is a didactic work of sorts (it teaches Nicholas as much as Updike's George Caldwell teaches his students), but it is one that teaches not directly but "through . . . metaphor." And the lesson, the goal, is nothing but the literary act itself—the exile that is a metaphor for nothingness/freedom.

The Magus, therefore, looks at the same action—teaching—that John Updike presents in *The Centaur.* But as Derrida subverts Levinas by grounding discourse not in a substantive Other but in faceless Being, so Fowles subverts Updike by portraying his teacher as an absence and his lesson as nothingness.

First, however, Fowles introduces the apprentice. Like most *Bildungsromane*—and unlike *The Centaur,* which founds itself on substantive otherness—*The Magus* begins with the young person who needs education.

Nicholas Urfe, the young man who narrates the story (at least until the novel's final chapter), is the second Fowlesian protagonist who has not been terribly appealing to readers. Although he is not as overtly horrendous as Frederick Clegg, Nicholas is a mean-spirited cynic, and as much as Clegg, he is a cold-blooded collector of women (though he accomplishes his purpose not by chloroforming them, but by tricking them into pitying his existential angst, his "solitary heart" [23]). But perhaps Nicholas does not need to be appealing. He is more a device for introducing Fowlesian themes than an interesting character in his own right (despite his Oxford education, for instance, his prose lacks the peculiar lyricism of Clegg's); Fowles himself, in the foreword to the revised edition of the book, calls him "a partial Everyman of my own class and background" who is made to pursue, in Greece, the "*domaine sans nom* of Alain-Fournier" (9).

Alain-Fournier romanticism is not the only familiar Fowlesian motif represented by Nicholas. Part 1 of the novel contains a variation on the Camusian metaphysical rebel theme; Nicholas tries to carve out space for his own freedom by rejecting religious beliefs and British social expectations. And he does so in a way that echoes Fowles's own rebellion as he describes it in *The Tree* and that also must remind us of Peter Caldwell's struggle for autonomy in *The Centaur:* Nicholas rejects his father. Unlike the mercurial George Caldwell, however, who will find his counterpart in the surrogate father Conchis, Nicholas's father is a representative of rigid authority (and, in a sense, of authoritative texts, the kind of texts that *The Magus* will dismantle). He is a brigadier who embodies the superego at its most blindly authoritarian: Nicholas's dutiful mother "never argued with him and always behaved as if he were listening in the next room, even when he was thousands of miles away" (17). And linguistically he is a mindless literalist; lacking the Derridean notion—which Nicholas will learn from Conchis—that the only way to curb the violence of words is to ironize them, negate them, Nicholas's father uses words with naive, aggressive faith: "In lieu of an intellect he had accumulated an armoury of capitalized key-words like Discipline and Tradition and Responsibility. If I ever dared—I seldom did—to argue with him, he would produce one of these totem words and cosh me with it, as no doubt in similar circumstances he quelled his subalterns" (17). Fowlesian hazard frees Nicholas from these oppressive parents;

they are killed in a plane crash during his second year at Oxford. So as the novel begins, Nicholas is, like Peter Caldwell, familially and even metaphysically alone, atheistic, an isolated self.

At the university, Nicholas continues his rebellion against what his father stood for in a more carefully defined intellectual way; just as Updike's Peter became a self-consciously avant-garde artist, Nicholas, along with a group of college friends, takes up French existentialism. Indeed, the name the group chooses for itself—"Les Hommes Révoltés" (19)—is simply the plural form of the French title of Camus's *The Rebel,* the book that spells out ideas that are central to Fowles's thought. But Nicholas is not yet an authentic Fowlesian rebel. His existentialism is all chic form: "We . . . drank very dry sherry, and (as a protest against those shabby duffel-coated last years of the 'forties) wore dark-grey suits and black ties for our meetings. There we argued about being and nothingness" (19). Nicholas's problem, interestingly, is the same as his father's; he has not yet learned irony. He treats existential literature literally rather than as a Derridean play of metaphors, and the result is not freedom but an enslavement to the ridiculous: "We didn't understand that the heroes, or anti-heroes, of the French existentialist novels we read were not supposed to be realistic. We tried to imitate them, mistaking metaphorical descriptions of complex modes of feeling for straightforward prescriptions of behaviour. We duly felt the right anguishes. Most of us, true to the external dandyism of Oxford, simply wanted to look different. In our club, we did" (19).

In fact, Nicholas begins to use his own excessively literal language as violently as his father used those capitalized words. As I have already mentioned, Nicholas employs existential jargon to seduce—and accumulate—women. In the process, however, he does seem, after only a few chapters, to achieve freedom, which will be the goal of the entire novel. He escapes from all his love affairs unscathed, and he even manages to leave the attractive Alison without feeling the loss. But this is a shallow, empty freedom, a freedom founded, again, on literal concepts rather than on truly deconstructed metaphors. Nicholas, as much as his most gullible lovers (and a great deal more than Alison), believes in his own literarily existential self-image; after constructing, for example, a highly artificial farewell letter to Alison, Nicholas relishes his own anti-heroic "feeling of emotional triumph. A dry feeling; but I liked things dry" (50). He is as alone in a self-enclosed totality as Peter Caldwell at his most solipistic; as Peter took perverse pleasure in picking at his psoriasis, so Nicholas carefully nurses his own isolation.

But *The Centaur* is about the way George Caldwell's reality breaks through Peter's self-enclosure. And Nicholas, too, now encounters something that he cannot possess, cannot literalize. He goes to Greece and falls in love with a woman, but it is only a metaphorical woman, and the metaphor refuses to accommodate itself to literal explication: "I fell totally and for ever in love with the Greek landscape from the moment I arrived. But with the love came a contradictory, almost irritating, feeling of impotence, as if Greece were a woman so sensually provocative that I must fall physically and desperately in love with her, and at the same time so calmly aristocratic that I should never be able to approach her" (51). It is Greece—specifically, the small island of Phraxos, where he will teach (badly) at a boys' school—that is this Fowlesian hero's secret place, his Edenic "world before the machine, almost before man" (53). This is the beginning of the disruption of Nicholas's arrogant world by a kind of otherness. But the goal of this disruption will be not a relationship with the Other (as it is in *The Centaur*) but rather a genuine freedom for the self. So the otherness represented here by Greece, and later by Conchis himself, cannot be encountered in any truly personal way; it has no face.

For a while, despite Greece's disruptive influence, Nicholas fools himself into continuing and deepening his image of himself as existential poet ("The onanistic literary picture of myself I caressed up out of reality began to dominate my life" [60]). He writes as much as he can and conveniently curses the school for not giving him time to write more. But Greece will not abide this illusion for long, and he is forced to face the nothingness that he toyed with at Oxford; Nicholas suddenly realizes that all his poetry is undergraduate banality: "The truth rushed down on my like a burying avalanche. I was not a poet" (60). He discovers what Fowles calls, in *The Aristos,* the "nemo": "By this I mean not only 'nobody' but also the state of being nobody—'nobodiness'. . . . The nemo is man's sense of his own futility and ephemerality; of his relativity, his comparativeness; of his virtual nothingness" (*Aristoi* 47, 49). Nicholas concludes that he belongs "to nothingness, to the *néant*" and that all he can create is his own death (62). He takes a borrowed gun up to the hills to kill himself.

Already, in other words, after only a few chapters in a very long novel, we have reached the point that Frederick Clegg reached almost at the end of *The Collector.* Just as two alternate tendencies in Clegg, the idealistic and the necrophiliac, were in a dialectical tension that it seemed only suicide would mediate, so a similar clash in Nicholas between the existential/poetic and the literal (the "violent," in both Levinas's and Derrida's terms) has led him to the same choice. But where Clegg was called back to life by mere mechanical repetition (he sees another young woman to collect), Nicholas is called back by romantic mystery and music: "From the hills behind came the solitary voice of a girl. . . . It sounded disembodied, of place, not person. . . . [I]t seemed intensely mysterious, welling out of a solitude and suffering that made mine trivial and absurd. I sat with the gun across my knees, unable to move while the sound floated down through the evening air. I don't know how long she sang, but the sky darkened, the sea paled to a nacreous grey" (63). If Fowles were a straightforward Wordsworthian romantic, this might have been the virtual end of Nicholas's story; the girl's song, like that of the Solitary Reaper, might have been the breath of a healing Nature, a kind of naturalized version of God's grace, a presence that poured itself into the heart of the lonely and depressed wanderer. The novel's teacher, Conchis, would then merely offer a reprise of this grace-filled song that has called Nicholas to a romantic rebirth—and, indeed, shortly after encountering Conchis, Nicholas does call him the agent of "a sort of green stir" (105), a desire to live again.

But for all his ties to the romantic tradition, Fowles is more interested in the way the mystery of Greece dismantles romanticism, exposing it as mere metaphor; its haunting music exposes even Nicholas's attempted suicide as a foolish literalization of poetic imagery. As Clegg wanted to die like Romeo, Nicholas is posing as Mercutio: "More and more it crept through my mind with the chill spring night that I was trying to commit not a moral action, but a fundamentally aesthetic one; to do something that would end my life sensationally, significantly, consistently. It was a Mercutio death I was looking for, not a real one" (64). What Nicholas experiences here is less a presence than an absence ("It sounded disembodied"); instead of nudging him closer to a positive Other, it drives him into deeper negativity.

And as the seemingly positive romanticism of the song is undermined by its negating effects, so Conchis's role will ultimately be nihilative rather than constitutive. In his hands, Nicholas will feel not reborn but disintegrated: "I had had a sense of being taken apart, disconnected from a previous self—or the linked structures of ideas and conscious feeling that constitute self; and now it was like lying on the workshop bench, a litter of parts, the engineer gone . . . and not being quite sure how to put oneself together again" (393).

Like *The Centaur,* therefore, *The Magus* allows its *Bildungsroman* hero to be jolted from an emotional stagnation by a teacher and father (and, in this case, magus). Fowles's Nicholas Urfe, however, is brought not to relationship with a loving Other but to freedom, founded on nothingness—of which Conchis is a living embodiment.

The sin, so to speak, of which Nicholas accuses himself after his flirtation with suicide is that of aesthetic theism. His desire to die a "Mercutio death" was based, he realizes, on an inadvertant belief that his life story is being watched by an attentive, providential Author/God: "All the time I felt I was being watched, that I was not alone, that I was putting on an act for the benefit of someone" (64). And this belief in providence offends Nicholas's own atheism; he considers himself "intensely false; in existentialist terms, inauthentic" (64). He will not be able to act with true existential freedom, he implies, until he realizes—fully and experientially— that he is absolutely alone.

And then Conchis seems to show him the opposite; it initially appears that Conchis has entered the book precisely as an embodiment of Nicholas's not-aloneness. Roaming around the southern part of Phraxos, feeling that it is his private, "secret province," Nicholas is prodded into an awareness of someone besides himself. First he notices that smoke is coming from the chimney of the Bourani villa, and he is dismayed: "My first feeling was one of resentment, since the solitude of the south side of the island must now be spoilt and I had come to feel possessive about it" (70). Then, after noticing Bourani's barbed-wire fence, which he thinks "insulted the solitude," he has an eerie experience of a kind of presence: "I was staring up at the hot, heavy slope of trees, when I had the sensation that I was not alone. I was being looked at" (70). And then he discovers clear evidence of this fact—two footfins, a towel, and a poetry book with passages from Eliot, Auden, and Pound portentously marked. Conchis has entered Nicholas's life and Fowles's book.

But although Conchis seems to be the revelation to Nicholas of otherness, even of a kind of metaphysical providence—much as George Caldwell served as such a revelation for his son Peter in *The Centaur*—we should note how different Conchis's entrance into Fowles's novel is from George's entrance into Updike's. George, remember, roared into *The Centaur* with a resounding forcefulness; though his frequent metamorphoses made it impossible entirely to comprehend his being (he was, in other words, infinitely distant from the "same"), he was very much *there*. Conchis, however, is at first invisible, a collection of traces that attest as much to his present absence as to his absent presence. Nicholas begins to find out more and more about him from the villagers and from his coteacher Demetriades, but Conchis defers revealing himself as a real, living presence. Indeed, the path to Conchis's house is marked "*salle d'attende,*" "the waiting-room"; if George Caldwell supplied a kind of phenomenological representation of the Barthian God, Conchis so far seems more to suggest Godot.

Indeed, a Godot—an absence—is precisely what a teacher must be in this Fowlesian *Bildungsroman.* Even after he physically appears in the novel (and the chapter in which this occurs begins—surely not coincidentally—with the words "The absence"), Conchis does not teach Nicholas that he is ethically called out of the same (or the self) and into being by a Levinasian Other; he teaches him, rather, that Being is a Derridean dialogue within the same, a play of metaphors that repeatedly dismantle themselves because their telos—a positively present Other—is *not.* Like George Caldwell, he continually unforms the forms he presents— and, also like George, he does so by invoking Greek myth. But the effect of the unforming is different this time: Conchis is a paradoxical embodiment of is-not-ness.

Nonetheless, Conchis does possess attributes, not unlike George Caldwell's, that make him a good teacher: he is a brilliant storyteller, he has a flair for the dramatic, and he is a striking personality. He uses each of these attributes, however, in a self-negating way. There is no way to add them up and arrive at an integrated character; as Peter Conradi states, "No theory about him coheres" (48).

The second section of *The Magus* is filled with long monologues in which Conchis tells stories about his life; he describes his passion for a young woman named Lily, his realization of the atrocity of war, his relationship with a Sade-like aesthete, his observation of a wild mystic, his discovery of the terror of pure freedom. And although he claims to despise fiction (he says that he has destroyed all the novels he ever owned), he soon makes it clear that these stories about his life are carefully, calculatedly plotted— and, indeed, are frequently fictitious. The real message of the stories, in other words, is that there are no objective truths, even (or especially) about Conchis himself: "He clearly meant me not to be able to relate the conflicting sides of his personality. Things like the humanity in his playing of Bach, in certain aspects, however embroidered, of his autobiography, were undermined, nullified by his perversity and malice elsewhere. He must know it, therefore must want me to flounder" (196). Conchis himself spells out his Derridean message: "Let me pass on an axiom about our species, Nicholas: Never take another human being literally" (236).

The dramatic performances that Conchis stages have a similar intent: they are designed not to teach but, in a sense, to unteach.

Seeing the beautiful Lily now, at Bourani, shatters Nicholas's belief in the Lily whom Conchis supposedly loved half a century earlier; and then seeing another, identical Lily, right after he has kissed the first one, shakes Nicholas's trust in the actual altogether. Much later, furthermore, Lily (or is it Julie?) carries him, via an intense experience of love making, into a kind of D. H. Lawrence novel— which is suddenly transformed, when Nicholas is dragged off to a dramatized "trial," into a novel by Kafka. The trial itself is first established as an ancient ritual: the participants are all disguised as mythic creatures. But it suddenly turns into a modern scientific experiment as the actors remove their bizarre costumes and become cool psychological researchers. All of these dislocations serve to obliterate Nicholas's faith in any substantive ground or center; far from anchoring his consciousness in an Other, they make him aware only of relativity, an interminable play (in the sense both of ludus and of drama) of difference.

Then there is Conchis's personality itself. And although Nicholas does describe his new teacher with some particularity ("He was nearly completely bald, brown as old leather, short and spare. . . . The most striking thing about him was the intensity of his eyes . . . with a simian penetration" [81]), by the end of the novel the character has metamorphosed so often that this concrete description is obliterated. Fowles himself has claimed that Conchis exhibits "a series of masks representing human notions of God, from the supernatural to the jargon-ridden scientific." And Fowles makes it clear that what is behind all these masks is precisely an absence, not a presence; he describes the masks as "a series of human illusions about something that does not exist in fact" (*Magus* Foreword 10). Beneath all the masks and metamorphoses, however, one seemingly genuine personality trait does persist: Conchis's famed smile. But Nicholas explicates this smile as "the smile of dramatic irony" (150), which would make it a bodily expression, paradoxically, of Conchis's absence, his smug separation from the world. If Derrida's God, rather than being a substantive Other, is mere relativity, appearing "Within difference, and at bottom as Difference itself" ("Violence" 116), then perhaps the single concrete act this God can perform is to smile ironically. So, by perpetually wearing this smile, Conchis manages after all to wear a mask of Fowles's true God: the God-who-is-not. Though he grandly presides over the dramatics that dominate the novel, Conchis ultimately teaches Nicholas that, metaphysically, he is *not* being watched.

And if the teacher himself is so disintegrated, surely the goal of his lessons is not the conventional self-improvement of his pupil. In other words, the purpose of Conchis's godgame is essentially not psychologically or spiritually constructive but is negative, deconstructive.

Here I realize I am entering controversial territory. Some insightful readers of *The Magus* have seen the godgame as a ritual with real, substantive content and a positive psychological purpose. Robert Huffaker, for instance, sees Conchis as a psychotherapist and the godgame as an elaborate way of leading Nicholas through Jungian analysis. Huffaker describes Jungian technique in this way: "By encouraging the awareness that the unknowable, the mysterious, does exist within the human mind, and by allowing the individual person to retain his faith in the beauty and efficacy of his own irrational nature, Jung's method would bring the neurotic to harmony and creativity by reinforcing his individuality" (58). And Huffaker claims that the godgame quite directly uses this technique to lead Nicholas to psychological health: "By presenting Nick with aesthetic, mythic, and historical images from the human unconscious, the godgame applies Jung's 'individuation' process" (60). Ellen McDaniel even more ingeniously claims that Fowles has created an elaborate myth based on the Tarot: "The author grounds his novel in the intricacies of this ancient and mysterious pack of seventy-eight cards—the same number of cards as there are chapters in *The Magus*—and draws a deliberate parallel between the quest of Nicholas Urfe in *The Magus* and the journey of the Fool through the graduated levels of the Tarot" (249).

But although I see such readings as good ways of entering into the novel's complex play of imagery, I think they mistakenly see the imagery itself as having an absolute value (Huffaker, for instance, speaks of Lily/Julie as an embodiment of Nicholas's anima, and McDaniel meticulously enumerates the references to the Tarot). In fact, I see the *play* of images to be more important than the images themselves. The godgame, then, does not help Nicholas create a personal myth (as Jungian analysis would); rather, it teaches him to demythologize—to deconstruct any myth. I agree, in other words, with Simon Loveday, who sees the long central episode of the novel as "a phoney." The narrative, Loveday says, is compelling, but the content is "subverted and ironised": "we must not be taken in by 'The godgame' " (32).

More to the point, *Nicholas* is taught not to be taken in by the godgame. As I have mentioned already, Conchis loads his stories and dramatizations with indications of their own artificiality, and he causes Nicholas to feel not—as he would in a Jungian or a Tarot ritual—a sense of deep, mysterious power; he feels, instead, that the normal world has been obliterated: "I had no feeling of the supernatural. . . . That does not mean I was not frightened; but my fear came from a knowledge that anything might happen. That there were no limits in this masque, no normal social laws or conventions" (204). Conchis himself calls his ritual a "meta-theatre," designed to help participants see through conventional-ities—first in the game, and then in life itself:

> "The object of the meta-theatre is precisely that—to al-low the participants to see through their first roles in it. But that is only the catastasis."
> "I'm afraid I don't know what that word means."
> "It is what precedes the final act, or catastrophe, in classical tragedy." He added, "Or comedy. As the case may be."
> "The case depending on?"
> "Whether we learn to see through the roles we give ourselves in ordinary life." (415)

This emphasis on seeing through roles, which Conchis himself describes as crucial to the godgame, explains why the game must conclude with what is called a "disintoxification" (529)—a free-ing of Nicholas from bondage to the game by a final, indubitable revelation of the game's artificiality. Indeed, disintoxification has been a part of the very fabric of the game from the beginning, but it is at the end of the game that, in Derridean terms, the game truly does violence to itself much as it has been (sometimes literally) doing violence to Nicholas. One can write, Derrida says, "by crossing out, by crossing out what already has been crossed out" (112), and, during the disintoxification, the godgame crosses out what has already been crossed out.

Nicholas's disintoxification includes his discovery that "Julie" is a fraud; his attendance at the fierce trial, during which he sees himself and his adventure reduced to the simplest Freudian terms; his viewing of a silly "blue" movie, followed by an act of on-stage intercourse between Lily and her black lover; and especially his tour of the "Earth," the caverns under Bourani that hold the godgame's dramatic props and scripts. And this tour, presented in chapter 65, represents Fowles's most overt and playful use of discourse's violence against itself. Not only does Conchis decon-struct his "meta-theatre" by allowing its actor and audience to see its artifices, but Fowles himself deconstructs his novel—which for one chapter, at least, is truly a metanovel—by revealing and meditating on its fictionality.

Nicholas's visit to the Earth (this is the word, by the way, from which Fowles derived Nicholas's surname [*Magus* Foreword 9]; we are, therefore, entering the very source of the protagonist's existence) begins with a new entrance into Bourani. More than ever it appears to be a secret place, a place that can be visited only by those in *author*ity: "a new notice covered the *Salle d'attente* sign. It said in Greek, *Private property, entrance strictly forbidden*" (556). Nonetheless, Nicholas enters Bourani, opens the hidden trapdoor, and descends to the caverns. There he finds an extensive theatrical wardrobe (some of the costumes he has seen during the Bourani dramatics, some he has not), and papers covered with sketched-out scenes and lines from the godgame. And he finds novels that have been placed there not by Conchis but by Fowles, and that have marginal comments referring not to the godgame but to a novel, *The Magus:* "There were a dozen or so Edwardian novels. Someone had pencilled notes on the flyleaves. *Good dialogue*, or *Useful clichés at 98 and 164. See scene at 203,* said one. *'Are you asking me to commit osculation?' laughed the ever-playful Fanny.* (557). Naturally, Nicholas does not comment on these notes, since they do Derridean violence to the very discourse that constitutes him.

This metafictional moment shows that the entire text is structurally teetering on the brink of self-obliteration. But a fairy tale that Nicholas finds in the Earth sums up thematically the meaning of disintoxication—and of the entire strategy of the godgame. The tale is called "The Prince and the Magician," and it describes a prince in a quest for truth; specifically, he wonders if islands, princesses, and God exist. But he discovers that truth is not to be had; all he gets are conflicting stories from two men, his father the king and a "man in evening dress," both of whom turn out to be magicians—magi. He is caught, in other words, within the space of difference between two opposing viewpoints; there is no wholly other, no God or teacher or Centaur, who can break through his isolation with any genuine revelation. The best the prince can do is existentially resign himself to the relative, to living in that space of nothingness which Derrida calls "creative imagination" ("Force" 8) and within which, according to this fairy tale, the self can work magic:

> "I must know the real truth, the truth beyond magic."
> "There is no truth beyond magic," said the king.
> The prince was full of sadness.
> He said, "I will kill myself."
> The king by magic caused death to appear. Death stood in the door and beckoned to the prince. The prince shuddered. He remembered the beautiful but un-

real islands and the unreal but beautiful princesses.
"Very well," he said. "I can bear it."
"You see, my son," said the king, "you too now be-
gin to be a magician." (562)

It is this concept of creative imagination—which Derrida likens to
exile or separation—that is, I think, really at the bottom of Fowles's
famed idea of the Few or the Elect (which I discussed in relation to
The Collector, and which is frequently brought up in *The Magus* as
well). For Fowles, those who are authentic enough to accept the
exile of the self from any metaphysical Other (either in the
Levinasian phenomenological sense or, more importantly, in the
positively religious sense), those who accept the absolute aloneness of the conscious self—and, indeed, the nothingness of this
Sartrean Being-for-itself—are the Elect, the Few. This is why the
godgame finally demands that its teacher, far from revealing a face,
must abscond, imitating the *deus absconditus.* And as Nicholas
stands with Alison at the end of the novel, he accepts this, and
therefore becomes one of the Elect: "There were no watching eyes.
The windows were as blank as they looked. The theatre was empty.
It was not a theatre. . . . It was logical, the perfect climax to the
godgame. They had absconded, we were alone" (667). As Fowles
himself writes, in a section of *The Aristos* called "The Godgame":
"If there had been a creator, his second act would have been to
disappear" (19).

So the teacher Conchis's lesson in this book has been not
substantive but strategic. He has, by artificially orchestrating his
own obliteration, used the violence of discourse against itself in
order to create a metaphor (or antimetaphor?) for the nothingness—the lack of absolute, authoritative otherness—that is his
(and Fowles's novel's) essential vision. *The Aristos* describes the
strategy: "Put dice on the table and leave the room; but make it
seem possible to the players that you were never in the room" (19).
The Magus, therefore, is a massive tour de force that simply creates
a space, a nothingness.

But although the movement of the book is a construction of
nothingness (which may make it less daring in this skeptical,
postmodern era than Updike's attempt to found a *Bildungsroman*
not on a pinprick of consciousness but on a solid Other), *The
Magus* is not an exercise in nihilism. As Clegg canceled himself out
in *The Collector* to generate space for Miranda's potential freedom,

so Conchis and his novel cancel themselves out to give Nicholas a real freedom; as I said earlier, Fowles possesses a residual devotion to existentialism that leads him to see freedom as a positive thing that must not be deconstructed. Although he does not believe in freedom in any absolute sense (he is not even sure that it is not an illusion), he considers it something that needs to be treasured, nurtured, striven for. During an interview, he said, "I think there's a tiny modicum of free will if you keep yourself open. I think occasionally you can make a decision which is possibly free. . . . All my novels are about how you achieve that possible—possibly nonexistent—freedom" (Singh 185). The often sadistic machinations of *The Magus* are an elaborate self-canceling strategy that creates the space in which Nicholas can, if only for a moment, experience freedom.

I have already, in my discussion of *The Collector,* argued that Fowles's nothingness, like Sartre's, is precisely freedom itself ("freedom," as Sartre puts it, "in its foundation coincides with the nothingness which is at the heart of man" [568]). *The Magus* even more than *The Collector* is filled with reflections on freedom, which is seen both as a grand fact about the human self and as a specific attribute of important existential moments in a person's life.

The most grand reflection on freedom occurs in the fifty-third chapter, the only chapter with a title (the title spells out, in Greek letters, the word for freedom—*eleutheria*). This is the chapter in which Conchis tells how he was branded a German collaborationist during World War II. During the war, he had been appointed mayor of the Phraxos village, and he had been forced to participate in the roundup of several Greek guerrillas. It was one of the guerrillas who proclaimed the simple, invincible fact of freedom; under torture, and even when Conchis had been told to beat him to death with an unloaded gun, the man simply roared "that same word, that one word: *eleutheria*. There was nothing noble in it. It was pure savagery, as if he was throwing a can of lighted petrol over us" (434–35). While others groped for "the non-existent pity of a *deus vindicans*" (437), this guerrilla affirmed the absence of such a God; he affirmed that the hole in Being left by God's absence is the space that guarantees human beings' power to make their world themselves. This guerrilla, then, is Camus's metaphysical rebel par excellence, and he demonstrates that the rebellion which Fowles so admires is founded on absence/freedom: "He was not God, because there is no God we can know. But he was a proof that there is a God that we can never know. He was the final right to deny. To be free to choose. . . . He was every freedom, from the very worst to the very best. . . . He was something that passed beyond

morality but sprang out of the very essence of things—that comprehended all, the freedom to do all, and stood against only one
thing—the prohibition not to do all" (441).

The guerrilla very nearly embodies freedom in the abstract, and
the fact that he himself is not a morally admirable figure demonstrates that freedom is not moral or immoral; founded on nothing,
it simply *is*. But this important chapter also illustrates another
dimension of freedom considered in this book: freedom is something experienced by an individual in an event that Conchis calls a
"fulcrum" (111). This is a moment that arises simply by chance, by
hazard (if such a moment were a providential gift, as it tends to be
in Updike's fiction, then it would for Fowles exemplify not freedom
but the denial of freedom). Standing over the guerrilla, ready to
beat him to death (unless he did so, he condemned a group of
innocent Greeks—and, he thought, himself—to death), Conchis
experienced such a fulcrum precisely because he felt what Sartre
calls the "anguish" of freedom: there was, quite literally, nothing
that separated him from the action he was about to undertake, and
that nothing was his freedom (see Sartre 71).

It is exactly such a fulcrum that the deconstructive strategies of
the godgame have been preparing Nicholas for (he entered the
game after a sort of fulcrum, the almost-suicide—but he did not
then understand the implications of the experience). First of all,
the game creates for Nicholas several artificial fulcra. Early in the
game, for instance, Nicholas is allowed to choose whether or not to
swallow what he thinks is hydrocyanic acid after betting his life on
a roll of dice; and then, much later, he is given the chance to punish
Julie/Lily with a whip, after learning that she has been in cahoots
with Conchis all along. Such moments obviously are not genuine
Fowlesian fulcra, because they have been engineered by a conscious (Conchis) creator. Still, in each case the metaphors that
Conchis uses are not positive but negative, deconstructive; they
teach Nicholas about the essential negativity of fulcrum experiences precisely by negating themselves. In the first case, Conchis
loads the dice and substitutes ratafia for poison—to illustrate, by
contrast, the difference between artificially manipulated reality
and true, godless hazard. And the second case takes place near the
end of the trial, in which Conchis has metaphorically canceled
himself out by illustrating his own lack of an absolute point of
reference (his lack of genuine otherness)—his existence, or nonexistence, in the gap of difference between the mythic and the
scientific (the same gap in which Clegg a great deal less consciously resided). Then, after these metaphorical absences have
prepared Nicholas for a fulcrum, he genuinely experiences one at

the end of the novel—after the teacher, the representation of God, has truly absconded.

Those critics who read *The Magus* as a positive parable of individuation tend to see the final chapter, in which Nicholas confronts the long-lost Alison, as a depiction of Nicholas's mature, psychologically integrated ability to embrace the real. In her discussion of the book's Tarot imagery, for example, Ellen McDaniel says with a matter-of-fact authority: "The world card of the Tarot, the last card, signifies synthesis and creation, and with Alison, Nicholas will create a new life founded on the lessons he has learned and the riddles he has solved" (259). Robert Huffaker, harking back to the tale of the Prince and the Magician, similarly describes the conclusion as a substantive celebration of Nicholas's new psychological wholeness: "Accepting that there is no truth beyond magic is accepting that there is no truth beyond the hazard and mystery of reality. Nick, like the prince, accepts two-dimensional reality: both conscious and unconscious perceptions" (69–70).

There is material in the novel to support such an interpretation. If Conchis is not an Other in the true, Levinasian sense, it sometimes seems that Alison is. Again and again, Nicholas refers to Alison as a kind of anchor of reality in the midst of the dislocating games that Conchis is playing with him. During an idyllic visit to Mount Parnassus, for instance, Nicholas thinks that Alison, unlike the people at the Bourani villa, is not a mere play of metaphors: "On Parnassus of all mountains, it occurred to me, her unsubtlety, her inability to hide behind metaphor, ought to offend me; to bore me as uncomplex poetry normally bored me. And yet in some way I couldn't define she had, had always had, this secret trick of slipping through all the obstacles I put between us; as if she were really my sister" (271–72). And much later, after the disintoxification, Nicholas, thinking that Alison is dead, mourns the loss of her "quotidianeity": "Only Alison could have exorcised her [Lily]. I remember those moments of relief at Monemvasia and on the ship coming back to Phraxos, moments when the most ordinary things seemed beautiful and lovable—possessors of a magnificent quotidianeity. I could have found that in Alison. Her special genius was her normality, her reality, her predictability; her crystal core of non-betrayal; her attachment to all that Lily was not" (564). Real, beyond metaphor, honest, lovable: Alison seems to have precisely what the Conchis company lack—a "face."

But of course, this is all a sham. Those who see Nicholas's reunion with Alison as an unequivocal embracing of the real have failed to consider how deeply ironized Alison has become. She has been playing Conchis's godgame herself, pretending to have committed suicide and then coyly allowing Nicholas to see her at a distance before disappearing again. The fact that Nicholas may deserve this torment does not change the fact that Alison has been playing with absence even more ruthlessly than Conchis himself.

In any case, the deeply ambiguous ending of the novel does not have Nicholas truly facing (in Levinas's sense) Alison or anyone else. Rather, it has Nicholas frozen in the moment that the entire novel has, through all its negations, been constructing (or deconstructing): his fulcrum, his moment of nothingness and freedom.

The chapter begins with the first of those authorial intrusions for which Fowles has become famous. A new voice breaks through Nicholas's first-person narrative and reflects on the impossibility, in these skeptical times, of definitively ending a novel: "So ten more days. But what happened in the following years shall be silence; another mystery" (656). Simon Loveday has aptly pointed out that this device subverts Nicholas's credibility as narrator and even as character (39); Fowles has bluntly reminded us of this young man's fictionality. But I think that the purpose of the intrusion is more Conchis-like (and Derridean): Fowles is trying not so much to subvert Nicholas as to subvert himself as creator. He is using discourse to cross itself out—to suggest, metaphorically, its absence, and the absence of Fowles (the creator) himself.

And then he leaves Nicholas in that frozen moment, at the "fulcrum": "All waits, suspended. Suspend the autumn trees, the autumn sky, anonymous people. . . . fragments of freedom, an anagram made flesh" (667–68). Fowles must now stop writing about and even stop looking at Nicholas; to pursue Nicholas's story beyond this fulcrum would be to continue to create—to be god, an Other who addresses the self and even acts providentially upon it—when the point of the novel is that Nicholas has escaped such otherness. Alison herself, at this moment, is not permitted to invade Nicholas's freedom; instead of facing Nicholas, she shows merely "The bowed head, the buried face" (667). Nicholas, we are made to see, is free because he is alone—without God, without Conchis, without Fowles. He is even, in a sense, without himself, since Being-for-itself has no substance; it is nothingness.

Teacher as Other

The Centaur, like *The Magus,* ends with a kind of frozen image— but it is an image not of the self but of the Other. The book's epilogue comically but genuinely establishes George Caldwell in heaven, in infinity, as a sign of the Zodiac: "Zeus had loved his old friend, and lifted him up, and set him among the stars as the constellation Sagittarius. Here, in the Zodiac, now above, now below the horizon, he assists in the regulation of our destinies, though in this latter time few living mortals cast their eyes respectfully toward Heaven, and fewer still sit as students to the stars" (222). As I have noted, the similarity of Updike's and Fowles's imagery is remarkable—Updike's teacher metamorphoses into a Zodiacal figure, and Fowles's into a figure from the Tarot. And in both *Bildungsromane,* the protagonist is educated not by ideas or even by experiences so much as by encountering an almost superhuman teacher/centaur/magus; in each case, the lesson is the revelation of the very otherness of the teacher himself.

But the ways the two writers use their imagery and the revelations that the respective apprentices receive are remarkably dissimilar; the novels are vastly different because they present radically different notions of that focal issue, otherness, and correspondingly different notions of the solidity of the self. The entire movement of Updike's *Bildungsroman* is to establish the self of the young protagonist as something that attains its substantiality from an ethical encounter with the unassimilable but substantive—absent but present—teacher/other. Fowles's book, on the other hand, is an elaborate exercise in antiwriting—an obliteration of the teacher/other, and even of the narrative, in order to create an empty space of freedom for the protagonist's substance-less self. *The Centaur* asserts that otherness *is* (in phenomemological terms, it repeats Karl Barth's theological assertion that "God is *God*") and that the self itself therefore has actuality and positive content. *The Magus,* on the other hand, because its other is thoroughly an absence and because the narrative itself cancels itself out, leaves the self in exile—even from any substantive, authoritative story about itself.

With these two novels, Updike and Fowles began with the same materials—the *Bildungsroman* form, lonely and atheistic narrators, charismatic teachers who exhibit a Greek godliness—and used these materials to constitute their respective philosophical and aesthetic worlds. And although the worlds they create are radically, even ontologically, different, the books' similarities reveal again the surprising bridge connecting these two quite dissimilar writers, one English and one American, and an even more surprising bridge connecting the two literary *viae*—the *negativa* and the *affirmativa*—that I have been describing. After looking at the two writers' sexual subversions of traditional novelistic narrative in *Couples* and *The French Lieutenant's Woman,* I will end this study by examining the way in which Updike and Fowles, much later in their careers, have made the two *viae* almost (but not completely) meet.

6

Sex as a Subversion of Convention:
Couples and
The French Lieutenant's Woman

Couples

Time has improved *Couples.* When it was first published in 1968, it gained notoriety for its sexual explicitness and for little else. Years later, however, the novel's sex seems quite unshocking and even a bit dated (now that we are in the era of AIDS—the 1990s—and the sexual revolution has been declared dead). The sex is essential to the book, surely, but it now seems not so much to be what the book is about but rather to be a part of a larger strategy, something that Updike uses both to energize and to ironize the narrative form and content that he has chosen to work with.

More than any other book Updike has written, *Couples* has the feel of a grand old Victorian social novel; a number of critics have compared it to *Middlemarch,* and the comparison is apt. As Robert Detweiler notes, this is a book not with one hero (though Piet Hanema does emerge as a dominant character, a sort of college-educated Rabbit) but with a "Composite Protagonist" (109): the protagonist is the town of Tarbox itself, just as the protagonist of *Middlemarch* is Middlemarch. But Updike opens up a big gap of difference between himself and George Eliot, and between the twentieth-century novel and the novel of the nineteenth century— and he does this, formalistically, by utilizing the kind of narrative discourse that previously had been relegated to pornography.

If the sex allows Updike to subvert a conventional form, it also successfully subverts the content. Like so many Updike novels, especially the Rabbit series, *Couples* is drenched in the textures of real American society at a very particular time. Updike himself has said that the novel's action "could have taken place only under Kennedy; the social currents it traces are as specific to those years as flowers in a meadow are to their moment of summer" (Plimpton

444). But this historical, sociological, very public texture is under-cut by the novel's obsessive interest in private, genital activity, which ultimately points toward an even more radically private event that each human self undergoes—death.

In this double way *Couples,* beneath its rather straightforward storytelling, looks to be covertly postmodernist—in a way that John Fowles might approve of. Just as Fowles deconstructs conven-tions in order to open up a space for the autonomous, utterly unencumbered self, so Updike here seems to be doing the same. His subverted Victorian novel seems to leave the human self alone with nothing but its own death, freed from any external god or society, a metaphysical rebel. (Indeed, we will see that in *The French Lieutenant's Woman,* the Fowles novel that best pairs up with *Couples,* Fowles employs a strategy just like Updike's: he too uses sex to subvert the Victorian novel form.) Nonetheless, in *Couples* the negative movement ultimately is itself ironized (as it is not in *The French Lieutenant's Woman*). The sexual subversion of the social- novel form and the American-suburbia content fails, at least partially. And radical existential freedom is qualified by repetitions—in this case, of God, of marriage, and of the social-novel form itself—of the sort that give Updike's books a foundation in substance rather than nothingness. For all its pretensions at exploding the traditional in order to usher in "*the post-pill paradise*" (58), *Couples* is finally a novel about the world's stuff, its substance, rather than about (sexual/genital or cemetery) holes.

Insofar as Updike assumes the narrative persona of a confident nineteenth-century novelist like George Eliot, he speaks with a kind of omniscient authority; he analyzes the behavior of the residents of Tarbox with the cool, though benign, rationality of a social scientist. Before describing the first experiments of the Applebys and the little-Smiths with partner swapping, for example, the narrator places the two couples in a larger sociological context (I quote at some length to capture his discursive style and sweep-ing breadth):

> Raised amid these national trials [the Great Depression and World War II] and introduced as adults into an in-dulgent economy, into a business atmosphere strangely blended of crisp youthful imagery and underlying de-personalization, of successful small-scale gambles car-ried out against a background of rampant diversification

and the ultimate influence of a government whose taxes
and commissions and appetite for armaments set limits
everywhere, introduced into a nation whose leadership
allowed a toothless moralism to dissemble a certain
practiced cunning, into a culture where adolescent pas-
sions and homosexual philosophies were not quite yet
triumphant, a climate still *furtively* hedonist, of a country still too overtly threatened from without to be
ruthlessly self-abusive, a climate of time between, of
standoff and day-by-day, wherein all generalizations,
even negative ones, seemed unintelligent—to this new
world the Applebys and the little-Smiths brought a modest determination to be free, to be flexible and decent.
(113–14)

This is Updike self-consciously rejecting the relativism of modernist and postmodernist literature, which can present only the
impressions of a single consciousness, or which explodes the
integrity even of the single consciousness itself. In fact, in his *Paris
Review* interview, Updike explicitly expresses an attraction (nostalgia?) for such an omnisciently certain narrator, and he describes
it, tellingly, as a kind of God who can load a narrative world with
substance:

The account of things done minus the presiding, talkative, confiding and pedagogic author may be a somewhat
dead convention; that is, like anybody who takes any
writing courses, I was told how stale and awful it is
when authors begin to signal, as Dickens did, over the
heads of the characters to the reader. Yet I feel that
something has been lost with this authority, with this
sense of the author as God, as a speaking God, as a chatty
God, filling the universe of the book. (Plimpton 448–49)

But this wisely analytical narrator (George Hunt finds his
persona downright avuncular [117]) is not the only voice in the
novel; it is surely not the voice that made the book, in the late
1960s, a kind of literary *cause célèbre*. Rather, the more famous
Updikean voice in *Couples* is the lyrically sexual one (the characters being described here are Piet and Angela, but in some ways it
hardly matters):

She tugged her gown to her throat and the bones of her
fingers confided a glimmering breast to his mouth,
shaped by an *ah* of appreciation; when with insistent
symmetry she rolled onto her back to have him use the

other, his hand discovered her mons Veneris swollen
high, her whole fair floating flesh dilated outward toward a deity, an anyoneness, it was Piet's fortune to have
localized, to have seized captive in his own dark form.
The woman's beauty caressed the skin of his eyes; his
shaggy head sank toward the ancient alleyway where,
proud queen, she frothed most. (205)

Such a passage could hardly have been written by a George Eliot,
let alone a Charles Dickens. Nor could it have been written by a
sociologist; it is important to note that Updike the eroticist is really
Updike the romantic—a romantic very much in John Fowles's
terms, undercutting the analytical, even mechanical, dimensions
of his text with a celebration of the private, the fleshily organic, the
frothy, even the sacred. Formally, then, the graphic sex serves to
break apart the public, social-scientific positivism of the omniscient narrator, to replace the mundane with the romantic (in the
way that Rabbit tries to do in, for instance, his early excursion
south).

So it seems that Updike uses his romantic/sexual voice to
shatter the book's solid, public, traditional discourse—but to what
end? Is he celebrating, in a Fowlesian way, the freedom created by
the act of rebelling, or is he bemoaning the sterility of a modern
world in which public, traditional values have been replaced by
radically private, romantic/sexual ones? As I have already suggested, I see the book, like other Updike fiction, engaged with
worldly substance rather than with existential nothingness/free-
dom, but it certainly does not take this position in a facile,
unambiguous way. It does, however, contain yet another form of
discourse that points toward an overall tendency, discourse that is
also quintessentially Updikean: existential meditations on death.

In addition to adopting the cool objectivity of the social analyst
and the hot sensuality of the romantic, Updike also slips into the
stream of consciousness of Piet Hanema, the character who most
strikingly lives the tension between the novel's public suburban
world and private sexual one. And in these passages Updike often
bombards us with fragmentary death images: "Revolving terror
scooped the shell of him thin. A translucent husk emptied of seed,
Piet waited to be shattered. "The Chinese knife across the eye. The
electric chair dustless in the tiled room. The earthquake that snaps
cathedral rafters. . . . Puffy-tongued dehydration. Black-faced as-
phyxia. Gentle leprosy. Crucifixion. Disembowelment. Fire. Gas in
the shower room" (273). The litany goes on and on. The harshness
and brokenness of these sentence fragments undermines both the

rationality of the George Eliot voice and the erotic lyricism of the D. H. Lawrence voice. When we enter the isolated consciousness, the book seems to say (and we enter Piet's thoughts, meditations, and even dreams quite frequently), we quickly come up against images of the most isolating event of all, death. Indeed, Freddy Thorne, the novel's "king of chaos" (78), the most articulate and coolly rational philosophizer among the couples, a dentist drawn to decay, suggests that death is the only fundamental reality, and that the couples' public activities and relationships, and especially their private sexual shenanigans, are futile attempts to deny this fundamental fact: "The funny fact is, you don't get better, and nobody gives a cruddy crap in hell. You're born to get laid and die, and the sooner the better. Carol, you're right about that nifty machine we begin with; the trouble is, it runs only one way. Downhill" (255).

But Freddy Thorne's is not the only, or even the most convincing, voice in the book; his morbid position is immediately countered by a character who has had plenty of intimations of mortality of his own, the erotic Piet Hanema: "Freddy . . . I think you're professionally obsessed with decay. Things grow as well as rot. Life isn't downhill; it has ups and downs. Maybe the last second is up. Imagine being inside the womb—you couldn't imagine this world. Isn't anything's existing wonderfully strange?" (255). The argument between Freddy and Piet can stand as a model for the formal tension I have been describing. The discourse of rationality clashes in this novel with the discourse of eroticism, and a third discourse—that of death—opens up beneath both. But we must turn from the novel's form to its content, its story, to see whether *Couples* does eventually find a *via affirmativa* through this potential nihilism (analogous to Piet's affirmation that perhaps "the last second is up"). We must look at the couples—their relationships with each other and with their larger society—and at the Piet-Angela-Foxy triangle to find the resolution of these ambiguities.

Just as Updike disrupts the authoritative, rational language of a traditional social novel with that of the pornographic romance, so does he use sex to problematize a traditional social story. Although the setting is parochial twentieth-century New England rather than parochial nineteenth-century England, Updike comes very close to describing the sort of small, self-enclosed community that Jane Austen chose to write about: "3 or 4 Families in a Country Village is the very thing to work on," Austen wrote to her niece Anna (Honan 359), and Updike has expanded Austen's scale only slightly. *Couples* presents a world of visiting and parties and game-playing that neatly mimics Austen's, and it even has something like

Austen's neoclassical decorum: the couples interact according to ritualized patterns and rules. The men play the sports of the season; then the men and women together gather at some couple's house for drinks, and they play eccentric but rigorously designed games. The analytical narrator describes the regularity of these get-togethers; the couples, we are told again and again, have founded their own secular church, and their rituals follow a kind of athletically liturgical calendar: "With these two men [Matt Gallagher and Piet Hanema], the Irishman and Dutchman, . . . began the round of sports—touch football, skiing, basketball, sailing, tennis, touch football again—that gave the couples an inexhaustible excuse for gathering: a calendrical wheel of unions to anticipate and remember, of excuses for unplanned parties" (116–17).

And Updike uses the point of view of an outsider to the group, that of newcomer Foxy Whitman, to create much the same effect that Jane Austen creates by thrusting inexperienced young women into the ritualized social worlds of her novels. Because Foxy—like Catherine Morland, say, or Emma Woodhouse—does not know the prescribed forms, she is at first at sea; her integration of herself into the community requires that she learn to read the forms correctly. So we have Foxy at the book's first dinner party learning her place ("Namecards in a neat round hand had been arranged" [30]), learning the empty liturgy ("Foxy waited instinctively for grace. Instead there was the tacit refusal that has evolved, a brief bump of silence they all held their breaths through. Then Bea's serene spoon tapped into the soup, the spell was broken, dinner began" [30]), and learning the roles of each group member (she infers, for example, that Freddy Thorne's loathsomeness "served as a unifying purpose for the others, gave them a common identity, as the couples that tolerated Freddy Thorne" [37]). Later, when Foxy goes to the Hanemas to watch the men play basketball (her attendance, she discovers, is a mistake, the sort that naive Austen heroines often make: the couples' code dictates that basketball is for men only), she learns—by observing the most trivial behavior—more about the complicated dynamics of this group: "The patterns of union," she realizes, "were many" (75).

The most stylized, ritualized way in which the couples interact is also the most Austen-like: they play parlor games. Two of them, "Impressions" and "Wonderful," are depicted at length in the novel, and Alan T. McKenzie has analyzed in some detail the way these games mirror the parlor games in Austen's *Emma;* in each book, McKenzie says, "formal exchange under intentionally ambiguous circumstances is . . . skillfully exploited to reinforce the implications of other passages in the novel" (53). McKenzie's main intention is to show that *Couples* is not just a sex novel, so his analysis of the parlor games mostly emphasizes the ingenious way in which Updike embeds complex characterization within a seemingly trivial description of game playing. But I think the fact that games—highly ritualized and codified forms of entertainment—are the couples' primary form of recreation has a more intrinsic importance in this book: it precisely establishes the couples' community as a traditional and formalized one, like the communities depicted by Jane Austen.

Of course, there is a difference, just as there is a difference between George Eliot's rational analyses and the discourse of this novel. And, once again, the difference is the sex.

Unlike Jane Austen heroines, who have to learn to read the characters and motivations of the people with whom they interact in their communities in order ultimately to become a part of that public world by marrying, Foxy Whitman struggles primarily to read the private, adulterous intertwinings of her new Tarbox friends. When her husband Ken speculates that the antagonism of Frank Appleby and Harold little-Smith has to do with money, Foxy counters with, "Ken, you're so work-oriented. I felt it had to do with s-e-x" (43). And Foxy is right. Work, a public, communal activity, is not the current beneath the couples' friendships and activities. It is s-e-x, and Foxy gets better and better at reading sexy secrets beneath the seemingly banal. When she hears Georgene Thorne and Piet, for example, exchanging "words puzzling in their grave simplicity," Foxy solves the puzzle handily; she reads the sex beneath the game:

> "How are you?"
> "So-so, dollink."
> "You've been on your sunporch."
> "Yes."
> "How was it? Lovely?"
> "Lonely."
> Overhearing, Foxy was rapt, as when a child she listened to her parents bumbling and grunting behind a closed door, intimacy giving their common words an exalted magic. (79)

And soon enough Foxy herself is playing the game. The hidden meaning behind the first depicted parlor game, "Impressions," has to do with Foxy herself: "Foxy began in fatigue and confusion to cry; and it was clear to all of them, except Angela and Ben, that as they had suspected she was seeing Piet" (195).

It may not on the face of it be obvious why adultery so radically deconstructs the Austen decorum of Tarbox; if anything in the novel seems to have rigid, neoclassical rules of decorum, it is adultery itself. Early in the book, for example, we are told that adulterous lovers Piet and Georgene follow a scrupulous etiquette: "The politeness was real. Lacking marriage or any contract, they had evolved between them a *code of mutual consideration*" (57, my italics). As other critics have pointed out, Piet in all his affairs — and especially in his affair with Foxy — is the courtliest of lovers; he is Tristan courting his Iseult with sublime *politesse*. Indeed, virtually all of the spouse swapping, at least early in the book, is a genteel, carefully choreographed ballet — or at least a stylized game in which, for instance, the Applebys and the little-Smiths become the Applesmiths, and the Saltzes and the Constantines become the Saltines. It seems, in fact, that adultery is these couples' way not of subverting the formal but of reintroducing it in an increasingly sloppy, chaotic society.

But in the end, this reading of the sexual carryings-on does not wash. Yes, adultery has been formalized in Tarbox, but the book demonstrates repeatedly that it is a form that unforms itself, precisely because it is founded not on substantial, willed, disciplined, generous love but on what Denis de Rougemont calls "passion."

Updike wrote an ambivalent but admiring review of de Rougemont's two discussions of love and passion, *Love in the Western World* and *Love Declared,* and it is a critical commonplace that *Couples* is at least partially a meditation on de Rougemont's ideas (de Rougemont, for example, bases his discussion on an analysis of the Tristan and Iseult story, which, as I have suggested, Piet and Foxy's affair mirrors). For de Rougemont, passion is not love at all; it is tied to self rather than other. The self, possessed by passion, is in love simply with the hedonistic experience of being in love: "Tristan and Iseult do not love one another. They say they don't, and everything goes to prove it. *What they love is love and being in love.* . . . Tristan loves the awareness that he is loving far more than he loves Iseult the Fair" (41). This is a radically antisocial form of Eros; it exists not in a community (even a community of two) but rather in utter solitude: "Iseult does nothing to hold Tristan. All she needs is her passionate dream. Their need of one another is in order to be aflame, and they do not need one another as they are. What they need is not one another's presence, but one another's absence" (41–42).

Robert Detweiler has shown as well as any critic the way the book's sexual affairs are founded on this Eros of absence:

> The double narcissism that de Rougemont seeks to ex-
> pose in Tristan and Iseult as the fallacious basis of love
> also affects Updike's characters. Piet is a modern Courtly
> Lover and a "secret dandy." The couples play at illicit
> sex because they have made the egotistical thrill of be-
> ing desired a goal in itself and do not grasp the founda-
> tion of a sound marital union. For example, after the
> affair between Piet and Foxy is exposed and Piet is left
> alone, "what he felt, remembering Foxy, was a nostalgia
> for adultery itself—its adventure, the acrobatics its de-
> ceptions demand, the tension of its hidden strings, the
> new landscapes it makes us master." (113–14)

Obviously, then, the scrupulously stylized forms that govern the couples' behavior, especially their sexual behavior, are forms that have been emptied of shared content. This is the way the couples have broken away from the Jane Austen world. For Austen, social rituals are only valuable if they are a form founded on a solid content: a vision of moral human action that is shared by a community and that in fact creates community. Indeed, having defined "virtues" as "those goods by reference to which, whether we like it or not, we define our relationships to those other people with whom we share . . . purposes and standards" (191), the moral philosopher Alasdair MacIntyre describes Austen as "the last great representative of the classical tradition of the virtues" (243). In the increasingly relativistic world of Austen's England, MacIntyre says, the realm of virtue has shrunk to the communities of marriage, family, and small village—but these are true human commu-
nities, predicated on people's presence to each other, precisely what Updike's adultery games deny.

For all the novel's interest in what ought to function as MacIntyre's realm of virtue—American society, history, and politics—
Couples seems bent on undercutting the communal, public, hu-
manly shareable aspects of even these things in much the same way that it undercuts the communal aspects of love-and-friendship rituals. This is a sociological novel that undoes its own sociology. The men's professions, for example, are presented with vivid detail, but the detail negates itself: the jobs are roles the men take on, extrinsic to their real selves, their couples selves (which are largely founded on passionate isolation rather than on community). When Carol Constantine criticizes Piet's work as a builder, she is entering proscribed territory: "One of their unspoken rules was that professions were not criticized; one's job was a pact with the meaningless world beyond the ring of couples" (246). As

Edward Vargo puts it: "Outside happenings deflect off the plea-sure-seeking lives of these couples" (129). Even John F. Kennedy, the very public figure whose presence looms over the book, is negated as statesman and reborn as narcissistic reflection of the couples themselves.

The president, like the residents of Tarbox, is from Massa-chusetts, and he is very much identified as a part of a couple: Jackie Kennedy is mentioned in the novel almost as frequently as her husband. And John Kennedy, like the members of Updike's couples, is athletically promiscuous; the book is littered with comments about Kennedy's adulterous escapades. The "latest Kennedy joke," for instance, depicts him sneaking into the White House in the middle of the night with his collar "all rumpled and . . . lipstick on his chin" (105); and when Foxy asks her mother, who lives near Washington, about the Kennedys, she is explicitly asking about just another couple:

> "Speaking of couples," Foxy asked, homesick for
> Washington, "how are the Kennedys?"
> "People say, better than they used to be. He used to
> be notorious, of course."
> "She looks less anxious in the newspapers lately. At
> her Greek beach." (292–93)

Indeed, two of the couples specifically pass the time by discussing "the similarity of JFK's background to their own" (148).

The couples' seemingly neoclassical etiquette, therefore, serves to formalize not community but narcissism, and even public affairs become, for these people, just a mirror of their own private "affairs." Alasdair MacIntyre surely would say that these couples lack any of the shared, teleological values that constitute vital communities, and the writers of *Habits of the Heart,* a fine socio-logical study of the contemporary United States that is indebted to MacIntyre's moral traditionalism, would say that Tarbox is not a community at all but only a "lifestyle enclave," a world founded on virtually nothing:

> Though the term "community" is widely and loosely
> used by Americans, and often in connection with life-
> style, we would like to reserve it for a more specific
> meaning. Whereas a community attempts to be an inclu-
> sive whole, celebrating the interdependence of public
> and private life and of the different callings of all, life-
> style is fundamentally segmental and celebrates the nar-
> cissism of similarity. . . . For this reason, we speak not of

> lifestyle communities, ... but of lifestyle enclaves. ...
> They involve only a segment of each individual, for they
> concern only private life, especially leisure and con-
> sumption. (Bellah et al. 72)

So far it seems that the content of *Couples* supports my thesis no
better than its form seemed to. In both cases, it appears that
Updike is not celebrating the world's substance, the "inclusive
whole" of true community, but is exploding it: the book's sexual
descriptiveness undercuts the objectively authoritative narrator,
and its obsession with sexual activity vaporizes the communal
rituals and worldly textures that seem to give the couples a
solidity. Perhaps the early naysayers were right, and in this book,
all is erotic narcissism.

But I propose that there is another dimension to the novel, that
Updike finds substantive humanity and even the possibility of
substantive community precisely by means of something that, on
the surface, might have seemed to give the book its most nihilistic
dimension (it would not seem an adequate foundation for community to Alasdair MacIntyre, an Aristotelian opponent of existentialism): its existential preoccupation with death. Death emerges
again and again as the couples' experience of an other, a reality
beyond narcissism; it is death that even makes the couples' hedonism seem poignant rather than selfish; and it is death that ushers
in the slight, tentative, but real providential repetition (in the
Kierkegaardian sense we have already seen) at the book's conclusion. These things to some degree ironize the book's irony and
allow Updike to resubstantiate the suburban world that he has
seemed all along to be negating.

A survey of all the references to death in *Couples* would be as
overwhelming as a survey of all the references to sex, since death
dominates the book almost as much as sex does. And the characters
who are most interested in (and obsessed with?) death are the two
men who, as we have already seen, establish the philosophical dialectic that envelopes the couples: Freddy Thorne and Piet Hanema.

I need to add very little to my earlier description of Freddy's
view. For Freddy, decay is all; he takes a rather vicious delight in
being a living embodiment of the Freudian death wish (which
perhaps makes him an oxymoron). But it is important to note that
for Freddy death and sex are inextricably intertwined—Freddy's
Eros *is* Thanatos. Indeed, his one explicit sex scene (he is in bed
with, of all people, Piet's wife Angela) is a grotesque celebration of
death. He is, not surprisingly, impotent, and it is "Big Man Death,"
not Angela, who finally arouses him:

"We die. We don't die for one second out there in the
future, we die all the time, in every direction. Every
meal we eat breaks down the enamel."

"Hey. You've gotten bigger."

"Death excites me. Death is being screwed by God.
It'll be delicious."

"You don't believe in God."

"I believe in that one, Big Man Death. I smell Him between people's teeth every day." (387)

Even after this arousal, Freddy surely cannot have sex with Angela;
he cannot connect with a living human being. He waits until
Angela falls asleep, and then he masturbates—having sex, perhaps,
with the Big Man himself.

Freddy, then, seems to be Updike's literary embodiment of
another key de Rougemontian claim about passion. For de Rougemont, passion is not only narcissism; it is also a longing for
annihilation, death: "The love of love itself has concealed a far
more awful passion. . . . Unawares and in spite of themselves, the
lovers have never had but one desire—the desire for death! . . . In
the innermost recesses of their hearts they have been obeying the
fatal dictates of a wish for death; they have been in the throes of *the
active passion of Darkness*" (46). But Freddy is not the main
character of *Couples;* if the novel has a central protagonist, it is
Piet. And for Piet, the connection between sex and death is
considerably more ambiguous.

Haunted by the deaths of his parents in a violent car crash, Piet
is, in his way, as obsessed with death as Freddy. Early in the novel,
for instance, when his daughter's hamster has been killed by a cat,
Piet's thoughts (presented in that fragmentary, stream-of-con-
sciousness fashion) seem as despairing as Freddy's. Death, for Piet,
seems to be an absence that consumes the world's substance: "He
felt the slow thronging of growth as a tangled hurrying toward
death. Timid green tips shaped like weaponry thrust against
nothing. His father's green fond touch. The ungrateful earth,
receptive. The hamster in an hour of cooling had lost weight and
shape to the elements. All that had articulated him into a presence
worth mourning, the humanoid feet and the groping trembling
nose . . . , had sunk downward toward a vast absence" (85). Piet
fears death—"It's not practical death I'm worried about, it's death
anytime, at all, ever" (284)—and even dreams about it: "The plane
streamed straight down. The liquid in Piet's inner ear surged,
froze. He knew there could be no pulling from this dive and awoke
in darkness, convinced of his death" (269).

But unlike Freddy Thorne, the decay-loving dentist, Piet is a builder who professionally battles decay and rot: "I want the foundation damp-proofed, I want polyethylene under the slab, I want lots of gravel under the drain tiles as well as over it, I want you to wrap felt around the joints or they'll sure as hell clog. . . . People have a nose for the rotten and if you're a builder the smell clings" (92). For much of the novel, Piet is vigorously attempting to fight death; he is a kind of Camusian metaphysical rebel, and he defiantly sets his own freedom against the limitations of death by constructing buildings that are as permanent as possible, by attending church and seeking a God who transcends death, and by having lots of sex. For Piet, therefore, sex is not a death wish but a life wish, desperate perhaps ("with each woman his heart was more intimidated by the counterthrust of time" [352]) but a life wish all the same. So Piet's story suggests that *Couples* is not just Updike's literary presentation of de Rougemont's ideas; it is also Updike's *answer* to de Rougemont. In his review of de Rougemont's works, Updike suggests that Eros can be life-affirming, and his comments could stand as a direct gloss on Piet:

> Might it not simply be that sex has become involved in the Promethean protest forced upon Man by his paradoxical position in the Universe as a self-conscious animal? Our fundamental anxiety is that we do not exist— or will cease to exist. Only in being loved do we find external corroboration of the supremely high valuation each ego secretly assigns itself. This exalted arena, then, is above all others the one where men and women will insist upon their freedom to choose—to choose that other being in whose existence their own existence is confirmed and amplified. ("More Love in the Western World" 299)

Indeed, invoking this passage from the de Rougemont review, Donald Greiner asserts that, for Updike, adultery itself is founded on a desire "to confirm one's life in the face of annihilation by death," not on a de Rougemontian death quest at all: "A fundamental anxiety in [Updike's] marriage novels is . . . recognition that the individual will die. Love and even adultery offer value in the cave of existential despair. . . . Choosing a lover outside the ceremony is more than insisting on the freedom to choose; it is selecting a partner who through sexual consummation validates the existence of the self" (103).

Rebel Piet does tenaciously validate "the existence of the self," maintaining that death is not all. As we have already seen, he asserts to Freddy that perhaps "the last second is up," and in a later passage pain itself—from canker sores, something with which dentist Freddy would be quite familiar—leads him to affirm his faith in (or at least hope for) a Providence: "His cankers hurt, especially the one his tongue had to stretch to reach, low and left on the front gum, at the root of his lip. A maze of membranes, never could have evolved from algae unassisted. God gave us a boost" (326).

Piet so far seems to be finding death to be an occasion only for personal rebelliousness; his adulterous activity in the face of death is just an assertion of personal freedom. Death, then, seems to be a kind of Fowlesian liberating absence, hardly a positive providence. (And, as Greiner points out, even the liberation is deeply ambiguous. The infinite freedom that the Updike adulterer opens up for himself turns out, Greiner says, to be debilitating because, lacking the constraints of the marriage vow, "increased options ironically immobilize the transgressor with the anxiety of choice. Freedom leads to despair" [120].) As I said earlier, however, death also has a more softly affirmative dimension in *Couples*. Though death at first arises in the novel as a private, existential ache, an awareness of death eventually brings many of the characters together in a painfully real way; it breaks through the "lifestyle enclave" and turns Tarbox into, if not a community, at least a substantive world. It is Foxy herself who ushers in this richer understanding of death when she tells Piet, in a letter, that his desperate fear of death is really the beginning of a genuine faith, an experience thrust upon him of a reality beyond himself: "*Sometimes I think you underestimate God—which is to say, you despise the faith your fear of death thrusts upon you*" (279–80).

And shortly afterwards, death is thrust upon all the couples—as upon all of the United States. The president, that young, vigorous man with whom the couples felt they shared a lifestyle, is assassinated.

On the surface, it seems that the couples are perversely untouched by the death of President Kennedy; Edward Vargo, for instance, sees the assassination sequence as yet another indication of the couples' shallow narcissism: "Even the death of President Kennedy cannot put a halt to their weekly party" (129). But the party at the Thornes' contains glimpses of a poignant, powerful external reality that these people can no longer easily ignore. Even though it is Doris Day's romantic singing that floods the room, news flashes erupt from beyond: " 'What's happening now?' Roger's deep voice inquired. 'Oh,' Foxy said, 'mostly old film clips. What are really heartbreaking are the press conferences. He was so

quick and sassy and, I don't know, attentive. He somehow brought
back the fun in being an American' " (320). This death is one of
those experiences that cuts through self-enclosed enclaves, that
links private Tarbox with the larger polis (and even, perhaps, with
the eternal). "Yesterday," Angela Hanema says, "he was just our
President way down in Washington, and now he belongs to all of us.
He's right here. Don't you feel him?" (322). Even Freddy's parody of
the Eucharist (" 'Take, eat,' he intoned, laying each slice [of ham]
on a fresh plate a woman held out to him. 'This is his body, given for
thee' "[334]) is, in an uncanny way, seriously communal rather
than frivolously blasphemous. For better or worse, it appears that
death has driven away Tarbox's easy hedonism.

It certainly drives away the easy hedonism of Piet and Foxy. If
the first two-thirds of the novel have Piet and Foxy enacting the
roles of narcissistic adulterers Tristan and Iseult, the final section
of the book, ushered in by President Kennedy's death, has them
enacting the roles of friends and finally of husband and wife. It is
not so much the president's death, though, that forces reality upon
them. It is a death much closer to home: Foxy's abortion.

Ironically, Piet is on the verge, he thinks, of achieving a kind of
perfect existential freedom, a liberty from the confining stuff of
the world, an escape into pure nothingness (or into Camusian/
Fowlesian rebellion). He has sex with Foxy for what he assumes
will be one last time, and then he flees this increasingly complex
relationship: "His palms tingling against the wheel, he backed the
truck around and headed toward the center of Tarbox. Through
the leafless trees peeked a gold weathercock. As the cab warmed,
he whistled along with the radio music, exhilarated once again at
having not been caught" (351). But Updikean providence, of a sort,
thrusts the world back at Piet. Foxy is pregnant with Piet's child,
and Piet and Foxy decide they must arrange an abortion. Aborting
the child is hardly the easy way out for them; this new confrontation with death drags them into and through a painful reality. For
Piet this encounter with the real ranges from a shameful collabora-
tion with his adversary Freddy (only the dentist knows where to
get an abortion) to an encounter with a "snuffly bum" (393)
outside the abortionist's office ("Piet gave him a quarter. 'Gah-
blessyafella.' Angel in disguise" [393–94]); for Foxy, of course, the
experience is intrinsically, bloodily painful; and for both of them, it
ultimately leads to ugly, wrenching divorces. Adultery itself, that
attempt to elude the dully actual by "giving yourself adventures"
(359), has ushered in the actual with a vengeance. Death and
divorce awaken Piet's belief in an Other beyond lifestyle enclave
and even beyond human community: "He believed that there was,

behind the screen of couples and houses and days, a Calvinist God Who lifts us up and casts us down in utter freedom, without recourse to our prayers or consultation with our wills" (434). This God, in fact, burns to the ground a foolish but essentially harmless little Tarbox church in an exhibition of raw, powerful otherness.

The harshness of this Other is tempered in the book's final pages, but its otherness is not. *Couples* ends with a series of repetitions (another death, a remarriage, a return to couples life) that providentially re-establishes the ordinary—and that ironizes and very nearly contains the deconstructive energy that sex has unleashed in the novel.

The illness and death of John Ong, a brilliant scientist who has been a member of the couples, tame death for Piet (and for all the couples). If death has been like the lightning bolt that destroys the Tarbox church—a transcendent force that has reminded the couples of a world beyond their narcissistic enclave—it now, as he looks into John Ong's eyes, seems to Piet ordinary, worldly, quaintly suburban: "The drug-dilated eyes, eyes that had verified the chaos of particles on the floor of matter, lifted and dragged Piet down into omniscience; he saw, plunging, how plausible it was to die, how death, far from invading earth like a meteor, occurs on the same plane as birth and marriage and the arrival of the daily mail" (448). Death, which has wrenched Piet away from the day-to-day and which he has resisted with all his rebellious energy, now opens Piet's eyes precisely to the value of the day-to-day: "Nothing," the narrator tells us, after describing Piet's visit to the dying John Ong, "was too ordinary for Piet to notice" (449).

Death remains a terrible, unassimilable mystery in this novel, as it does throughout Updike's work; the description of John Ong's actual death has a sense of transcendent awe: "She [Bernadette Ong, John's wife] had been beside the bed when he died. One moment, there was faint breathing; his mouth was human in shape. The next, it was a black hole—black and deep. The vast difference haunted her, gave the glitter of the mass a holocaustal brilliance" (475). But the mystery of death's "vast difference," its otherness, is dialectically balanced at the end of *Couples* by its equally mysterious ordinariness.

And Piet's relationship with Foxy eventually has this worldly ordinariness too. After the passionate romance of their secret affair, and after Piet's nearly melodramatic showdown with Foxy's husband Ken, Piet and Foxy find that at their best they are close, intimate friends. Their ultimate relationship is best embodied in a long, prosy letter from Foxy to Piet at the end of the book; the letter lacks the fire of their affair, but it contains perhaps the key insight of the novel—that sex is a search not for death, or even for life and freedom, but just for companionship: "*After weeks of chastity I remember lovemaking as an exploration of a sadness so deep people must go in pairs, one cannot go alone*" (473).

In a speech delivered only a year after the publication of *Couples,* Updike suggested that the relaxing of sexual mores in the post-Freudian era is killing off the novel as a genre; previous sexual proscriptions, Updike claimed, created a tension that cannot be duplicated in modern times:

> The Novel's Victorian heyday has passed. If my impression is correct, that capitalism put sex in a treasure chest, the chest, after so many raids upon it, is battered to the point of collapse. The set of tensions and surprises we call *plot* to a great extent depends upon the assumption that bourgeois society discourages and obstructs free-ranging sex. . . . Freud, misunderstood or not, has given sex the right to be free, and the new methods of contraception have minimized the bail. Remove the genuine prohibitions and difficulty, and the three-dimensional interweave of the Novel collapses, becomes slack and linear. The novels of Henry Miller are not novels, they are acts of intercourse strung together with segments of personal harangue. ("The Future of the Novel" 37–38)

In a sense, *Couples* is a lengthy meditation on this Updikean proclamation that the novel is dead. Updike seems consciously to have shown how free sex deconstructs both the form and the content of the traditional novel: sex tears apart the coherent analyses of the book's confident sociological narrator, and it also subverts the social rituals that shape the characters' actions. To those critics who have found the book two-dimensional or slack, we could retort that this is precisely Updike's strategy—that *Couples* is not a novel but an antinovel, a radical declaration of independence from novelistic conventions. And Updike's portrayal of a society in which adultery rather than marriage, chaos rather than order, has become the norm does in fact lead Donald Greiner to see Updike not as a realist but as a modernist or even postmodernist: "In detailing the breakdown of the marriage agreement and all that the dissolution through adultery signifies, the novelist also breaks his agreement with the reader that both observe a socially agreed-on set of conventions. Not realism but ambiguity is the result" (48).

I have demonstrated, however, the ways in which *Couples* subverts its own subversion of the novel genre. The pursuit of sex here is a desperately religious act; sex in this novel is sometimes a pursuit of death and sometimes a flight from it, but death always looms beneath it, introducing an otherness that breaks open the couples' narcissism. This subversion of the subversion ultimately allows Updike to regain and redeem the ordinary. David Lodge has explained how much the book is constituted by Updike's "remarkably precise, sensuous notation of the physical texture of ordinary experience," a texture that is perhaps ironized (revealed as weak and fragile) but is never obliterated:

> The descriptions of Tarbox, its couples and their way of life—the neglected beauty of the landscape, the comfortable elegance of the expensively remodelled homes, the casual entertaining, the ball games and parlour games, the plentiful food and drink, the intimate uninhibited conversations, as the children watch the blue flickerings of the TV bring meaningless messages of remote disasters and upheavals in the outer public world (only the assassination of J. F. Kennedy . . . disturbs the couples' calm assumption that 'news happened to other people')—all this is exquisitely rendered, so that we feel the charm, the allure of this way of life, and also its weakness, its fragility. ("Post-pill" 243)

So the book finally is a vivid novelistic—not antinovelistic—portrait of the American suburbs of the early sixties.

And the book ends with a reaffirmation—a repetition—of the traditional narrative form: the narrator manages to wrap up this volatile novel with a gently ironic but satisfying summary statement about each character, making *Couples,* in Updike's own words, "in some ways an old-fashioned novel": "I found the last thirty pages—the rounding up, the administering of fortunes—curiously satisfying, pleasant. Going from character to character, I had myself the sensation of flying, of conquering space" (Plimpton 449). This is a good description of the way the novel works at the end; although Updike has been spending most of his time with Piet Hanema and his women, Angela and Foxy, he will not let them leave the stage until he has also rounded off the tales of all the other couples, giving all his plots the sort of closure that Dickens, for instance, gives in his densely populated novels. So we are told of the death of John Ong, the dissolution of the business partnership of Piet Hanema and Matt Gallagher, Bea and Roger Guerin's adoption of a black child (" 'Roger and I have integrated Tarbox!' Bea exclaimed breathlessly" [475]), a new affair between faithfully Catholic Terry Gallagher and her teacher's husband and a near-affair between Janet Appleby and stolid Ken Whitman, and the retreat of the couples from sexily psychological games to bridge. The book ends with a very conventional wrapping-up paragraph in which the narrator chattily puts the novel's events into the past ("Now, though it has not been many years, the town scarcely remembers Piet") and eases us out of the book, placidly leaving Piet and his new wife Foxy in a new city "where, gradually, among people like themselves, they have been accepted, as another couple." Even the profusion of commas in that final phrase gives it a leisurely, vaguely archaic, nineteenth-century feel.

So for all its sexual extravagance, for all its skepticism about the viability of the novel form and about the possibility of community in the United States, *Couples* is yet another Updikean celebration of the ordinary, the suburban. Although sex seems about to usher in Updike's radical literary freedom and his characters' radical existential freedom, the nothingness that constitutes freedom is replaced by a return of a substantial otherness, a Something. In the decades following the publication of *Couples,* Updike would vigorously scrutinize (some say negate) this Something in a series of explicitly theological novels; in *Couples,* though, he tentatively but genuinely embraces the Something.

The French Lieutenant's Woman

Fowles's *French Lieutenant's Woman,* published in 1969, only a year after *Couples,* was almost as sensationally successful as Updike's book. And its strategy (which perhaps accounted for much of its commercial success) is very similar to that of *Couples:* Fowles uses sex to celebrate a radical freedom from older novelistic conventions and from existential restraints on the individual.

If the protagonist of *Couples* is the town of Tarbox as a whole, the protagonist of *The French Lieutenant's Woman* may well be not one of the story's characters but rather its narrator, its voice. "In a real sense," Peter Conradi argues, "this voice is the book's true hero: its heroic work is no less than the simultaneous Faustian reclamation of an imagined historical epoch as well as the exposure of its own compositional resources and historical premisses" (67). The speaker tells a story about a Victorian love triangle, and he talks like a chatty, intrusive, nineteenth-century narrator; "Fowles's debts," Linda Hutcheon says, "to Scott, George Eliot, Thackeray, Arnold, Dickens, Froude, and Hardy are perhaps more or less evident" (120). And yet he opens up a gap of difference between himself and his Victorian subject matter not quite (as Updike does) by using the language of pornography, but certainly by talking frankly about sex.

His book's plot itself is also frankly sexual: Fowles, like Updike, uses sex to disrupt the content as well as the form of his novel. The story's primary actor, Charles Smithson, is a kind of Darwinist rebel against Victorian conventionality, but he is initially a rather conventional rebel; in the solid Victorian tradition of Eliot, Arnold, Huxley, and others, he has transferred his faith from a Christianity in which he cannot believe to Duty, Culture, and Science. But sexual passion breaks open Charles's conventional unconventionality. A passionate attraction to Sarah Woodruff, the book's mysterious title character, wrenches Charles away from his lovely Victorian fiancée and into the arms of—well, not necessarily of Sarah.

As he usually does, Fowles ultimately parts from Updike. Although Fowles's strategy here is remarkably similar to Updike's in *Couples,* the textures of the novels are remarkably different. The texture of *Couples* is ordinary suburban detail, which, as we have seen, the novel finally celebrates, however ambiguously; but the texture of *The French Lieutenant's Woman* is constituted by the very playfulness of the narrator, who is a kind of reincarnation of the existential philosophizer of *The Aristos.* And what Fowles's novel finally celebrates is not the ordinary and conventional, but it is not the passionately sexual either: it is, rather, the gap of freedom itself, opened up in this case by sexual passion but ultimately deconstructing not just the ordinary but the erotic as well. So Fowles, like Updike, ends up ironizing his own ironic device (sex); he does so, however, not to fill a void but to allow it—to demand it—to gape.

Updike, as we saw, has in an interview described the way he used, in *Couples,* a "presiding, talkative, confiding and pedagogic" narrator, one who "signal[s], as Dickens did, over the heads of the characters to the reader," one who creates the "sense of the author as God, as a speaking God, as a chatty God, filling the universe of the book" (Plimpton 448–49). But Updike's words here describe Fowles's narrator in *The French Lieutenant's Woman* more exactly than they describe Updike's in *Couples*. Fowles's novel opens with a description of the Cobb, the quay at Lyme Regis, in 1867, and his speaker is more like a garrulous old history professor ("presiding, talkative, confiding and pedagogic") than like a post-Jamesian novelistic narrator:

> It is quite simply the most beautiful sea rampart on the south coast of England. And not only because it is, as the guidebooks say, redolent of seven hundred years of English history, because ships sailed to meet the Armada from it, because Monmouth landed beside it . . . but finally because it is a superb fragment of folk art.
>
> Primitive yet complex, elephantine but delicate; as full of subtle curves and volumes as a Henry Moore or a Michelangelo; and pure, clean, salt, a paragon of mass. I exaggerate? Perhaps, but I can be put to the test, for the Cobb has changed very little since the year of which I write, though the town of Lyme has, and the test is not fair if you look back towards land. (9–10)

"I," "you": the book's point of view, technically, is third person, I suppose, but this is actually a first-second-third-person novel.

Not surprisingly, this narrator will, when his characters come on the scene, "signal, as Dickens did, over [their] heads . . . to the reader." We are told at length (some early critics complained that it was at *tedious* length, as if Fowles should have skipped the analyzing and gotten on with his novel; but the analyzing *is* the novel) how Charles, Ernestina (his fiancée), Sarah, and others embody or dismantle the sociological/political/philosophical facts of the Victorian Age. Here, for instance, is the narrator's early description of the conventionally Victorian Ernestina: she has "exactly the right face for her age; that is, small-chinned, oval, delicate as a violet. You may see it still in the drawings of the great illustrators of the time—in Phiz's work, in John Leech's. Her gray eyes and the paleness of her skin only enhanced the delicacy of the rest. At first meeting she could cast down her eyes very prettily, as if she might faint should any gentleman dare to address her" (26–27). And here is a complex (and perhaps preachy) sociological analysis of Charles's formal, cumbersome wardrobe for paleontology expeditions:

> If we take this obsession with dressing the part, with being prepared for every eventuality, as mere stupidity, blindness to the empirical, we make, I think, a grave—or rather a frivolous—mistake about our ancestors; because

it was men not unlike Charles, and as overdressed and overequipped as he was that day, who laid the foundations of all our modern science. Their folly in that direction was no more than a symptom of a seriousness in a much more important one. They sensed that current accounts of the world were inadequate; that they had allowed their windows on reality to become smeared by convention, religion, social stagnation; they knew, in short, that they had things to discover, and that the discovery was of the utmost importance to the future of man. (44)

Probably the most relevant and telling part of Updike's description of the old-fashioned narrator is his final claim that such a narrator generates the "sense of the author as God"—an omniscient controller of a created universe. And in *The French Lieutenant's Woman,* Fowles himself (or his narrator) seems to adopt Updike's traditional stance, declaring that novelists have one primary reason for writing: "*We wish to create worlds as real as, but other than the world that is*" (81). In addition, Updike says that a particularly satisfying experience of this creative power was, during the writing of *Couples,* the achievement of a closed ending with its traditional "rounding up, . . . administering of fortunes" (Plimpton 449). Fowles bestows precisely such an authoritative ending on *The French Lieutenant's Woman:*

And so ends the story. What happened to Sarah I do not know—whatever it was, she never troubled Charles again in person, however long she may have lingered in his memory. . . .

Charles and Ernestina did not live happily ever after; but they lived together, though Charles finally survived her by a decade (and earnestly mourned her throughout it). . . .

Sam and Mary—but who can be bothered with the biography of servants? . . .

Now who else? Dr. Grogan? He died in his ninety-first year. (264–65)

Fowles even indulges in the most showily godlike of authorial tricks, assigning the obnoxious Mrs. Poulteney to hell: "Then she fell, flouncing and bannering and ballooning, like a shot crow, down to where her real master waited" (266).

Anyone even marginally familiar with the novel, however, knows that this is not the book's real ending, its final ending (in this case, those words are not redundant); nor is authoritative pedagogy Fowles's primary purpose in the body of the book. Fowles undercuts his novel's conventional Victorian form and the seemingly godlike powers of his own narrator. He does this most flamboyantly by playing postmodernist games with alternate endings, but we will back up and see first how he ironizes his apparent nineteenth-century form throughout the novel by disrupting it with one of the great secret things for both Fowles and Updike, sex.

The nineteenth-century conventionality of Fowles's chatty, personal narrator is smashed by the fact that the narrator is aware of twentieth-century events and mores; as Conradi puts it, Fowles "makes it clear that he is divided between the desire to write a Victorian novel and the desire to expose the pretence on which such an ambition must be based: between inhabiting the literary pieties of the old tradition and demonstrating a felt obligation towards the ironic and self-conscious wisdom of his own age" (59–60). And the narrator is at his most ironic and self-conscious when he talks about sex. Fowles pedantically, but also archly and wittily, tells us facts about the Victorian Era that he knows no Victorian novelist could acknowledge:

> What are we faced with in the nineteenth century? An age where woman was sacred; and where you could buy a thirteen-year-old girl for a few pounds—a few shillings, if you wanted her for only an hour or two. Where more churches were built than in the whole previous history of the country; and where one in sixty houses in London was a brothel (the modern ratio would be nearer one in six thousand). . . . Where there is not a single novel, play or poem of literary distinction that ever goes beyond the sensuality of a kiss, where Dr. Bowlder . . . was widely considered a public benefactor; and where the output of pornography has never been exceeded. (211–12)

Fowles's point, as always in this book, is not simply to ridicule Victorian sexual repression; it is, rather, to show that the libido is a disrupter of all cultural systems, a relativizer of all dogmatic claims about human nature and society. In the face of sex, all discourse becomes metaphor: "I have seen the Naughty Nineties represented as a reaction to many decades of abstinence; I believe it was merely the publication of what had hitherto been private, and I suspect we are in reality dealing with a human constant: the difference is a vocabulary, a degree of metaphor" (212).

Sexual discourse, in fact, even obliterates (if only temporarily) the talky and self-assured narrator himself. When it comes time to describe Charles's escapades in a red-light district, Fowles playfully puts down his pen and allows his text to be taken over by an anonymous pornographer:

> What particularly pleases *me* about the unchangingness of this ancient and time-honored form of entertainment is that it allows one to borrow from someone else's imagination. I was nosing recently round the best kind of secondhand bookseller's—a careless one. Set quietly under "Medicine," between an *Introduction to Hepatology* and a *Diseases of the Bronchial System,* was the even duller title *The History of the Human Heart.* It is in fact the very far from dull history of a lively human penis. It was originally published in 1749, the same year as Cleland's masterpiece in the genre, *Fanny Hill.* The author lacks his skill, but he will do. (240)

Fowles proceeds to quote from this eighteenth-century text— "The first House they entered was a noted Bagnio, where they met with a Covey of Town Partridges . . ." (240)—for about two pages, and *The French Lieutenant's Woman* for a while is absorbed into that larger system of Books About Sex. Sex, it seems, can dismantle even the myth of authorial authority.

Sexual discourse, then, cuts across this narrator's cozy Victorian analyses with some of the same deconstructive energy that such discourse possesses in *Couples.* Furthermore the novel's story mirrors its discourse again as in *Couples:* if sexual descriptiveness ironizes Fowles's Victorian-narrator pose, so an encounter with erotic passion destroys Charles Smithson's Victorian gentility. And the person who arouses this erotic passion in Charles is the book's central enigma, the mysterious woman whom Fowles has thrust into his novel even though the Victorian Era cannot accommodate her: Sarah Woodruff.

As most Fowles critics have noted, Sarah is a mystery. Charles and his sometime mentor Dr. Grogan (the smartest characters in the book) never quite figure her out, and it is she who provokes Fowles to talk about his own limitations as an author precisely because even he does not (he says) understand her, his own creation. "Who is Sarah?" the narrator asks at the end of chapter 12. "Out of what shadows does she come?" (80). And chapter 13 (the "unlucky" chapter [82]), the chapter in which Fowles first talks very explicitly about the existentialist philosophy undergirding his novel, begins with Fowles's answer to these questions: "I do not know" (80). Indeed, the impossible quest to know Sarah is, according to Conradi, the action that drives both Charles Smithson and the narrator: "Sarah is a subjectivity wholly unknowable, and . . . the object of a quest which is as explicitly that of the narrative voice as it is that of Charles" (70–71). Fowles himself, in an essay on the writing of this novel, has claimed that the image of Sarah began for him as an enigmatic, dreamlike experience: "It started four or five months ago as a visual image. A woman stands at the end of a deserted quay and stares out to sea. That was all. This image rose in my mind one morning when I was still in bed half asleep. It corresponded to no actual incident in my life (or in art) that I can recall" ("Notes on Writing a Novel" 88). Within the context of the novel, however, the mystery of Sarah — although never solved (she must remain a kind of cypher, a naught) — is more precisely placed than this original image. It is Sarah who jars Charles out of his conventional Victorian unconventionality, and she does this largely by awakening his interest in and passion for sex.

Charles, as I have already mentioned, is to a certain degree a Victorian rebel from the beginning. Having toyed with religion and hedonism, he has become a committed Darwinist; now a fairly skilled paleontologist, he is also "a quite competent ornithologist and botanist into the bargain" (44) — a real intellectual ally of his creator. Sexually, however, Charles is as conventional as a Jane Austen hero; his courtship of Ernestina Freeman consists of the kind of repartee that witty Austen lovers engage in (though without Austen's solid communal foundations the repartee seems a bit empty and lifeless, especially since we already know that Ernestina is a rather frivolous creature):

> "Shall you not go converse with Lady Fairwether?"
> "I should rather converse with you."
> "I will present you. And then you can have an eyewitness account of the goings-on in the Early Cretaceous era."
> He smiled. "The Early Cretaceous is a period. Not an era."
> "Never mind. I am sure it is sufficiently old. And I know how bored you are by anything that has happened in the last ninety million years. Come." (69)

Charles makes up his mind quite easily to embrace the legitimate (conventional?) pleasures of married life: "Everything had become simple. He loved Ernestina. He thought of the pleasure of waking up on just such a morning, cold, gray, with a powder of snow on the ground, and seeing that demure, sweetly dry little face asleep beside him — and by heavens (this fact struck Charles with a sort of amazement) legitimately in the eyes of both God and man beside him" (70). And this all leads to a conventional "interview with Ernestina's father" that is "brief, and very satisfactory" (70), and a first kiss "with lips as chastely asexual as children's" (71). Our radical Darwinist does not know that he himself, with his Victorian respectability, is among the most outdated and endangered of species.

And the instrument of destruction, of extinction, is Sarah, whose initial stare cuts through Charles's respectable engagement to Ernestina with a power that combines a kind of Freudian libido (it is not, in Victorian terms, a feminine stare at all) and an annihilating Sartrean "look":

> She turned to look at him—or as it seemed to Charles, through him. It was not so much what was positively in that face which remained with him after that first meeting, but all that was not as he had expected; for theirs was an age when the favored feminine look was the demure, the obedient, the shy. . . . [I]t was an unforgettable face, and a tragic face. . . . There was no artifice there, no hypocrisy, no hysteria, no mask. . . .
>
> Again and again, afterwards, Charles thought of that look as a lance; and to think so is of course not merely to describe an object but the effect it has. He felt himself in that brief instant an unjust enemy; both pierced and deservedly diminished. (14–15)

Fowles's description of this stare is so drenched in negativity, it is almost impossible not to connect it with the "look" described by Sartre in *Being and Nothingness,* a look from another that steals the self from itself, envelops the self in nothingness, and yet also grants the self a profound (and shameful) awareness of its own being: "We are dealing with my being as it is written in and by the Other's freedom. Everything takes place as if I had a dimension of being from which I was separated by a radical nothingness; and this nothingness is the Other's freedom. . . . "Shame reveals to me that I *am* this being, not in the mode of 'was' or 'having to be' but *in-itself*" (Sartre 351). It might be argued that Sarah's look, however it deconstructs Victorianism and "nihilates" Charles, is not explicitly libidinous. But as the novel progresses, Sarah's destructiveness is more and more clearly linked with her sexuality. She is, for one thing, a woman with a "past": she is not Sarah Woodruff, she is the French Lieutenant's "Woman" (a cozy euphemism for "Whore"). And—horror of horrors—she has the impropriety to go walking in the "Undercliff," a kind of sensual Garden of Eden, the sort of organic, romantic, mysterious paradise that Fowles celebrates throughout his writings (especially in his autobiographical work *The Tree*): "In summer it is the nearest this country can offer to a tropical jungle. It has also, like all land that has never been worked or lived on by man, its mysteries, its shadows, its dangers" (59). And when Charles finds Sarah there, innocently asleep, as un-selfconsciously sensual as Hardy's Tess when she crawls through a gooey garden to listen to Angel Clare's harp-playing ("She went stealthily as a cat through this profusion of growth, gathering cuckoo-spittle on her skirts, cracking snails that were underfoot, staining her hands with thistle-milk" [*Tess of the d'Urbervilles,* ch. 19]), the narrator tells us that "the whole Victorian Age was lost" (63).

Charles's initial conscious attitude about Sarah, as he begins secretly to associate with her, is "not sexual, but fraternal, perhaps paternal" (62), but such condescension cannot last long—not in the presence of her deconstructive *look.* It is not long before he is linking her face "with foreign women—to be frank (much franker than he would have been to himself) with foreign beds" (99). And he becomes "a little obsessed with Sarah . . . or at any rate with the enigma she presented" (106), while he begins to wonder if his choice of a fiancée is "only too conventional" (107). The section of *Couples* in which Updike's Piet Hanema is most overcome by sexual passion is entitled "Thin Ice," and Fowles uses the same term to describe the Victorian dilemma that Charles is experienc-ing (his problem, of course, is "terror of sexuality"), and which he tries to escape by a typically Victorian retreat into "stiffness": "When one is skating over so much thin ice—ubiquitous economic oppression, terror of sexuality, the flood of mechanistic science—the ability to close one's eyes to one's own absurd stiffness was essential" (119).

It does not work, however. None of the Victorian categories (the townspeople's cruel euphemism "the French Lieutenant's Wom-an," Dr. Grogan's clinical "Melancholic," Charles's own "Woman in Distress") can enclose the mystery of Sarah—or stem the sensual passion that she (and especially her *look*) provokes in Charles:

> Destiny.
> Those eyes. (189)

Against Dr. Grogan's orders, Charles goes to her, they kiss (not, apparently, "with lips as chastely asexual as children's"), and "the moment overcame the age" (199).

This kiss is followed by a fierce act of intercourse in an Exeter hotel, during which Charles is overcome by a hunger "not merely sexual, for a whole ungovernable torrent of things banned, romance, adventure, sin, madness, animality" (274). To say that this sexual encounter leaves Charles "deconstructed" is to expose the euphemistic quality of that word; it leaves him *destroyed* — "like a city struck out of a quiet sky by an atom bomb," the narrator says, using anachronism to illustrate the extent to which Charles is no longer a Victorian gentleman (275). And Charles's English gentility is further eroded when his shamed state induces his manservant Sam defiantly to resign ("If you wishes for hattention, pray ring for one of the 'otel domestics" [303]), when he is forced by Ernestina's angry father to sign a document declaring that he has "forever forfeited the right to be considered a gentleman" (324), and when he leaves England and finds himself more at home in the United States. Sarah and sex have cut Charles off from himself — from any kind of self that has defined content.

Ironically, though, Sarah even cuts him off from sex itself. As it was in *Couples,* sex in *The French Lieutenant's Woman* is strategic rather than substantive. The sex scene in this novel is as brief as it is explosive, and it paradoxically makes Sarah seem less sexually oriented at the very moment that Charles finally has sex with her. As Conradi puts it: "Charles discovers that, despite having played the role of fallen woman, Sarah was in fact a virgin. She thus combines both halves of the Victorian typology: at exactly the point when she ceases to be a virgin she begins for the first time *to appear to have been one*" (65). This paradox makes Sarah a rather fine embodiment of Derridean difference. She is neither virgin nor whore (both words have been emptied of their applicability at the same moment); she is the play of difference between these two concepts, the nothing between the two somethings.

But Sarah has in fact admitted this to Charles much earlier. "The French Lieutenant's Whore," she has told him, is not who she is, intrinsically; it is merely a role she has adopted, a mask she has donned: "I did it so that people *should* point at me, *should* say, there walks the French Lieutenant's Whore — oh yes, let the word be said. So that they should know I have suffered, and suffer, as others suffer in every town and village in this land" (142). Her courting of misery leads the clinical Dr. Grogan to declare Sarah a pathological masochist (a more enlightened view than that of the townspeople, who simply see her as a perverse sinner), but Sarah herself has a more existentialist explanation for her role playing: "I knew no other way to break out of what I was.... Sometimes I almost pity them [other women]. I think I have a freedom they cannot understand. No insult, no blame, can touch me. Because I have set myself beyond the pale. I am nothing, I am hardly human any more. I am the French Lieutenant's Whore" (142). "I have a freedom . . . I am nothing" —as we have seen, these phrases are for Fowles very nearly synonymous, and they explain, I think, Sarah's role playing. She becomes "the French Lieutenant's Whore" precisely because that is what she is *not*. Her real self is that which is different from her persona; we can say nothing more substantive about Sarah than that.

So Sarah is even more enigmatic than she originally appeared. Not only does her passion for Charles cut her off from her Victorian society, but her freedom cuts her off even from her passion. Conradi suggests that Sarah is less Charles's lover than his teacher, a sort of erotic/anti-erotic Conchis: "Like Conchis . . . she is finally unknowable; and her resistance to interpretation is connected, like Conchis's, with her capacity to educate" (64). And Linda Hutcheon makes it clear what lesson this female Conchis (like the original Conchis) is trying to teach: Sarah's role, Hutcheon asserts, is "creating fictions and thereby granting freedom" (129). Sarah, then, is finally not, as some critics have suggested, some sort of embodiment of the Jungian anima or of the sensual seductress or of the twentieth-century feminist (see Huffaker 110, 112); these interpretations grant her too much positive content. She is more like Hardy's Well-Beloved, a perpetual absence that is perpetually pursued. Her sexuality is a mask for this absence—this freedom.

This nothingness/freedom beneath sexuality is perhaps what most clearly sets Fowles's strategy in *The French Lieutenant's Woman* apart from Updike's in *Couples*. Both novelists use sex, in these books, in a deconstructive way: to undermine the conventions of the nineteenth century, the Golden Age of the Novel. But Updike, as we have seen, finds not absence but death beneath sexuality, and then he finds a Kierkegaardian repetition—a return of the ordinary (suburban) world. Updike, still following his *via affirmativa,* affirms substance. Fowles, however, affirms absence; his *via* remains *negativa.* Freedom of self from all content (Sarah is not whore or victim or melancholic or feminist or even woman) seems to be Sarah's governing principle. And it is certainly her lesson to Charles, who for all his rebellion is, as I have noted, initially quite Victorian. Let us conclude this comparison of *The French Lieutenant's Woman* with *Couples* by looking at Fowles's narrative structure—at the way in which his novel's design reflects not only a deconstructive strategy (which he shares with Updike) but also, at its core, a dedication to pure existential freedom, to nothingness (which Updike does not share).

There are many narrative tricks in *The French Lieutenant's Woman,* but none is more striking (or more frequently discussed) than the book's multiple endings. Indeed, the multiple endings of this novel are, by his own admission, what first provoked David Lodge to "give any extended thought" to the subject of "alternative or ambiguous endings" ("Ambiguously" 143, 154). Lodge has come to see such endings as a key feature of postmodernist fiction, with its rejection of an absolute order:

> Even this kind of ending [the modernist open ending] . . . can seem too comfortable or consoling in its endorsement of the commonplace that life, somehow or other, goes on; and insufficiently self-conscious about its own conventionality. The open ending, like the closed ending, . . . asserts the existence of *an* order; and it still makes a claim for the fiction's realism, verisimilitude, or 'truth to life'. These claims have been strongly challenged by many contemporary novelists sometimes designated postmodernist. Instead of the closed ending or the open ending, we get from them the multiple ending, the false ending, the mock ending or the parody ending. (154)

The French Lieutenant's Woman, Lodge says, "belongs to this [postmodernist] category" (154). I agree, though I think that Fowles puts a kind of existentialist spin on his postmodernism: Fowles's novel does assert a single order, but it is Sarah's order, an order without content—the order of freedom itself.

I have already discussed the novel's first, and falsest, ending— the closed ending in which, as Lodge puts it, we "get what Victorian novelists and their publishers called 'the wind-up'—a brief resumé of the subsequent lives of the principal characters" (143). This ending has Charles dutifully suppressing his passion for Sarah and returning to Ernestina (and, as we have seen, it has Mrs. Poulteney spending a well-earned eternity in hell). What Charles rejects in this version of his story is not Sarah so much as freedom. He has reached a Fowlesian "fulcrum"—a pivotal moment at which he can choose either freedom (the Fowlesian secret place) or dreary routine (the Fowlesian suburbs); he chooses, according to this first ending, the routine:

> Charles felt a sense of sadness and of loss, of having now cast the fatal die. It seemed to him astounding that one simple decision . . . should determine so much. Until that moment, all had been potential; now all was inexorably fixed. He had done the moral, the decent, the correct thing; and yet it seemed to betray in him some

> inherent weakness, some willingness to accept his fate,
> which he knew ... would one day lead him into the
> world of commerce; into pleasing Ernestina because she
> would want to please her father. (261)

But then Fowles jettisons this ending, though in a somewhat misleading way. He claims that the ending occurred in Charles's imagination: "The last few pages you have read are not what happened, but what [Charles] spent the hours between London and Exeter imagining might happen" (266). In fact, however, this false ending is a textual, narrative trick rather than a bit of stream of consciousness. Fowles has used the Derridean device that I discussed in relation to *The Magus;* he has made discourse "*do itself violence,* ... negate itself in order to affirm itself*" (Derrida "Violence" 130). Fowles has written an ending in order to unwrite it, because the unwriting and the nonending are his contentless content.

This explains the two showy appearances of the novelist as a character in his fiction (in the first appearance he is on a train with Charles, trying to decide how to resolve the story; in the second he is a clownish magician who turns back time in order to usher in an alternate ending), the intrusiveness of the narrator throughout the book, and the much-discussed double ending itself. Fowles is using Derridean play to unwrite, to negate, so that his narrator, his characters, and his book will seem to evaporate and leave us with utterly free nothingness. By calling attention to himself and his own godlike powers within the novel's universe, and then subverting those powers by denying himself the ability even to end his own story authoritatively, Fowles is doing for us what Sarah does for Charles (and what Conchis does for Nicholas in *The Magus*): he is dramatizing the *deus absconditus,* the absent god—or really Absence-as-God—which frees the self from any restrictions on its freedom.

I reject, then, all the authoritative claims by critics as various as Huffaker, a traditionalist, and Conradi and Lodge, postmodernists, that the book's final ending is its *real* ending. Yes, it does seem too sentimental, given the novel's rebellion against the conventional, to see the "happy" ending (in which Sarah and Charles are brought together by an unexpected, providential gift, a baby girl conceived during their single sexual encounter) as a genuine resolution of the story. The "sad" ending, the final ending, is more toughly modern; Sarah resists to the end Charles's overtures—an early feminist, she permanently asserts her own freedom. By itself, though, this ending is as authoritative as the first; in Lodge's terms, it asserts one clear order in which Sarah is feminist teacher and Charles is wounded learner. In other words, it gives Sarah and Charles solid, unshakeable content. What the two endings do together, however, is resonate with each other—and with that first, aborted ending—to dissolve all substantial plot-content and leave Charles, and us, in a kind of vacuum. Charles is neither the man who wins Sarah nor the man who loses her; he exists forever in the gap of difference between those two substantive propositions. The creator of that gap is a god who creates nothing, who is nothing. And *The French Lieutenant's Woman* is the nothing that this not-god has not-created.

I am not saying that *The French Lieutenant's Woman* is nihilistic, at least not in the generally accepted sense of the word. The book is an existential affirmation—of freedom—just as *Couples* is an affirmation of human relationship. It is striking how similarly both novels reach their affirmations: by using sexual content, and even (to a greater or lesser degree) the language of pornography, to break down the traditional content and form of the English-language novel. But it is equally striking how different the affirmations are; they are as different as a dark forest from sunny suburbs, as empty space from teeming community, as Sartrean freedom from Christian providence.

7

Nothing/Something

I could pursue this comparison between Fowles's self-canceling fiction of nothingness and Updike's substance-affirming fiction of somethingness by looking at some of the works they wrote in the decade following *Couples* and *The French Lieutenant's Woman.* Fowles's romantic tales in *The Ebony Tower,* retreats from the ordinary modern world, could be effectively juxtaposed with a selection of Updike's realistic suburban *New Yorker* stories; and Updike's experiment with multiple endings in *Marry Me* could be compared with Fowles's similar literary tricks. The writers' respective portraits of successful, established artists would serve as an interesting comparison, too: Fowles's *Daniel Martin* is self-reflective (it is deeply autobiographical) and self-reflexive, while Updike's Bech books are other-reflective (the Jewish Bech is more Saul Bellow than John Updike) and often rambunctiously extroverted. But rather than belabor my thesis, I want to skip ahead to the 1980s and look at two pairs of novels by these respective authors that resonate with each other in new and surprising ways: a Fowlesian dyad, *Mantissa* and *A Maggot,* and the last two entries of Updike's "*Scarlet Letter* trilogy," *Roger's Version* and *S.*

Like the other novels compared in this study, these books are neatly matched formalistically. *Mantissa* and *Roger's Version* are very distinctly novels of ideas; as they move into the latter parts of their careers, both Fowles and Updike seem drawn again to look at their own theories in schematic ways. And *A Maggot* and *S.* are both narratively eccentric examinations of religious movements that the respective authors themselves do not subscribe to. The real connections between Updike and Fowles, however, are more than formal this time; as if to validate my linking of them, the novelists in these later writings have drawn closer together thematically and ideologically. Updike has returned to his most explicitly religious existentialism, which burns in these books with a kind of metaphysical rebelliousness; and Fowles has in a sense moved beyond his own existentialism, atheistic as it was, toward a kind of heavily qualified spirituality. In *Mantissa* and especially in *A Maggot,* Fowles embraces a kind of modified deconstruction, perhaps even comparable to the affirmatively theological deconstructive strategy that I have ascribed to Updike; Fowles now seems to be pointing not toward the absolute nothing-ness-that-is-freedom but toward *something,* however unnameable. And Updike's three-novel homage to *The Scarlet Letter* (the first of the trilogy is 1974's *A Month of Sundays,* which I will discuss in some depth as an introduction to the series) subverts the marriage theme of the Rabbit trilogy. Even more than *Couples,* these later Updike novels are not so much about marriage as about the breaking open of marriage by adultery; adultery in these books is a vehicle for transcending—negating, turning into nothing-ness—the earthly and ordinary.

These pairs of novels, then, challenge the neat antinomies I have established throughout this study. And it is a welcome challenge. I have been arguing that Updike and Fowles are prototypal novelists, whose careers suggest that the novel as a genre exists within the tension between something and nothingness; it seems that some novelists (too often sloppily tagged "realistic") gravitate toward one of the poles and some (the "romantic"?) gravitate toward the other. But I would not be so foolish as to claim that the poles are absolutely exclusive. We have already seen, for example, the way existential nothingness has always been an important dimension of Updike's fiction; his most famous character, Rabbit Angstrom, has been plausibly called a "Nothing-man." We have also seen that Fowles is a storyteller, a creator of rounded characters and plots, and not just a Sade-like destroyer. These later works merely show that as each of these writers matures, he reaches beyond himself to encompass even more fully the pole—aesthetic, philosophical, theological—that is opposite to his own basic standpoint.

In any case, the growing similarity of Updike's and Fowles's works does not undermine the essential validity of my schema. In fact, I intend to argue here that, despite these increasing resem-blances, Fowles's remains a *via negativa* (the heroine of *Mantissa* does not exist, at least in any operational sense of the word, and the hero of *A Maggot* is a mystic who is radically absent from the text) and Updike's a *via affirmativa* (transcendent adultery may be the emphasis of the *Scarlet Letter* novels, but the books' grounding is a return to—a repetition of—the ordinary, marriage). So even in these most ambiguous works, the visions of Updike and of Fowles are slanted toward, respectively, something and nothingness.

Mantissa and *A Maggot*

In many ways, *Mantissa*—even more than Fowles's earlier works—is a novel that is insistently about nothing, no thing. The title, Fowles reveals in a footnote, means "An addition of comparatively small importance, especially to a literary effort or discourse" (188); he is saying, in other words, that *Mantissa* adds essentially nothing to his literary corpus. Fowles's narrative strategy here, more than ever before, is self-canceling. Each successive section of the novel in a sense dissolves the reality that has been proposed in the section preceding it. The book is peppered with offhand references to deconstruction, and it seems almost an exercise in demonstrating how one can, in that Derridean way described in my discussion of *The Magus,* use language "to write by crossing out."

The book begins with a Sartrean revision of the Cartesian discovery of the cogito: rather than a thinking substance, the self in this novel is born as a conscious *non*substance. At its most primal, this consciousness is not an "I think" but rather an "It is conscious"; here is Fowles's first sentence: "It was conscious of a luminous and infinite haze, as if it were floating, godlike, alpha and omega, over a sea of vapor and looking down; then less happily, after an interval of obscure duration, of murmured sounds and peripheral shadows, which reduced the impression of boundless space and empire to something much more contracted and unaccommodating" (3). Only later does this "sense of impersonality" give way to the "unwilling deduction" that It is "an I of sorts" (4). And although the I slowly accumulates substance—"not just an I, but a male I" (4)—and it is even assigned a name, Miles Green, and a wife, these facts are extrinsic. In itself, It has "No name. Nothing. No past, no whence or when" (5). Anything beyond this pure point of insubstantial consciousness is merely a cacophony of signifiers that have no solid signifieds: "Names, people's names, street names, place names, disjointed phrases. . . . He had perhaps heard them before, as words; but he had no idea what relevance they were supposed to have" (5). If it is possible to make Nothing the protagonist of a novel, Fowles seems bent on doing so.

As this first chapter progresses, though, Fowles does seem temporarily to have a real narrative to spin. Miles Green, it appears, is an amnesiac bedridden in a gray, padded hospital room, and the women who face him appear to be a doctor and a nurse attempting to cure him with sexual shenanigans ("Bonds. A whip. Black leather. Whatever you fancy" [23]). The doctor explains the Freudian theory behind her "therapy": "Memory is strongly attached to ego. Your ego has lost in a conflict with your superego, which has decided to repress it—to censor it. All Nurse and I wish to do is to enlist the aid of the third component in your psyche, the id. Your id is that flaccid member pressed against my posterior. It is potentially your best friend. And mine as your doctor" (26). For a while this encounter with the women seems to be Fowles's attempt to invoke the Updikean/Barthian idea that a real, substantive self comes to be only when it faces an other: as Miles "inadvertently [digs] his nails into the nurse's bottom," a moral being rather than a mere point of consciousness seems to emerge: "Yet somewhere inside his blinded psyche an entire moral being continued to protest at this abject surrender to animality, this blatant pandering to the basest instincts. It was seconded by an aesthetic being, a person of taste, a true if temporarily lost Miles Green" (32).

But this is all a hoax, as Fowles hints from the start by naming the doctor "Dr. Delfie"; the doctor and the nurse are not flesh-and-blood, autonomous characters at all, but mere literary devices. Furthermore, the self that Miles finds during this supposed therapy is not a real self but a coy sexual joke—at the height of arousal, Miles has a flash of inspiration that he is a "Member of Parliament" (pun definitely intended): "No silent Member, he: he would catch Mr. Speaker's eye and rise, nothing could stop him rising, with aplomb and dignity and full force, to his most solemn and convincing height" (34–35). And if "Miles" and "Dr. Delfie" are not people but shams, their encounter is even more thoroughly exploded. This has been not an interaction between substantive self and substantive other but rather a bit of linguistic play. There are suggestions of this fact sprinkled throughout the chapter: as Miles reaches orgasm, for instance, and Dr. Delfie begins to talk as if he is actually giving birth, she describes his birthing/climaxing as "Right to the very last syllable" (41). Then, at the end of the chapter, the nurse announces to Miles what sort of child he has borne: "It's a lovely little story. And you made it all by yourself" (44).

And the story, the baby, the non-thing that these non- persons have been involved in producing, is nothing but the first chapter of *Mantissa* itself: "She bent her pretty capped head to read the top page, using a finger to trace the words, as she might have touched a newborn nose or tiny wrinkled lips. ' "It was conscious of a luminous and infinite haze, as if it were floating, godlike, alpha and o-me-ga" ' " (44). So the book's vivid, tour-de-force opening chapter has after all consisted of nothing more than text as text playing with text.

But the chapter ends, literally, with a "CRASH!" (45). Into Miles's hospital room stomps someone who seems to have a new and very vital autonomy, a genuine rather than sham otherness, which might serve—in the Levinasian way of the Other that bursts into Updike's *The Centaur*—to break open the self-enclosed text of the novel's first part. The person who enters certainly seems to be quite *other* than the sterile literary devices of chapter 1:

> There stands an infinitely malevolent apparition straight out of a nightmare; or more accurately, straight out of a punk rock festival . . . black boots, black jeans, black leather jacket. Its gender is not immediately apparent. . . . The only certain thing is that it is in a towering rage. Beneath the black jacket, which is festooned with out-size safety-pins (another hangs from the left earlobe) and swastika badges, can be glimpsed a white T-shirt with a pointing pistol printed on it. The splintered shocks of hair above are also white, a staring albino white. . . . (49)

This creature—a woman, we discover—makes the doctor and nurse evaporate and makes "each sheet of paper" of *Mantissa*'s first chapter dissolve into "nothingness" (51)—though in a sense it was already a kind of nothingness anyway. By deconstructing the deconstructions of the book's first chapter, in other words, this vivid creature seems perhaps to be ready to introduce some real substance into the novel.

But then the book deconstructs the deconstruction of the deconstruction, and the otherness of this woman, it now appears, is as illusory as everyone else's. It turns out that she is Erato, the Muse of love poetry, an externalization of novelist Miles Green's own creativity. Her identity, we discover, is utterly fluid and insubstantial; she was both the doctor and the nurse, she then becomes this punk rocker, and she proceeds to become a radical feminist, a traditional goddess, an invisible voice, an "infinitely compliant" (190) Japanese lover, and finally just a silence. Of course, as I have shown in my discussion of George Caldwell in *The Centaur,* fluidity of form can be an artistic way of rendering not a character's nothingness but rather his or her ungraspable other-ness, "alterity," and I intend to argue that Erato does exhibit some traces of alterity. But most frequently, it seems that Erato is so fluid because she does not exist at all in any substantive way. She is a mere bubble in Miles/Fowles's free artistic imagination, and she changes color and shape at his whim precisely because she is nothing and his creativity is bounded by nothing. "I'm just," Erato complains, "one more miserable fantasy figure your diseased mind is trying to conjure out of nothing" (85). She later gripes about her non-status—"The sexual exploitation's nothing beside the ontological one. You can kill me off in five lines if you want to" (94)—and she bemoans the fact that her novelistic creator can toss her "back to nothingness, like an old boot" (94).

Erato's transformations, then, are largely representations of her nothingness. From this point of view, it can be argued that Erato is not a character and that she certainly is not a goddess; she is, rather, a kind of negative palimpsest—a series of erased forms drawn over the same space of blank paper. She is the book's primary embodiment of the Derridean concept of writing by crossing out.

So in a sense, Erato is yet another example of a Fowlesian nothingness, a Sartrean "nihilation." Indeed, she is very much the sort of self-canceling figure that Frederick Clegg was in *The Collector:* just as Clegg was a self-canceling clash between mechanism and romanticism, so do Erato's clinical personae (the doctor and the nurse, who always speak a reductively rationalistic, scientific language) clash with her emotive and/or divine personae—and leave nothing. This nothingness is, again, the empty space that constitutes, and is, freedom. Drury Pifer, in a canny discussion of deconstruction in this novel, has suggested that the following statement by Derrida (already quoted in relation to *The Magus*), "might well serve as a gloss on *Mantissa*": "To grasp the operation of creative imagination at the greatest possible proximity to it, one must turn oneself toward *the invisible interior of poetic freedom*" (Pifer 163, my italics). So this time, it seems, the freedom that Fowles is invoking by his negations is not so much existential as it is artistic or textual: it is the freedom of the artist, or of language itself, to be bound by nothing. More than any of his previous works, then, *Mantissa* is a metanovel.

Indeed, the book is downright heavy-handed in its insistence that it is about nothing but the artistic process itself that occurs in the author's imagination. I have already noted that this is a novel of ideas; most of the book's text consists of a literary-critical dialogue. But it could be called a monologue; the entire book, we discover, takes place in—in a sense it *is*—the space, the freedom, of the writer's mind:

> "I bet you haven't even cottoned on to what these grey quilted walls really stand for." He pauses . . . and looks at her. She shakes her head. "I knew you hadn't. Grey walls, grey cells. Grey matter?" He taps the side of his head. "Does the drachma begin to drop?"
> "It's all . . . taking place inside your brain?"
> "Brilliant." (115–16)

Miles proceeds to give Erato a very theoretical lecture on modernism and postmodernism; the lecture, among other things, seems to erase Miles and Erato's existence as narrative characters and turn *Mantissa* entirely into a critical work. The "reflective novel," Miles maintains, is "sixty years dead"; the novel is now a "*reflexive* medium*," which means that "serious modern fiction has only one subject: the difficulty of writing serious modern fiction" (118). To a large extent, this really is what *Mantissa* is about; in fact, Drury Pifer feels that the novel ultimately swallows up its characters, its images, and itself into a kind of self-reflexive black hole: "On its final pages the novelistic figment, Miles Green, is supposedly knocked unconscious and attended by Nurse Cory. But by now the reader's disbelief is no longer suspended. He knows there is no Green, no nurse, nothing here but a text for explication. All literary substance has been deconstructed and the verbal shards that remain are shuttled past in the final paragraphs. . . . You close the covers on a world that has swallowed itself. Your return there is unlikely" (174–75).

So Erato, the ever-changing, ultimately vanished Muse, seems to be nothing more than the personification (or un-personification) of what Fowles, in his discussion of Hardy's *The Well-Beloved,* describes as the absence—the "permanent state of loss"—that haunts the literary imagination and keeps it repetitively searching for those always-deferred embodiments of the Well-Beloved, "the maternal muses who grant the power to comprehend and palliate the universal condition of mankind, which is, given the ability of the human mind to choose and imagine other than the chosen or the actual course of events, a permanent state of loss" ("Hardy and the Hag" 40).

And yet, despite all the negating that goes on in *Mantissa,* there is an undercutting of this negation that—although it may not, alas, save the novel from being a literary failure—suggests a slight movement in Fowles's vision, a movement away from an existential glorification of pure nothingness/freedom and toward an embrace of a kind of psychological/mystical/archetypal almost-something. "Everyone's so dreadfully serious these days," Erato says (117) as Miles launches into his hyper-serious peroration on self-reflexive literature, and Erato's complaints, confusions, and touches of sarcasm suggest that *Mantissa* is supposed to be as much a spoof of a self-reflexive narrative as it is an example of one. Indeed, while the book mostly insists on Erato's non-existence, it also suggests the opposite: Erato's autonomy and refusal to be swallowed up into a deconstructionist maelstrom. The "CRASH!" with which she shatters the games of chapter 1 and the punch in the face with which she flattens Miles at the end of chapter 2 do give her at least an aura of autonomy. And the claims that she is a mere product of Miles's creative freedom are at least partially balanced by suggestions that she is a limitation on that freedom (a real other). In a coy reference to *The French Lieutenant's Woman,* for instance, Miles says that far from being wholly controlled by his own will, his fiction has been molded by Erato according to *her* whims:

> "I was going to follow in Joyce and Beckett's footsteps. But oh no, in you trot. Every female character has to be changed out of recognition. She must do this, must do that. Every time, pump her up till she swamps the whole shoot. And in the end it's always the same bloody one. I.e., you. Again and again you've made me cut out the best stuff. That text where I had twelve different endings—it was perfect as it was, no one had ever done that before. Then you get at it, and I'm left with just three." (127–28)

Eventually, Erato herself—in her guise as Dr. Delfie—explains her own ontological foundations fairly straightforwardly: "I happen to be a female archetype with an archetypally good sense, developed over several millenia, of deeper values" (140). Yes, she grants that her physical presence is "purely illusory, a mere epiphenomenon" (140), but she implies that she does have an essential reality, a somethingness, non-physical though it may be.

Fowles is, of course, invoking Carl Jung here, for whom he has acknowledged admiration. But until *Mantissa* and especially *A Maggot,* Jung has, I think, merely provided Fowles with archetypes to play with and deconstruct; Fowles has backed off from granting the Jungian psychic archetype any ontological grounding, because such actuality would threaten his commitment to atheistic existential freedom. Now, however, Fowles is at least toying with the Jungian idea that the ineffability of archetypes—their tendency to defer themselves, to metamorphose indefinitely—is an epistemological but not ontological issue. Certainly Jung, a good Kantian, does admit that, from the perspective of our limited consciousness, archetypal images are a mere play of phenomena; sounding faintly deconstructionist, Jung asserts that the essence of an archetype remains elusive, deferred:

> Every statement going beyond the purely phenomenal aspects of an archetype lays itself open to . . . criticism.
> . . . Not for a moment dare we succumb to the illusion

that an archetype can be finally explained and disposed
of. Even the best attempts at explanation are only more
or less successful translations into another metaphorical
language. (Indeed, language itself is only an image.) The
most we can do is to *dream the myth onwards* and give
it a modern dress. (160)

Such ambiguous, relativized archetypal images and metaphors are
rather different from the straightforward, "solid archetypal model" that is the first term in what J. Hillis Miller calls "Platonic"
repetition, the basis of unambiguously mimetic narrative (*Fiction
and Repetition* 6). Nonetheless, Jung is ontologically not a rela-
tivist; he affirms that "an *unconscious core of meaning*" (156) lies
beneath an archetype—that an archetype is founded on an unnameable something, which confronts the ego with a genuine
otherness. The center may be essentially beyond our grasp, but for
Jung there assuredly is a center.

It is difficult to measure how far Fowles has gone, in *Mantissa,*
toward an affirmation that such an archetypal something exists
beyond and in relation to the conscious freedom/self. Certainly
this self-reflexive novel of ideas in many ways demolishes all
content outside "the invisible interior of poetic freedom"—the
book's radically deconstructive ending especially accomplishes
this demolition. However, there are suggestions that Fowles is
moving, in a very qualified way, toward the possibility that a
mysterious something does face his cherished Sartrean nothingness.

It is indicative of just how firmly nothingness grips Fowles's
works that the novelist's breakthrough to substance is *A Maggot.*
Although I do suggest that this book affirms something beyond the
self's private and non-substantial freedom, *A Maggot* is hardly a
Dickensian banquet celebrating life's plenty. The novel's title, for
one thing, is as negative as that of *Mantissa* (indeed, the similar
titles lead me to assume that Fowles considers the two books to be
companion pieces). And the plot is almost as shadowy as that of the
previous work.

Fowles himself, in a brief prologue, explains his title this way: "A
maggot is the larval stage of a winged creature; as is the written
text, at least in the writer's hope. But an older though now obsolete
sense of the word is that of whim or quirk." But Julian Moynahan, in
a rather snide *New Republic* review, suggests that the title is even
more annihilating: "Incidentally, aren't maggots the larval stage of

the common or carrion fly? Rather remote from the Nabokovian butterfly, one might say. This title may be even more self-depreca-tory than that of Fowles's *Mantissa* (1982), which means a trivial addition to a preexisting literary corpus. The French have a phrase for it: *mauvaise honte*" (48). And if the title threatens to annihilate the book, the plot (for some readers, at least) completes the job. No, this is not a story in which the characters turn out to be merely nothingnesses in an absent writer's mind, but it seems almost as insubstantial—a story about not finding out what happened. Set in 1736, it begins with "a forlorn little group of travellers" who are crossing "a remote upland in the far south-west of England" (1). But they are not who they seem to be, and after one of them does or does not commit suicide, we spend several hundred pages with an investigator trying to find out where they were going and what they were doing, and we are left only with mystery and with the absence of the protagonist (an unnamed young lord—a *deus absconditus*?). My examination of the book's initial narrative sections, and of its dramatizations of the investigator's attempts to pull the truth out a parade of witnesses, will reveal how much this novel is yet another example of Fowlesian textual play, a tension between competing texts that leaves an empty space. But I will also show that the empty space this time resonates with echoes of *something* rather than sheer nothingness; although Fowles clears away his space largely to make room, yet again, for existential freedom, this time it is freedom grounded on a kind of political, archetypal, and—dare I say it?—religious substantiality.

The novel's first fifty pages, its only extended narrative section (the rest of the book is mostly presented as a transcript of the investigator's interrogations—there is no omniscient narrator to tell us the unambiguous truth), introduce the male protagonist, a young lord who is trying to plumb the mysteries of the cosmos. Although Fowles's cool narrative objectivity keeps the lord enig-matic, an absence even during his only physical appearance in the book, readers of Fowles will recognize that this is yet another Fowlesian existential rebel. His face is described as brooding and aristocratic, but also confident and able to will freely: "Unmistaka-bly [his face] suggests will, and an indifference to all that is not will" (16). And to his companion Lacy, an actor he has hired to pretend to be his uncle, he speaks of his present mission in a highly Fowlesian way: "Hazard" (not providence) has brought him to a "Rubicon" (17)—like the fulcrum that Conchis speaks of in *The Magus,* the sort of moment of truth that Charles reaches near the end of *The French Lieutenant's Woman*—and he must either steal his freedom now or lose his chance to rebel metaphysically against dead social conventionality: "I am born with a fixed destiny. All I told you of my supposed father I might have said of my true one—and much worse, for he is an old fool; and hath given birth to another, that is my elder brother. I am, as you might be, offered a part in a history, and I am not forgiven for refusing to play it. . . . I have no liberty, Lacy, unless I steal it first. If I go where I will, as now, I must go as a thief from those who would have me do as they want" (37–38). There is, in addition, a theatricality about his present enterprise that links the lord directly with Conchis: this adventure, he tells Lacy, "is truly like a tale, why, one of your play-pieces" (39), and he himself, he implies, is writer and director. Furthermore, it is a morally ambiguous theatricality, as Conchis's was. The lord's exertion of freedom has a Sade-like ferocity; there is a woman in the lord's small entourage, the whore "Fanny" who is actually Rebecca, the novel's heroine, and the lord possesses, dominates, collects her as forcefully as Clegg did Miranda: "Mr Bartholomew [the lord's pseudonym] stares down into her eyes a long moment. There seems something demonic now in that face beneath the bald head; demonic not in its anger or emotion, but in its coldness, its indifference to this female thing before him. It speaks of a hitherto hidden trait in his character: a sadism before Sade" (43). As if to tip us off that nothingness is, once again, the foundation of this assertion of pure freedom, Fowles gives the lord a sort of mystical double, a valet named Dick Thurlow (his death apparently by suicide will spur the book's eventual investigation), a handsome deaf mute whose silence becomes a metaphor for the lord's own secret self, his profound nothingness:

> The deaf-mute servant comes into the room, and closes the door. He stands by it, staring at his master by the fire-place, who looks back. . . . It is such a look as a husband and wife, or siblings, might give, in a room where there are other people, and they cannot say what they truly feel; yet prolonged far beyond that casual kind of exchange of secret feeling, and quite devoid even of its carefully hidden hints of expression. It is like turning a page in a printed book—and where one expects dialogue, or at least a description of movements and gestures, there is nothing: a *Shandy*-like blank page, or a gross error in binding, no page at all. The two men stand in their silence, in each other's looking, as in a mirror. (39–40)

More even than his Fowlesian predecessors, the hero of *A Maggot* remains undisclosed, a textual gap—"a *Shandy*-like blank page, or a gross error in binding, no page at all."

Rebecca, the book's heroine, will also be enigmatic, but we will nonetheless hear much more from her in the book's later dramatic sections. Suffice it to say for now that she, in the opening narrative section, is also a familiar Fowlesian type: she is part Sarah Woodruff (she is a notorious whore who has suffered from social prejudice and who now, under the spell of a man, is seeking a kind of freedom in a secluded, wooded place) and part the twin actresses in *The Magus* (the lord has recruited her to play a part in a strange theatre of the real). In any case, Rebecca and the lord are both romantic rebels against the conventional. And despite his distanced, camera-eye style in describing them, Fowles is quite willing to editorialize about this highly conventional world he has chosen to depict, England in the mid-eighteenth century, which he describes as having hit a rigid, reactionary slump between the English and the French Revolutions: "To us such a world would seem absurdly prescribed, with personal destiny fixed to an intolerable degree, totalitarian in its essence" (50). In the remainder of the book, Fowles will depict, in a deeply ambiguous way, the wrenching open of that world.

But before wrenching it open, Fowles will present the book's most vivid personification of totalitarian rigidity, Henry Ayscough, the barrister who works for the young lord's father and who is investigating the mystery of Dick Thurlow's violent death and of the lord's disappearance. We receive Ayscough's investigation flatly, objectively, in the form of legal transcripts; there is no room in Ayscough's world for emotion or subjectivity. Nancy Bishop Dessommes, in a piece published in *Southern Humanities Review,* claims that the "detached thinker" Ayscough is a reincarnation of "Nicholas Urfe, the aloof Oxford scholar of *The Magus*" and of "Charles Smithson, the self-assured Victorian scientist of *The French Lieutenant's Woman*": "Like his predecessors, he is the antithesis of a female figure whose presence invades his well-ordered world and who defies any definition he or society would impose on her" (291). Dessommes does qualify her equation of Ayscough with Urfe and Smithson, but even so her statement is inaccurate. The heroes of *The Magus* and *The French Lieutenant's Woman* are metaphysical rebels from the start—much more analogous to the young lord than to Ayscough. Ayscough, rather, is an unambiguous embodiment of the merely scientific side of Fowles, the obsession with pruning trees and collecting butterflies (and other living things), without any of the antithetical romantic dimensions that the earlier Fowlesian heroes, even Clegg, had. Ayscough is determined to get to the bottom of the young lord's tawdry affair; he is a man for whom the romantic and mysterious—the Fowlesian secret *domaine,* the dark and hidden—is at best foolish and at worst grossly immoral: "I'll not rest till all's laid bare" (97). And he does not want to understand the lord, but only to uncover the facts of his story: "I give no credit, except upon facts," he says, sounding proudly Gradgrindian (113).

Ayscough's rigid world and worldview—which, Fowles suggests, is fairly representative of the middle of the eighteenth century—is what the lord is rebelling against (and although the lord's language is familiar, in some ways an echo of *The Aristos,* it begins to appear that this is a rebellion founded on a more positive and substantive vision than we have seen before in Fowles). The actor Lacy, as conservative as Ayscough though more genial, describes with some dismay the lord's rejection of neoclassical ideas of order and stasis and his substitution of a kind of deconstructionist theology in which God is the invisible ground for a world of changing text. The young lord, Lacy reports, believes that

> God is eternal motion. . . . [The lord] said he did not
> deny the existence of such an Author, yet must beg
> leave to doubt our present notions of Him; for he said it
> would be juster to say we were like the personages in a
> tale or novel, that had no knowledge they were such;
> and thought ourselves most real, not seeing we were
> made of imperfect words and ideas, and to serve other
> ends, far different from what we supposed. We might
> imagine this great Author of all as such and such, in our
> own image, sometimes cruel, sometimes merciful, as we
> do our kings. Notwithstanding in truth we knew no
> more of Him and His ends than of what lay in the moon,
> or the next world. (144–45)

Ayscough, of course, is disgusted with the young lord for rejecting "all that Providence most plainly designs for him," and he explains the lord's behavior with a simple bit of naturalistic psychologizing: "he is not so much to blame for his perversity as some malign accident of nature" (182). But in one of the rare bits of narrative that are sprinkled among the legal transcripts, the narrator criticizes lawyer Ayscough as handily as Ayscough does the lord: "All ancient and established professions must be founded on tacit prejudices as strong as their written statutes and codes; and by those Ayscough is imprisoned as much as any debtor in the Fleet by law" (235).

It is Ayscough's legal transcripts that constitute the text of most of the novel after its introductory section, and the clash between the flat objectivity of the prose and the romantic, mysterious content that the prose attempts to disclose is the prevailing dynamic of the book; Ayscough is, so to speak, the text that the novel deconstructs. He does discover, however, some fairly straight-forward facts about what happened to the lord, Dick, and Rebecca just before Dick's death and the lord's disappearance: it seems that Davy Jones, the rather silly Welshman who had been enacting the part of the entourage's guard, followed the threesome into the forest. Davy reports to Ayscough that he saw them arrive at a cave in the woods, that they met a strangely dressed woman, and that all four (Rebecca now dressed as a May Queen) entered the cave. After a long while, Davy continues, Dick emerged—"his face wild, such as truly a man in a fit, with the greatest fear upon him" (227)—and ran off, and then Rebecca herself came out, naked and dazed. This is as much as we learn, objectively, about the climax of the story; these are the facts, and they are all but useless, explain-ing nothing about Dick's death or the lord's disappearance. It is up to Rebecca to provide the meaning—the truth?—behind the facts, and what she ends up doing is showing that meaning is ambiguous, dark, hidden, that mere objectivity cannot approach it. She gives two radically different explanations of the facts, and in doing so she spins two tales representing dissimilar literary genres, horror and science-fiction/fantasy. In other words, just as *The French Lieutenant's Woman* (and also, in a sense, *The Collector*) had two endings, *A Maggot* has two climaxes. In the remainder of my discussion of this novel, I will show the extent to which the clash between the two climaxes merely deconstructs Ayscough's objec-tive language system and leaves nothing, and the extent to which it points toward a substantive something.

In my discussion of *The Collector* I noted that Fowles is paying homage, in that novel, to Hitchcock's *Psycho;* similarly, Rebecca's first version of the story of the cave is a kind of tribute to *Rosemary's Baby*. We hear from Davy Jones that Rebecca has told him that the lord brought her to a Satanic ritual, which led eventually to her rape and seeming impregnation by the devil.

The ordeal began, Rebecca told Jones, at Stonehenge, where the lord had gone presumably to commune with the spirits of darkness before really meeting his Muse and his destiny at the cave. The lord told Rebecca to lie on one of the stones ("We may think of her," Julian Moynahan sneers, "keeping it warm for Tess Durbeyfield" [48]), and then "The King of Hell, . . . the Prince of Darkness" (252) appears. Despite his lack of education, Davy Jones manages to give the telling an appropriately Gothic flavor:

> Then there was all of a sudden a great rush or hurtle
> close in the night above, as of some great falcon that
> passed. And as a flash of lightning, so be it no thunder-
> clap warned of its coming; and tho' but in this great
> flash, she did see a figure that stood above her on a
> stone pillar as a statue might, next above where she lay,
> that seemed of a great and dark-cloaked blackamoor,
> which did gaze most greedily down upon her, like he
> was that falcon whose wings she heard, his cloak still aflut-
> ter from his falling, and so he would in an instant spring
> down further upon her, as a bird upon its prey. (251)

But this is only the prelude; the main event is the tale of the cave. Rebecca bore out Davy Jones's story, saying that she was forced to dress as a May Queen and that then a strange woman appeared, to whom the lord and Dick paid homage "as if they had met some great lady, a queen, sir. Tho' in all else she looked no earthly queen, no, most cruel and malevolent" (255). Then they entered the cave, where the strange woman joined two other frightening, witch-like women; and "behind these three stood one dressed in a dark cloak and masked, as it might be a hangman" (257)—the "blackamoor" (258), whom Rebecca knew to be Satan. Soon Satan "stood naked, proud in his demon's lust and would come down upon her" (259), and Rebecca fainted, was presumably raped, and then awoke to see the lord joined in "black wedding" to the strange demonic Muse. Then an orgy commenced ("Why, even the raven stood upon the cat, as though to cover her" [260]), after which Rebecca was drugged by one of the witches and fell into a very vivid dream in which she seemed to be walking with Satan down a long hall hung with great tapestries covered with pictures portraying "inhuman cruelty" (261). Among other things, she saw images of a pitiable beggar girl—whom she recognized as "her own self, as she was before her coming to London" (263)—and of "a fair corse of a young lady being gnawed by a seethe of maggots as it lay, unburied; and one of which was monstrous large, she could not forget it" (265).

Through it all, however, Rebecca told Jones she experienced not despair but rather "a great thirst, or so she put it, sir, she did mean it in her soul, a need for our Redeemer Christ" (262). And when she awoke and found herself alone, Rebecca did not sink into the cynical hopelessness of Young Goodman Brown (whose ordeal is similar to Rebecca's); rather, she was moved to return to her Quaker religion and to proclaim a Christianity of radical equality, a Christianity that flies in the face of Ayscough's rigid social order and that he roundly rejects as treason and dissent (which for him are synonymous). She spoke, Davy says, "of how Jesus Christ came into this world for such as she and I, to show us a path through its night. . . . [A]nd she said that the gentlemen who went to her bagnio were not better than us, but worse, for they did choose to live evilly when they might live well, while it was forced upon us, only to get our daily bread. That wealth was a great corruption in men's minds. . . . For there was no rank in Heaven, she said, save in saintliness" (270–71). This, startlingly, is the conclusion of Rebecca's version of *Rosemary's Baby*—the two are similar tales with wholly different ultimate revelations.

But for now, the ultimate revelation seems less important than the fact that Rebecca claims, when Ayscough interviews her directly, that these horrific events never occurred; she lied, she says, to Davy Jones because she wished "to lead him from meddling further" (306). It is true that she is pregnant, but she asserts now that the father is not Satan but Dick, the lord's deaf-mute servant, with whom she admits to having had sex at the lord's initiation. She proceeds to retell the story of Stonehenge and the cave; her second version is as otherworldly as her first, but this time the literary mode is not horror but fantasy (with an anachronistic touch of science fiction). Yes, she says, at Stonehenge she did experience "a great rush in the sky above" (327), but this ushered in an encounter not with Satan but with God: she saw an old bearded man beside a young carpenter, and then she smelled a sweet fragrance and saw a kind of Dantesque vision: " 'twas white as the summer sun, shaped as a rose" (330).

The incidents at the cave, furthermore, are similarly transformed. The strange woman now is not malevolent but sweet and comforting; indeed, the young lord's Muse, his Well-Beloved, is revealed to be an embodiment of no less than Holy Mother Wisdom, and she takes her place beside the Father and the Son as the Holy Spirit, the third person of a feminized Christian Trinity. And in the cave she leads Rebecca, as Satan did in the story's first version, to a vision of a maggot, but this time it is a sublime, transcendent maggot, a sort of chariot from heaven. Actually it is identifiably a spaceship from a distant galaxy; if the first version of the story resembles *Rosemary's Baby,* this time the model seems to be *Close Encounters of the Third Kind:* "Then came there a sigh from the floating maggot, and it did begin to fall, most slowly, like a feather; and came so until its belly rested nigh upon the ground; and from that belly now there stuck forth thin legs that had great dark paws, on the which it rested. No sooner that than of a sudden there appeared upon its side towards us an open door" (366). Rebecca boards the "maggot" and, just as she saw visions on a tapestry in her dreamy experience in the horror tale, so now she watches a sort of movie on a screen inside the ship; it is a movie about heaven—or the socialist Utopia—or some faraway paradisaical planet:

> Exceeding beautiful. . . . All built of white and gold, and gardens everywhere. . . . [People] Of many nations. Some white, some olive or yellow, some brown, others black as night. . . . [I]t seemed all did live in common, without distinction nor difference. . . . [S]aw I no poor, no beggars, no cripples, no sick, not one who starved. Nor saw I those who here parade more rich and magnificent, neither; 'twas plain all were content to be of a sameness in their circumstance. . . . (375–78)

It is to this perfect world that Rebecca claims the young lord has been whisked in the magical maggot.

As different as the two versions of the story are, it should already be clear that this second version leads to virtually the same vision of radical Christianity with which Rebecca ended the first, a vision of reenfranchisement of the disadvantaged: " 'Twas loving kindness and her [Holy Mother Wisdom's] mercy. None so sinful they may not be saved" (383). And, again, Rebecca claims to have been reconverted to Christianity, though now she has moved to an offshoot of the Quakers called the "Prophets," who believe that the Christ of the Second Coming will be a female Christ. Ayscough, of course, brushes these claims aside as treasonous and heretical, just like the claims Rebecca made to Jones at the end of her horror tale. The two stories are, for Ayscough, nonsensical and puzzling; he can accommodate neither—and surely cannot accommodate both—to his rationalism. But they leave him, and the book, with the image of a great eighteenth-century negator: Dissent. The two stories represent a subversion of the era's political and religious orthodoxy— and they even, with their supernaturalism and their irreconcilable factual contradictions, subvert Ayscough's solid rational discourse. Rebecca makes the latter point explicitly, claiming that her discourse uses a different "alphabet" from Ayscough's, and although Ayscough rejects this subversion—"Mistress, there is one and one only alphabet, that is plain English" (424)—his desperation and defeat are clear. Rebecca's tales are religious dissent as radical deconstruction of conventions.

And Fowles seems to be using Dissent as an eighteenth-century approximation of the existential nihilation that grounds freedom; Rebecca—whose child, we discover, will be Ann Lee, the founder of the radically unorthodox Shakers—seems a kind of proto-

Sartrean. In the novel's epilogue, Fowles asserts that "a convinced atheist can hardly dedicate a novel to a form of Christianity" (462). Nonetheless, he claims that Dissenters, by virtue of their act of radical rejection, were discovering freedom: "Unorthodox religion was the only vehicle by which the vast majority, who were neither philosophers nor artists, could express this painful breaking of the seed of the self from the hard soil of an irrational and tradition-bound society" (463). Fowles has planted hints in the novel that this is what Dissent represents; his description of Rebecca's eventual husband John Lee, a dissenting "Prophet," is a tribute to a spare, stripped-down rejection of worldly encumbrance — "as if [the Lees] have said to themselves: We have nothing, and so may be godly" (292). One of Rebecca's first statements to Ayscough, furthermore, is a defense of freedom, a refusal to allow "rank and respect" to "forbid our liberty of conscience" (304), and later she asserts that her Christianity is a rejection of every ironclad "must" (428). So it seems that Dissenters, for Fowles, prefigured both deconstruction and existentialism, and that Rebecca's deconstructive, logically incompatible stories function to dismantle Ayscough's objective, totalitarian discourse and to open up that space of nothingness which is freedom.

This is all familiar Fowlesian terrain. Once again Fowles has used language to cross out, in a Derridean sense, to cancel an oppressive presence and open up a liberating absence. This is, it seems, another Fowles novel about language's inadequacies—a novel that untells.

More, however, is going on this time. The strategy of the self-canceling narratives that we have seen again and again in Fowles's works does point toward existential freedom, but this time it embeds this freedom within a positive, even if hazy, vision rather than within a vacuum; just as Erato, in *Mantissa*, is a non-character who points, if only negatively, toward an archetypal something, *A Maggot* is an antinovel that sees as well as unsees. It is true that Rebecca acknowledges that her vision can be mediated only by *crossing out* the language of the flesh: "Unless we cross it [the flesh], we shall not be saved," Rebecca says (423), sounding like a merging of Derrida with St. Paul, and later she says that her maggot tales "are no more than words in this world" (431). She adds, though, that the words do have referents, however deferred; her words are "signs to greater than words hereafter" (431). Her negation of discourse is founded, in other words, on something new in Fowles, though hinted at in *Mantissa*: a vision not of freedom founded on nothingness but on some absent but archetypal vision. And that vision—nebulous, surely, and established not directly but only in the play of Rebecca's two wildly incompatible stories—has something to do with a Kingdom (whatever that is) of God (whoever that could be) founded on radical equality and love; the horror story and the fantasy both point toward this absent-but-present archetype. Indeed, Walter Miller, Jr., has suggested that Rebecca's two stories, for all their differences, have a common Jungian structure: "The fascinating central motif in this novel is the numinous female triad linked to a mysterious fourth— three witches and Satan (the lord transformed), or a female Holy Trinity joined by a harlot" (11). Miller goes on to say that such an archetypal union is, for Jung, "a token of growing maturity (Rebecca's or the satanic lord's)," and that the real point of the book, one that shatters Ayscough's rational discourse but that proposes instead not nothingness but myth, is that *both* stories are true: "The equivalence of the infernal and the celestial versions of the scene in the cave conform to Jung's psychology, and both versions of the cave scene are true" (11).

Although a thorough analysis of Jung's theories is beyond the scope of this study, I suggest that his theory of archetypes—which are, as we have seen, absent yet substantive—may be a fruitful bridge from postmodernist deconstruction founded on radical absence to a postpostmodernist deconstruction founded on a deferred but intuited something. In any case, Fowles seems to be moving in this direction. Indeed, he ends *A Maggot* with a near-Updikean introduction of substance; Rebecca receives a kind of providential gift—a baby, Ann Lee—and the narrative language suggests not pure existential freedom but a reaching beyond self to other: "Now Rebecca looks down at the tiny creature in her arms. There is something of a wonderment in her eyes, at this other, this intruder into her world; she bends and very gently kisses its pink and wrinkled forehead" (459).

The book's final sentence, before the epilogue, begins with the words of the lullaby Rebecca sings to the baby: "*Vive vi, vive vum, vive vi, vive vum, vive vi, vive vum*" (460). And although Fowles asserts that "they are not rational words, and can mean nothing," he uses the word "nothing" ambiguously here. This nothing is not the self dwelling in its own vacuum of freedom; it is addressed to a real other. Fowles's final analysis of Dissent in the book's epilogue, furthermore, is a passionate appeal not just for freedom but also for justice and equality, for a moral subordination of self to other: "We grow," he says, "too dominated by the Devil's great I, in Shaker terminology" (467). And he pays tribute to a Logos that, though lost (deferred) and a mere maggot (a whim, a nothing), nonetheless *is,* and is "almost divine"—"the lost spirit, courage, and imagination of Mother Ann Lee's word, her Logos; its almost divine maggot" (467).

The Scarlet Letter Revisited

So John Fowles, whom I have been discussing as a poet of existential nothingness, seems to be moving toward a tentative, heavily qualified, but nonetheless affirmative religious vision. Meanwhile Updike, whom I have discussed as a novelist whose theological vision is grounded in a reverence for the world, for things, has later in his career been branded as a nihilist.

In a now infamous review of *Roger's Version* published in the *New York Review of Books,* Frederick Crews asserts that the later Updike "has radically divorced his notion of Christian theology from Christian ethics" (7), that he has given up his idea of a providential God and instead "has come to take morbid satisfaction in God's imagined indifference to our goings-on" (8), and that even his decision to build novels around Hawthorne's *The Scarlet Letter* rather than around real worldly experience shows that "he no longer feels at home in the here and now" (14). Yes, Crews admits that Updike remains interested in Christian theology, specifically that of Karl Barth, but Crews says that Updike's "adaptation of Barthianism" is mainly notable for "its pugnacity and its grim coldness," and that Barth's notion of a God who is " 'Wholly Other' from us" has allowed Updike to abandon any notion of a providential or ethical God (8). Crews concludes that the "primary" Updike, the one who exists beneath "the worldly satirist of the Bech stories, the genially urbane *New Yorker* essayist, the light versifier, the Red Sox fan, or the critics' sacramental sage," is actually "morbid and curmudgeonly, starved for a missing grace, playing an unfunny hide-and-seek with his readers, reluctant to confide his anguish yet driven to express both a lurking nihilism and a doctrinal obsession that barely keeps that nihilism at bay" (14).

Although I will eventually explain why I reject Crews's argument, it is stated so vigorously and intelligently that it must be attended to; Crews does, albeit in a mean-spirited way, raise some legitimate issues. And Ralph Wood, a scholar of religion and literature, develops Crews's ideas in more detail in a very smart, sensitive essay on Karl Barth published in *Books and Religion,* which even more deeply challenges my claims that Updike portrays a world imbued with substance and providential presence. Wood challenges Crews's suggestion that Updike's increased nihilism is tied to his "reliance on Barth's antinomian theology" (29); rather, Wood claims that Updike misreads Barth. Wood says that

Barth's God is profoundly gracious and ethical, deeply involved in the human world: "For Barth, the glad news that God has not left human life hanging perilously in the balance, but that He has graciously justified and sanctified it in Christ Jesus, is the real impetus for ethical endeavor. Far from snapping the cords of the moral life, divine grace blesses the tie that binds us to each other and to the world" (29). But Wood does agree with Crews's major premise, that the later Updike has become a prophet of nothingness. He argues that this is because Updike, with his portrayals of a radically other God and of humans groveling in increasingly kinky adultery, has abandoned Christianity altogether and become a kind of Gnostic:

> What no one seems to have discerned is that Updike is the advocate not of a Barthian so much as a Gnostic sexuality. Far from being a heedless worldling bent on celebrating all the glories of the flesh, Updike at his worst is a Gnostic with an angelic disregard for God's good creation. The Gnostic, writes Hans Jonas, envisions ". . . an absolute rift between man and that in which he finds himself lodged—the world. In its theological aspect this doctrine states that the Divine is alien to the world and has neither part not concern in the physical universe; that the true God, strictly transmundane, is not revealed or even indicated by the world, and is therefore the Unknown, the totally Other, unknowable in terms of worldly analogies" (*The Gnostic Religion,* p. 327). (31)

Wood's claims particularly jar me because they make Updike sound theologically not at all like the Updike I have been describing but more like the Fowles who wrote *The Aristos,* a Fowles whose only god could be a *deus absconditus* ("If there had been a creator, his second act would have been to disappear" [*Aristos* 19]). Even putting aside for a moment Crews's and Wood's charges that Updike is ethically nihilistic, at the very least such an Updike would aesthetically be a poet of nothingness rather than of something, a follower of the literary *via negativa.*

John R. May, however, would probably deny this. In a response to my own analysis of the Rabbit books, May has suggested that Updike's *Scarlet Letter* trilogy uses repetition in much the same way that I described repetition in the Rabbit novels: the repetition is Kierkegaardian, a positive experience of grace. May does note that while marriage is the form this repetition takes in the Rabbit books, in the *Scarlet Letter* books "ironically enough, repetition comes in the form of adultery, not marriage. Updike is after all the master of reversal." Adultery, May goes on to say, is for Updike "an emblem of the human condition and the ground of transcendental experience" (15). But both Frederick Crews and Ralph Wood would likely point out, quite correctly, that this change from repetitive marriage to repetitive adultery is extremely significant; it cannot be brushed aside as just a neat reversal. Kierkegaard's entire thesis is that grace comes in and through the ordinary, the familiar, and adultery is a breaking of the familiar in its root ("familial") sense. As Donald Greiner argues in his study of literary depictions of adultery, adultery in Updike's world generally represents, both morally and aesthetically, rebellion against the ordinary, not a repetition of it (see Greiner 44–48, 104–6). The God of adultery really does seem to be different from the God of marriage — as different as Wood's Gnostic God is from his Barthian/Christian God.

So in this final look at Updike's novels, an analysis of the *Scarlet Letter* trilogy, I must examine the ways these later works show a new embrace of the nothing. Looking briefly at the sounding of the theme of adultery in *A Month of Sundays,* the first book of the series, and then looking more closely at the late 1980s books *Roger's Version* and *S.,* I will show how fiercely Updike challenges my thesis that his religious views are founded on a positive vision of the world of things, on a *via affimativa.* But I will also show that even in these novels, Updike finally curbs the negativity; even here he points, more than Crews and Wood acknowledge, toward a return to the ordinary. These adultery books do in fact ultimately affirm true Kierkegaardian repetition — founded on marriage, connection, presence rather than dissociation and absence — after all.

A Month of Sundays is, in more ways than one, an antinovel. It is formally a non-narrative; its major action is really just the journal writing of the first-person protagonist, Tom Marshfield (a twentieth-century Dimmesdale, a minister who has been sent from Massachusetts to a desert rehabilitation center because of scandalous sexual activities). He says he is writing for an audience, the mysterious and unattractive nurse Ms. Prynne (Hawthorne's Hester has certainly deteriorated in the modern era), but it seems that she is only an absence, that the book is about extreme self-involvement rather than communication.

More importantly, though, the book is thematically a kind of "anti"-novel: it seems to be anti-everything, a loud No to all the stuff of the world that Updike has so often celebrated. Tom describes himself as always having wanted to blast away the things, the "circumstances," of his life, even when he was a child: "I would put myself to sleep by imagining objects—pencils, hassocks, teddy bears—sliding over a waterfall. I loved shedding each grade as I ascended through school. Even the purgative sweep of windshield wipers gratifies me. A lifelong drive to disrobe myself of circumstances has brought me stripped to this motel" (139). Of course, Rabbit Angstrom has the same urge to run from his suburban clutter; nonetheless, *Rabbit, Run* and its sequels are narratively located in those suburbs—Rabbit's compulsion to negate is providentially countered by the narrative in which he is embedded. Tom's negations, on the other hand, exist in a kind of vacuum, a desert. The book offers no clear alternative to his loud No (though there may be traces of an underlying affirmation).

The book, first of all, says No to the American society of its time; this is Updike's Nixon book—Tom Marshfield's story is set "at some point in the time of Richard Nixon's unravelling" (7)—and Nixon decay is everywhere. As Tom puts it in one of the sermons sprinkled throughout the text, the quintessential contemporary American disease is anorexia, a spiritual desiccation: American parishioners, he says, are captives "of infertile apathy, of withering scorn, of—to use a strange Greek word suddenly commonplace—*anorexia,* the antithesis of appetite" (193). Not surprisingly, then, the book also says No to suburbia—more radically than the Rabbit books do. Rather than depicting ordinary suburban life, this novel has removed its protagonist from the suburbs and plopped him in the desert. Tom himself, in the same sermon from which I just quoted, claims that the desert—the nothingness—is quickly engulfing the suburbs, that the human world soon will be only desert: "The pavements of our cities are deserted, emptied by fear. In the median strips of our highways, naught blows but trash. In our monotonous suburbs houses space themselves as evenly as creosote bushes, whose roots poison the earth around" (193). And again and again the book says No to God. Indeed, Tom Marshfield's sexual affairs are very nearly founded on such a negation. The most chilling scene in the novel has Tom trying to stir himself to sexual potency by demanding that his lover blaspheme: " 'You dumb cunt,' I said, 'how can you be so dumb as to believe in God the Father, God the Son, and God the Holy Ghost? Tell me you really don't. Tell me, so I can fuck you. Tell me you know down deep there's nothing. The dead stink, Frankie; for a while they stink and then they're just bones and then there's not even that. Forever and ever' " (185). A writer whom I have been describing as the late-twentieth-century poet of America, suburbia, and Christianity seems, in this book, to say No to all three.

For our purposes, though, the most notable negation is the book's loud No to marriage. If America and its suburbs are a prison, marriage is, according to Tom, the shape that prison takes; the only freedom—the great annihilator of the constricting stuff of the world—is adultery: "Wherein does the modern American man recover his sense of worth, not as dogged breadwinner and economic integer, but as romantic minister and phallic knight, as personage, embodiment, and hero? In adultery. And wherein does the American woman, coded into mindlessness by household slavery and the stupefying companionship of greedy infants, re-cover her powers of decision, of daring, of discrimination—her dignity, in short? In adultery" (58). I must not be so flatfooted as to fail to note that there is grandly ironic humor here (Tom goes on to say that "Verily, the sacrament of marriage, as instituted in its adamant impossibility by our Saviour, exists but as a precondition for the sacrament of adultery"). But in light of all the negations in this novel, I must assert that there is something serious going on too. Adultery is, at least symbolically, being praised here because it is the great No to contemporary American imprisonment. Tom Marshfield describes adultery in downright Fowlesian/Camusian terms as the nakedness, the nothingness, that constitutes freedom: "The adulterous man and woman arrive at the place of their tryst stripped of all the false uniforms society has assigned them; they come on no recommendation but their own, possess no creden-tials but those God has bestowed, that is, insatiable egos and workable genitals" (58). If adultery in the *Scarlet Letter* novels really is, as John May claims, the form Updikean repetition takes, Updike's "emblem of the human condition and the ground of transcendental experience," then it really does seem that Updike has embraced the theological negativity, the Gnosticism, that Ralph Wood ascribes to him—a profound rejection of the world and an adherence to a God who is the negation of the world, who in a real way is *not,* a *deus absconditus* who can be approached only in the No of adultery.

Before examining the extent to which *Roger's Version* and *S.* also proclaim such an absence rather than a presence, I must look at slight traces of an alternate vision even in *A Month of Sundays,* the Updikean textbook on the theology of adultery. One trace is Tom's relationship with his clergyman father. Tom claims to have rejected his father's liberalism ("a smiling fumbling shadow of German Pietism, of Hegel's and Schleiermacher's and Ritschl's polywebbed attempts to have it all ways, of those doddering

Anglican empiricists" [31–32]) in favor of Barth, but his father's presence—and the stuff, the circumstances, the somethingness of that presence—gave him a conviction of God's presence that somehow sustains Tom's theism even in the desert:

> It was, somehow, and my descriptive zeal flags, in the *furniture* I awoke among, and learned to walk among, and fell asleep amid—it was the moldings of the doorways and the sashes of the windows and the turning of the balusters—it was the carpets each furry strand of which partook in a pattern and the ceilings whose random cracks and faint discolorations I would never grow to reach, that convinced me, that *told* me, God was, and was here, even as the furnace came on, and breathed gaseous warmth upon my bare, buttonshoed legs. Someone invisible had cared to make these things. (30)

And this appreciation of furniture also gives Tom a very unpostmodernist attachment to the presence of the world rather than to its absence, and to the ability of language to convey meaning (even of words such as "God") rather than to defer it:

> My intuition about objects is thus the exact opposite of that of Robbe-Grillet, who intuits . . . in tables, rooms, corners, knives, etc., an emptiness resounding with the universal nullity. He has only to describe a chair for us to know that God is absent. Whereas for me, puttying a window sash, bending my face close in, awakens a plain suspicion that someone in the immediate vicinity immensely, discreetly cares. God. Since before language dawned I knew what the word meant: all haggling as to this is linguistic sophistry. (32–33)

I am not sure what to do with such an affirmation of presence near the beginning of a novel that seems hellbent on negating, on blasting familial stuff with adultery and theistic substance with blasphemy. This book is, perhaps, more deeply at odds with itself than the earlier Updike works that I have analyzed (and hence, Crews's claims that the later Updike has become deeply conflicted may have some validity). But I must note that *A Month of Sundays* does structurally add one more "anti" that ends up being ironically affirmative: it becomes an anti-antinovel. After writing to nothingness, to silence, for twenty chapters, Tom is jarred by a startling revelation; it seems that someone, Ms. Prynne perhaps, has written a response in his journal—the word "Nice." Granted, the word has been erased—it is an *absent* presence—but there is at least a trace, evidence finally of a not-quite-absconded other (and, analogically, Other): "Bless you, whoever you are, if you are, for this even so tentative intrusion into these pages' solipsism" (198). And then the book ends with Ms. Prynne's actual appearance, which is directly linked with Tom's return from the desert, his rebirth ("I . . . was afraid, not afraid, afraid to be born again. Even so, come" [269]). His prose, in the final chapter, is interrupted in midsentence, and after an extended white space (which indicates not absence but a real visit from a real human being, Ms. Prynne), Tom writes, "Bless you," and then explicitly invokes an image of providence: "What a surprise" (270). What Tom Marshfield and Ms. Prynne have done, of course, is have sex, but this time it really does seem to be an experience of something rather than nothingness, a *via affirmativa:* "What is it, this human contact, this blank-browed thing we do for one another? There was a moment, when I entered you, and was big, and you were already wet, when you could not have seen yourself, when your eyes were all for another, looking up into mine, with an expression without a name, of entry and alarm, and of salutation. I pray my own face, a stranger to me, saluted in turn" (271). This encounter, and the other traces of an embrace of the real, cannot entirely save the book from charges of negativity, Gnosticism, and even nihilism. But these things certainly show that *A Month of Sundays* is not an unambiguous antinovel.

It is not *A Month of Sundays,* however, but rather *Roger's Version* that is the focus of Frederick Crews's claims that Updike is a nihilist and Ralph Wood's that he is a Gnostic. Crews calls *Roger's Version* the "coldest and most self-conscious" of Updike's novels, and he describes its plot as one that is founded on a chilly, even necrophiliac, "resentment of enthusiasm" (12)—a distaste for the messy, vital stuff of life that I have been arguing is always blessed in Updike's world. Crews says that Roger Lambert, the skeptical divinity-professor protagonist (analogous to Hawthorne's Roger Chillingworth), must destroy the computer student Dale Kohler both because of Dale's confident Christian faith and because of his youthful sexual energy (Dale, standing in for Hawthorne's Dimmesdale, will have an affair with Roger's wife, named not Hester but Esther). "Before the novel is over," Crews says, Dale "will have been not just silenced but shattered in spirit" (12). Wood, furthermore, carefully analyzes Roger's theological position and shows that it—and hence, he infers, Updike's—is not Barthian/Christian at all. Roger, according to Wood, founds his theology not on the positive revelation of God in Jesus Christ (the Barthian position) but on merely a *negative* proof: the experience of angst, "the vexed human consciousness—our inability to find an animal at-home-ness in the world" (30). And although Wood grants that the "early Barth may have made some noises" suggesting that his God, like Roger's, is "totally Other: a timeless transcendence, an eternal Absolute having commerce with neither history nor nature," Wood affirms that "it *is* God's presence and not his absence that Barth celebrates.... Hardly absenting Himself from time, space and causality, God indwells the world as Immanuel" (31).

Crews's and Wood's positions are, as I have acknowledged, compelling. There is more than a small strain of fiery negativity in *Roger's Version,* a novel that deconstructs God and sex, theology and pornography, a book that squeezes faith down to the tiniest of kernels—which ends up resembling the infinitesimal existential kernel that Fowles, in his Sartrean vein, celebrates as freedom. But there are also some distinct and significant strands of positive rather than negative faith—affirmations, even amid all the negativity, of the something rather than the nothing.

Crews and Wood and others have shown quite well how the novel functions to dismantle any belief in an immanent, present God and to replace it with a *deus absconditus,* a god of absence. The book's major dramatic conflict is between the icy divinity-school theologian Roger, who feels that religious experience must always be dark and negative ("I am a depressive. It is very important for my mental well-being that I keep my thoughts directed away from areas of contemplation that might entangle me and pull me down" [2]), and the blithely optimistic Dale, who thinks that God is revealed clearly in the created world and that science is on the verge of unequivocally proving God's existence: "The most miraculous thing is happening.... The physicists are getting down to the nitty-gritty, they've really just about pared things down to the ultimate details, and the last thing they ever expected to happen is happening. God is showing through. They hate it, but they can't do anything about it. Facts are facts" (9).

Dale, a friend of Roger's niece Verna, has come to Roger to see if Roger's divinity school will give him a grant to analyze these facts and prove God's existence on his computer. What he is unprepared to discover is that Roger finds this project distasteful and even blasphemous. The book, especially in its early sections, is filled with Roger's erudite theological proclamations that the true God can only be a God of absence; he bases his argument on Barth, but as I have noted Ralph Wood makes a convincing case that, lacking the Christian element of divine *presence,* Roger's version of theology is more Gnostic than Barthian.

Roger begins by arguing that the physical universe is simply too massive — in Sartrean terms, far too much is *de trop* — to have some immanent logos or telos; the sheer messiness of the universe's *something* suggests that the meaningful is outside this substance, is in fact nothing: "I suppose a fundamental question . . . about any modern attempts to relate the observed cosmos to traditional religion becomes the sheer, sickening extravagance of it. If God wished, as Genesis and now you tell us, to make the world as a theatre for Man, why make it so unusably vast, so horribly turbulent and, ah, crushing to contemplate?" (16). God, for Roger, must be radically apart from (*totaliter aliter*) these scientific facts, this mess of worldly stuff. This totally other deity, as he describes it, hardly has the benevolent, morally inviting face that it has in Updike's Christian/Levinasian meditation on the Other, *The Centaur;* although Roger invokes Barth, it is true that his emphasis on the *deus absconditus,* however striking, sounds very Gnostic (and Fowlesian):

> [God's] objectivity must be of a totally other sort than that of these physical equations. . . . I . . . see a problem with His facticity, as it would be demonstrated to us. We all know, as teachers, what happens to facts: they get ignored, forgotten. Facts are *boring.* Facts are inert, impersonal. A God Who is a mere fact will just sit there on the table with all the other facts: we can take Him or leave Him. The way it is, we are always in motion *toward* the God Who flees, the *Deus absconditus;* He by His apparent absence is always with us. (235)

Perhaps most relevant to my own claims about the works of Fowles and Updike is Roger's explicit discussion of the *viae* to God. And not surprisingly, he does not endorse a *via affirmativa.* In fact, he does not even endorse a *via negativa;* for Roger Lambert — and he again invokes, even quotes, Barth — there is *no* human way to God:

> I seized the moment to look up the Barth quote. It involved, I remembered, a series of *via*s, each discounted as a path to God. It was almost certainly from *The Word of God and the Word of Man.* . . . And at last, just as I had abandoned hope, the loose, scribbled pages opened to the page where, in triple pencil lines whose gouging depth indicated a strenuous spiritual clutching, my

youthful self had marginally scored, in "The Problem of
Ethics Today," where one would least think to find it:

> There is no way from us to God—not even a *via neg-*
> *ativa*—not even a *via dialectica* nor *paradoxa.* The
> god who stood at the end of some human way—even
> of this way—would not be God.
>
> Yes. I closed the book and put it back. *The god who*
> *stood at the end of some human way would not be*
> *God.* (41–42)

By itself, of course, this is merely good Protestant theology, an
affirmation that sinful humans do not earn grace by their own
works but only receive it providentially from the generous God.
But in light of Updike's novel's suggestions that there is no God
who dwells providentially within creation, this sounds like yet
another proclamation of God's radical, absolute absence from the
human world. When Roger describes his faith as his "hot Barthian
nugget insulated within layers of worldly cynicism and situation
ethics" (193), we may be ready to sketch the measurements of that
nugget: like the Sartrean consciousness, and like the freedom that
constitutes that consciousness, it is a single geometrical point—a
nothing suspended in empty space. Indeed, Roger is so concerned
to free God from Dale's scientific categories that he says he is
determined to "free Him, even though He die" (84).

This Gnostic theology is not just a detached theory that is
discussed in *Roger's Version.* A kind of Gnostic, deconstructive
absenting of things present and presenting of the absent is a large
part of the novel's very linguistic and narrative design. Almost as
prominent as the book's theological and scientific discourses,
which exist at least partially as a Derridean play of difference, is its
discourse dealing with sex (and, as in *A Month of Sundays,* it is
always *adulterous* sex). This discourse, too, is played off the theological in an ironic way that displaces, absents, even cancels, each.

Roger himself draws attention to the relation between the two
modes of discourse: "I always feel better—cleaner, revitalized—
after reading theology, even poor theology, as it caresses and
probes every crevice of the unknowable. Lest you take me for a
goody-goody, I find kindred comfort and inspiration in pornography, the much-deplored detailed depiction of impossibly long and
deep, rigid and stretchable human parts interlocking, pumping,
oozing" (42). Roger does, admittedly, claim that "what eventuates
from these sighing cesspools of our being, our unconscionable
sincere wishes," are "cathedrals and children" (42–43); he seems,

in other words, to suggest that the transcendent is immanent in the most deeply carnal—not a Gnostic idea at all. Later Roger proceeds, in the book's most impressive tour-de-force segment, to demonstrate the relation between pornography and theology by using explicitly pornographic narrative to illustrate the theologian Tertullian's claims about the human soul's need for the body; once again it appears that the point is to bring together (in a providential way, perhaps), rather than to divorce, the bodily and the transcendent. But such a Christian, Incarnational interpretation would be too facile. The fact is that the ironic juxtapositions of the sexual discourse with the theological tend to annihilate both, to empty both of substance.

Roger certainly does not depict Tertullian as a theologian who reveres the physical. Rather, Roger's Tertullian has a revulsion for the carnal (especially the feminine carnal); as Roger tells his wife Esther, Tertullian "was a heretic because he was a Puritan, a purist, called a Montanist in those days. . . . He was too good for this world" (128–29). And Tertullian, Roger goes on, told his wife that after his death she was "to remain chaste, *not* to remarry, *even* to a Christian. Also, he thought that women, whether married or unmarried, should remain veiled" (129). This Gnostic, flesh-hating context ironizes from the start Roger's explication of Tertullian's defense of the doctrine of the Resurrection of the Body in *De resurrectione carnis* ("How incontrovertibly and with what excited eloquence does Tertullian build up his argument that the flesh cannot be dispensed with by the soul!" [160]). Despite the fact that Roger's Tertullian seems to be espousing a respect for the body, the images that Roger lingers over in Tertullian's text are frequently (and this is the source of the humor of the passage) grotesque; for Tertullian, Roger says, "the Heavenly mystery of the Logos was made to descend, by means of a Platonic scaffolding of degrees of ideality, down into reality via ultimate dependence upon that repulsive muscle housed among our salivating mouth membranes and rotting teeth—the eyeless, granular, tireless tongue. *De organo carnis* indeed" (161). And then Roger paraphrases Tertullian's criticism of the non-Christian condemnation of the body, but again it is the theologian's near-pornographic luxuriating in physical detail, and ultimately in death, that titillates Roger: it is heathens, not Christians, Tertullian says, who accuse the body "of being unclean from its first formation out of Earth's feces and then uncleaner still from the slime of its semen, of being paltry . . . , infirm, guilty . . . , burdensome, troublesome. And then (according to the *ethnici*), after all this litany of ignobility, falling into its original earth and the name of a cadaver, and from this name certain to dwindle into no name, into the death of all designation" (163). When Roger goes on to say that "Tertullian, like Barth, took his stand on the only ground where he could: the flesh is man" (163), this seems, as Ralph Wood has argued, less like a celebration of "all the glories of the flesh" than like a Gnostic condemnation of humanity to a slimy alienation from the divine.

And then, when Roger illustrates this pornographic theology with overblown theological pornography—he describes his vision, which turns out to be uncannily accurate, of Dale and Esther's adulterous sexual activities—the two modes of discourse explode against each other hilariously, ferociously:

> Esther's studious rapt face descends, huge as in a motion
> picture, to drink the bitter nectar and then to slide her
> lips as far down the shaft as they will go, again and
> again, down past the *corpus spongiosum* to the magnifi-
> cent twin *corpora cavernosa* in their sheath of fibrous
> tissue and silk-smooth membrane, their areolar spaces
> flooded and stuffed stiff by lust; her expert action shows
> a calculated tenderness, guarding against her teeth graz-
> ing, care on one side and trust on another emerging *per
> carnem,* her avid cool saliva making Dale's prick shine in
> the attic light. (163–64)

Frederick Crews's sarcastic comment about this passage—"*Huge as in a motion picture:* we scarcely know whether we are supposed to read the scene or to rent it" (14)—indicates a misapprehension of Updike's effect here. The theological context has drained the pornographic discourse of its eroticism (and hence, of its rentability), and the pornographic descriptions render ludicrous the earnest theologizing. All that is left is an ironic grin (and a satisfied one, I hope; this is brilliant black comedy), a kind of existential emptiness. The linking of adulterous sex with theology has, as it did in *A Month of Sundays,* effected not an integration of God and humanity but a rupture, a divorce.

Indeed, as the book's secular plot spins on, Roger explicitly achieves the divorce between the divine and the human that his play of language has celebrated. Near the end of the novel, after vividly imagining the sexual carryings-on of Dale and Esther and toying with the idea of an adulterous (and incestuous) affair of his own with his young niece Verna, Roger finally does have sex with Verna. Verna has just physically abused her little daughter Paula (Updike's version of Hawthorne's Pearl), and Paula's overnight stay in a hospital, perversely enough, has opened up the space for Roger to have his fling. And an act of adultery—a vigorous sexual

No to his suburban, familial ordinariness—has powerful theological significance for Roger, just as it did for Tom Marshfield; it is an
experience of God not as providential or moral but as absence:

> We lay together on a hard floor of the spirit, partners in
> incest, adultery, and child abuse. We wanted to be rid of
> each other, to destroy the evidence, yet perversely
> clung, lovers, miles below the ceiling, our comfort be-
> ing that we had no further to fall. Lying there with Ver-
> na, gazing upward, I saw how much majesty resides in
> our continuing to love and honor God even as He in-
> flicts blows upon us—as much as resides in the silence
> He maintains so that we may enjoy and explore our hu-
> man freedom. This was *my* proof of His existence, I
> saw—the distance to the impalpable ceiling, the im-
> mense distance measuring our abasement. So great a fall
> proves great heights. (302)

This is very nearly the definition of the *via negativa* as I have been
describing it both theologically and aesthetically. It seems that this
novel's explicit theological assertions, its linguistic strategies, and
its plot all operate negatively: Updike uses language and story to
cross out language and story and point toward the Derridean
absent center (or, in the case of the more theologically minded
Updike, the Gnostic absent God).

But, as in *A Month of Sundays,* I see an alternative movement
here, a crossing out of the crossing out, which points toward at
least the possibility of a return to the positive rather than the
negative. For one thing, even the deep negativity of the pornogra-
phy/theology section and of the adultery/incest scene is softened.
After the nastily funny, deconstructive ironies of the Tertullian-
and-sex prose, Updike and his protagonist suggest, in a moving,
sincere way, that the real insight of Tertullian and of those with
hefty libidos is that a resurrection of the *body*—a repetition of our
ordinary, fleshly selves, of something rather than nothingness—is
what we crave, what we consider salvation:

> *Rursus,* Tertullian goes heartbreakingly on, *ulcera et
> vulnera et febris et podagra et mors reoptanda?* In our
> bodily afterlife, are we to know again ulcers and wounds
> and fevers and gout and the wish for death—the re-
> newed wish for death, to give the *re-* its curious, heart-
> breaking force. And yet, my goodness, pile on the cavils
> as you will, old hypothetical heretic or pagan, we *do*
> want to live forever, much as we are, perhaps with some

> of the plumbing removed, but not even that would be
> strictly necessary, if the alternative is being nothing, be-
> ing nonexistent specks of yearning in the bottomless
> belly of *nihil.* (174)

Similarly, Roger comes to a more moderate, less fiercely negative
insight some time after his sexual encounter with Verna. He
realizes that his reveling in God's absence was heresy and that the
true revelation effected by this sordid act was simply a repetition, a
return to the "muddle and woe" of the human condition:

> From my corbelled limestone academic precincts I had
> been dragged down into that sooty brick parish of com-
> mon incurable muddle and woe from which I had es-
> caped twice before, in leaving Cleveland, and in leaving
> the ministry. . . .
>   Indeed, it has occurred to me that in my sensation of
> peace *post coitum,* of sweet theistic certainty beneath
> the remote vague ceiling, of living *proof* at Verna's side, I
> was guilty of heresy, . . . that of committing deliberate
> abominations so as to widen and deepen the field in
> which God's forgiveness can magnificently play. *Más,*
> *más.* But *thou shalt not tempt the Lord thy God.* (310–
> 11)

Most critics seem not to have noticed this softer side of *Roger's*
Version, the way the book is not only about a fierce gap between
God and humanity but also about finding God in the return of the
ordinary. This is perhaps because too many have focused solely on
the explicit theologizing of Roger Lambert and on Roger's acerbic
reflections rather than on the book as a whole. Frederick Crews
acknowledges that this is his slant on the novel; he says outright,
for example, that the debate between Roger and Dale is a fraud, that
Roger is Updike's mouthpiece: "The debate is labored and stilted,"
Crews says, "but it can be skimmed; we know that Roger the
Barthian has got to win" (12). But I suggest that although Roger's
voice encloses the novel and his voice is generally, in Ralph Wood's
terms, Gnostic, the overall impetus of the book shows Updike's
residual commitment to a theology and aesthetic that Wood would
consider genuinely Barthian and therefore Christian.

Although the plot has Roger crushing Dale just as his namesake
Roger Chillingworth crushes Dimmesdale, Dale—along with Verna—cannot be simply dismissed. If the main text of the novel is
Roger's destruction of Dale, the subtext is Dale and Verna's initiation of a repetition, an experience of grace and even faith for Roger.

This Chillingworth is hardly the book's hero; he is a self-described "dour, tweedy villain" (257) who needs to have the chill taken out of him, and Dale and Verna accomplish this feat to a certain extent.

Crews is simply wrong to say that Dale's statements in his debates with Roger can be disregarded. Dale's lengthy arguments that physics and biology reveal a world imbued with the miraculous rather than just a dead machine are powerfully developed. And his criticisms of Roger's safe academic gamesmanship are telling—indeed, they make Dale a better Barthian than Roger:

> "Anyway, what you call religion around here is what other people would call sociology. That's how you teach it, right? Everything from the Gospels to *The Golden Bough,* Martin Luther to Martin Luther King, it all happened, it's historical fact, it's anthropology, it's ancient texts, it's humanly *interesting,* right? But that's so safe. How can you go wrong? Not even the worst atheist in the world denies that people have been religious. . . .
>
> "Studying all that stuff doesn't say *any*thing, doesn't com*mit* you to anything, except some perfectly harmless, humane cultural history. What I'm coming to talk to you about is God as *fact,* a fact about to burst upon us, right up out of Nature." (18–19)

What Dale is affirming here is a very Barthian position: that God is *God,* not some intellectual curio. "God's face is staring right out at us," he says later (20), sounding as if he were making a commentary on Levinas and *The Centaur.* And when Roger expounds hotly on his *deus absconditus*—"I am absolutely convinced that my God, that anybody's real God, will *not* be deduced, will *not* be made subject to statistics and bits of old bone and glimmers of light in some telescope!"—Dale "mildly" makes a wisely devastating observation about *dei absconditi:* "Your God sounds like a nice safe unfindable God" (93).

Dale's strength in the novel, however, is vested not so much in his actual arguments (he does, after all, begin to crumble) but in the way he jars Roger out of his "nice safe" agnostic apathy. Dale ushers in a repetition of Roger's past self, the self that is not a New England intellectual (the novel's setting appears to be Boston) but rather an ordinary suburban Midwesterner; it is not Dale's theology project but rather his connection to Roger's hometown, Cleveland, and to Roger's half-sister Edna that draws Roger to him in the first place: "When this young man called me at the school and, requesting an appointment, named my half-sister Edna's daughter Verna as a friend of his, and he explained that he, like me, came from the Cleveland area, my wish to hang up was less strong than my curiosity" (1).

For all his intellectual resistance to Dale, Roger experiences him as a kind of double; Roger talks of the "odd and sinister empathy" (95) he feels with Dale. And in several key passages—passages that hum with the familiar Updikean sense of the sublime revealed in and through the mundane—Roger rediscovers a world of immanent grace by imaginatively placing himself within Dale's mind. Walking to and from Verna's apartment, for instance, Roger sees a chaos of urban ordinariness ("There were no more Volvos and Hondas, just Chevies and Plymouths and Mercurys, rusted and nicked, Detroit's old boats being kept afloat by the poor" [54]), but the image of Dale transforms it. A green puddle becomes not just an indication of a car that leaked antifreeze but "a marvel, a signifier of another sort, a sign from above" (55), a black dog turd is "an unvarnished wonder, an auspice" (57), and a ginkgo tree is a "flimsy trapdoor" into the beyond: "Peace descended, that wordless gratification which seems to partake of the fundamental cosmic condition" (78). Most striking, though, is the sense of the sacred that Roger achieves from contemplating, and then visiting, the plain lumberyard where Dale works: "A bare bulb burned thinly. . . . A circular saw blade gleamed. . . . Sawdust, its virginal aroma, permeated the crystallizing black air. . . . *Fear not.* I felt surrounded by a blessing, by a fragrant benignity" (159).

So Dale initiates a repetition of the faith-filled Roger, the innocent Roger from Cleveland, and he even reawakens Roger's interest in Esther, his wife: Roger's pornographic reveries about Dale and Esther are the sexiest thoughts he has had about his wife in ages. If the explicit plot of the novel concerns Roger's breaking down of Dale's faith, the implicit plot has Dale breaking *open* Roger's faith. Dale, in other words, is a sort of prophet; after describing Dale as an eccentric outsider to organized religion, Roger reflects, "If the salt lose its savor, wherewith indeed? Jesus Himself, John the Baptist: raggedy outsiders. Insiders tend to be villains. Like me, I would smilingly tell my incredulous, admiring students" (96). It seems foolish to maintain, in the face of passages like this, that Roger Lambert is Updike's mouthpiece and that Dale Kohler is merely Roger's straw man.

Even Verna is not merely the adulterous escape into nothingness that Updikean characters typically seek. Though Roger's single full sexual encounter with Verna is fiercely negative, Roger tells us repeatedly that Verna is attractive to him not because she is no one but because she is a kind of repetition of his half-sister Edna; even more than Dale, Verna carries with her the healing textures and scents of the suburban Midwest. When he first visits Verna's apartment, it is not lust but "inwardness"—in Kierkegaardian terms, the sense of grace-filled repetition—that Roger most vividly experiences: "The secluded squalor of this unnumbered apartment pulled at me as I left. Its musty aroma searched out some deep Cleveland memory, perhaps the basement where my grandmother had laid up canned peaches on dusty shelves and where she did the week's washing with a hand-turned wringer, amid an eye-stinging smell of lye. Verna's place had for me what some theologians call inwardness" (76).

It would be wrong to sentimentalize this novel, to deny that it is largely an elaboration of the negative theology of adultery put forward in *A Month of Sundays*. As the book ends, Dale, who has been experiencing a literal as well as Sartrean "nausea" (340), and Verna head back to a Cleveland that hardly sounds paradisaical — "that heartland muddle, that tangle of body smells and stale pieties, of parental curses and complacent mediocrity" (348)—while Roger stays with Esther for the less-than-inspiring reason that "Esther is part of my life. I once went to a great deal of trouble to make her part of it and I'm too old to do any more rearranging" (347). Nonetheless, the brush with Cleveland has given Roger's New England home at least a breath of the alive and new. Roger and Esther are, for a while, taking care of Paula, who is a repetition of the feminine and sexual in a very new way: "I had never before seen female genitals in so new a condition. They were sweet—two lightly browned breakfast rolls fresh and puffy from the oven" (351). Furthermore, long-loved half-sister Edna now exists again, at least potentially, as a gracious repetition of the ordinary "vulgar" past:

> One of these days, Edna must call, to discuss things. Her child, her grandchild. I have sent Verna to her as a message she must answer. Her voice will be roughened by all these years, but not in essence changed: vulgar, self-satisfied, platitudinous, sexy. Pleasantly pungent, like the smell of one's own body. Flat-tasting but oddly delicious, like the meals served up to me in our solitude by my mother, love-miserly Alma. The certainty of this contact, between now and death's certainty, felt to me like money in the bank. (353)

Esther herself is now alive for Roger again: when she is not at home, "her absence felt like a presence, an electrical charge of silence in the house" (352). Is this the book's definitive affirmation of absence, of a wife *abscondita?* Or is this primarily an affirmation

of presence, of marriage rather than adultery? There is no definitive answer in this very ambiguous book, but in any case, the
novel's final paragraphs do suggest that Updike wants to leave us
with at least the potential—heavily qualified and ironized though
it may be—for a repetition of presence and marriage rather than of
absence and adultery. Esther, we are told, has been at least comically reborn ("Whatever emotions had washed through her had
left an amused glint, a hint or seed" [354]), and she has regained
her presence, her otherness, her capacity to surprise:

> "Where on earth are you going?" I asked her.
> "Obviously," she said, "to church."
> "Why would you do a ridiculous thing like that?"
> "Oh—" . . . In her gorgeous rounded woman's voice
> she pronounced smilingly, "To annoy you." (354)

This may not be a ringing affirmation of marriage, but it is not quite
nothing either.

Some of the first readers of *S.,* the third installment in the *Scarlet
Letter* trilogy, seem to have considered this book very nearly to be
nothing. Christopher Lehmann-Haupt calls the book's story "nearly farcical," and he claims that the novel's apparent substantive
interest in religions—Oriental and Western—is a fraud, that religious ideas are presented merely to be evaporated: "Lest there be
any question of disrespect for the mishmash of faiths that are
invoked in the novel, Mr. Updike ends up pulling the rug out from
under his plot so the entire religious dimension turns out to have
been a joke to begin with" (16). And Anatole Broyard asserts that
although the book presents the religious journey of its title character, Sarah Worth, "it's hard to take Sarah's pilgrimage seriously—
even she doesn't after the first few days" (7). In addition, Broyard
says that Sarah herself is a kind of non-character, that the novel so
strips her of illusion that there is nothing left but Updike's technical experiment with a female voice.

Such critics' complaints are somewhat justified. *S.* is in some
ways Updike's most thorough antinovel. Its epistolary technique
flattens out the narrative, much as Fowles's dramatic technique
flattens out the narrative in *A Maggot;* Sarah Worth, the protagonist, is a kind of disembodied voice, potentially a no one, much as
Rebecca often seems to be a disembodied voice in *A Maggot;* and
the central revelation of the novel is that the book's premise is a
fraud, much as the climax of *A Maggot* is the seemingly self-

canceling clash of two contradictory climaxes. *S.* is in many ways Updike's most Fowlesian book, a retreat to nothingness—an exposure of the nothing behind religious ideas. And yet, also like *A Maggot, S.* does find a positive religious revelation after all; I am convinced that the book's religious interests are quite serious. Though this revelation is deeply qualified, it is a characteristically Updikean revelation, founded not (as Fowles's is) on an opening up of unspeakable mystery but rather on at least a potential embrace of the ordinary; the book shows at least a trace of a continued commitment to the *via affirmativa*. My study of these vastly different and yet provocatively similar novelists ends by looking at these alternate movements, the No and the Yes, in *S.*

Sarah Price Worth is the book's Hester Prynne—she is married to Charles Worth (a stand-in for Chillingworth), she has a daughter named Pearl, and she has an affair with a kind of religious minister, a Hindu/Buddhist guru, the Arhat who is really Art (the novel's odd version of Arthur Dimmesdale). Sarah seems, however, less like Hester than like a female Rabbit Angstrom, though her knowledge of yoga has already given her an Eastern vocabulary that Rabbit lacks. As the book opens, Sarah has run from her marriage and from all the burdensome suburban circumstances—the something, the matter, the *"prakriti"*—surrounding it; the stuff of the world, she writes to her husband Charles, has melted away, and her free nothing-self, her *"purusha,"* has slipped through the hole in the net:

> My spirit, a little motionless fleck of eternal unchanging *purusha,* was invited to grow impatient with *prakriti*— all that brightness, all that flow. I would look at the rim of the saucer of my fourth decaf for the day and feel myself sinking—drawn around and around and down like a bug caught on the surface of bathwater when the plug is pulled. . . .
>
> Let me become truly nothing to you, at last. I will change my name. I will change my being. The woman you "knew" and "possessed" is no more. I am destroying her. I am sinking into the great and beautiful blankness which it is our European/Christian/Western avoidance maneuver to clutter and mask with material things and personal "achievements." (10–11)

Like *A Month of Sundays,* Sarah's story is set in the desert, away from mundane suburbia; Sarah has left New England and gone off to an ashram in Arizona led by her guru/idol, Shri Arhat Mindadali ("Supreme Meditator"). Her purpose there is to achieve the goal of apophatic mysticism, the *via negativa:* "samarasa" (32), absolute, imageless, beatific unity—the nothing.

A large portion of the novel's first half is a presentation of the psychology and theology of nothingness, stated in Hindu/Buddhist terms—and for all the book's satirizing of the ashram, the ideas are presented with a forcefulness which suggests that they are truly being tested, held up to the light. Sarah vividly describes, for instance, the way the Eastern idea of letting go of the ego has a pure, peaceful negativity that makes it seem preferable to Western Freudianism:

> The notion of the subconscious as a pool of eddies (*vasanas*) that originate in memory and feed the conscious eddies (*chittavrittis*) and which certain exercises can eventually erase in a blissful motionless (*nirvana* = without wind) state of *samadhi* has—this way of putting things—a certain intimate, non-terroristic simplicity that appeals to me. . . . I mean, should the game be to referee between superego, ego, and id, or to relax the whole system, by letting the ego and its harassing entanglements just fade away? (112)

The Updike whom I have been describing throughout most of these pages would probably prefer the Freudian refereeing, but Sarah—at least temporarily—gives us compelling reasons to prefer the fading away. Likewise Sarah's idea of God, although she does use the word "something" rather than "nothing," is as far from Barth's as it could be; rather than a distinct personal Other, Sarah's God is hazy, foamy, a luxuriously vague mystery (like the God that Fowles would espouse at his most theistic moments): "The whole matter of whether God exists or not, which I always thought rather boring, is just plain tran*scend*ed, it seems so obvious that *some*-thing exists, something incredibly and tirelessly good, an outpouring of which the rocks and I and the perfect blue sky with its little dry horsetails are a kind of *foam,* the foam on the crest of all these crashing waves" (44).

But most apropos to this discussion of Updike's adultery trilogy is the theology of sexuality presented in *S.* Updike has once again created a society, this time a Hindu commune, in which religious proclamations are mixed with sexual shenanigans, and the Gnostic premises are stated outright. "There are no orgies here," Sarah writes to her mother. "There is just love in its many forms." And although Sarah's explanation of the ashram's free sex may partly be a comical rationalization, it is also at least partly plausible (especially in light of the ideas I have been analyzing in this study): "If you knew anything about yoga or Buddhism you would know the idea is to get out of the body for good, not to achieve physical pleasure. And the state we all strive for here is perfect indifference" (101). This Eastern variation on Gnostic indifference, sex that crosses out sexual desire, is utterly at odds, Sarah tells Charles, with marriage, which is loaded down by circumstances, substance, *prakriti;* once again, adultery is revealed as the ideal:

> Let go of . . . me. You have the houses and the New
> Hampshire land and all the silver that didn't come from
> either the Prices or the Peabodys—the Worth stuff is
> clunky but sterling and you could sell it on consignment
> through Shreve's if you're feeling so desperately poor.
> You have your profession and society's approbation. I
> have nothing but my love of the Arhat, and he promises
> me nothing. Nothing is *exactly* what he promises—that
> my ego will become nothing, will dissolve upwards.
> (67–68)

The Arhat even more explicitly declares that truly revelatory sex must be adulterous, that married sex is too ordinary, too much a repetition of the mundane; as he seduces Sarah, the Arhat says that it is best if the beloved "*is parakiya rati—the wife of another. That is why I so much like your Charles. We need him. Otherwise you are apakva, unripe. Otherwise you are samanya rati, ordi-nary woman. We must mentally conceive you into vishesha rati—woman extraordinary, divine essence of woman*" (196).

Throughout the text, the Arhat develops quite thoroughly the book's theology of sexuality as a road to nothingness, a use of the physical to negate the physical. In a transcript of a sermon which sounds like a Buddhist parody of Updikean sex-and-theology prose, the Arhat says that imageless beatific unity, samarasa—an immer-sion in a hole, a nothingness—can be achieved through and symbolized by sex: "The cock in the cunt. This is bliss, rasa. This is samarasa, the bliss of unity. This is Mahasukha, the Great Bliss. This is Mahabindu, the great point, the Transcendental Void. This is maithuna—fucking" (115). The Arhat goes on to develop the idea, not a particularly feminist one, that a woman is the nothingness in which a man must lose himself in order to snuff out his ego. He presents what Ralph Wood would call a Gnostic idea that matter, *prakriti,* can be used to negate itself, that a certain sort of pleasure can point toward the annihilation of all pleasure, all feeling:

> A man who is not enlightened has this fear of nothing-
> ness that comes from saying "I." When a man has this

fear he turns to woman. She is mother. She is common sense. She has no fear. She is prakriti before it thought "I." He turns to her. He makes love to her. He inhales her aroma. He looks into her black eyes and sees the redness of her mouth when she laughs. There is a poem that says, "Put away the idea of two and be of one body." The fear that he has goes away. She is maya, she is nothingness. (119)

Beneath all this sex talk, it is really the deconstructionist use of text to cross out text that is at the core of the Arhat's teaching. His most striking sermon is a rather lengthy story about the journey of Kundalini, "the female energy in things" (80); at the end, however, he dismisses his own narrative as a fraud: "The story of her journey is a very detailed lie, like the horrible cosmology of the Jains or the Heaven and Hell of Dante" (88). He maintains that the only valid use of details, of substantive narratives, is to burn away details, to reveal the nothingness beneath: "Details obstruct us from enlightenment, from samadhi, from surrender of ego. We must forget. We must drive out foolishness from our systems. We must use foolishness to drive out foolishness. . . . That is why I told you the fairy story of Kundalini, the little snake that lives at the bottom of our spine. While you were hearing it, no other garbage was in your heads or stomachs; little Kundalini burned it all away" (88–89).

This using of details to burn away details eventually seems to be not only the Arhat's purpose but Updike's as well. It turns out that Updike's story of the Arhat, like the Arhat's story of Kundalini, has been a "very detailed lie": the Arhat, Sarah discovers, is not a guru from India but an ordinary man from Watertown, Massachusetts. His real name is Arthur Steinmetz; he grew up in an agnostic Jewish-Armenian family, *"took off for India"* (241) after reading Alan Watts, Krishnamurti, Salinger, and Ginsberg, and then came back to the United States because *"this is the place to score. This is the place where duhkha translates into money"* (238). But Art's materialism (as the Arhat, he has accumulated a fleet of flashy cars and buckets of jewels) is really only one manifestation of a more thoroughgoing negativity. Art, an artist much like Fowles's Magus, has been manipulating a kind of stage play; he says that his performance as a fabulously successful guru has been strategic, that the *"Buddha Realm Bit"* was *"symbolism"* rather than acquisitiveness: *"You may or may not believe this, but I really don't give a shit about any of this material garbage. It's all external, it's all just semiotics. I am non-attached, that's not just bullshit"* (244).

Art says that the purpose of this show was *"enlightenment"* —
*"Stop people short for even a second, and you have that much
more of a chance of enlightenment fighting its way past the
aham and all that defensive furniture"* (244) — but it can only be
a radically contentless enlightenment, even emptier than the
freedom that Conchis leads Nicholas to in *The Magus*. Sarah herself
suggests that all Art's talk about nirvana really may mask a passion
for annihilation; how, she asks, does nirvana "differ from extinction?" (246). Why, she wonders, "have all this religion to attain just
what we're afraid we're going to get anyway? I mean utter death,
utter extinction" (247). And Art reveals himself to be even more of
a negator than the Gnostic/Hindu Arhat; Art's response to Sarah
truly uses sex to cross out the text, to obliterate substantive
concerns, leaving no genuine religious ideals — and not even respectable lust — but nothing. Sarah, Art says, still using Eastern
mystical language but draining it now of its resonance, must simply
become *shunya*, the void: *"You must become shunya. You must
become emptiness. Shunya also means a girl of low caste, a slut.
When you become an utter slut, then vajra* [thunderbolt; phallus]
*will shatter you. Buddha will fill you. . . . "Baby, all your ques-
tions — they are optical illusions of the mind. They disappear in
the right light"* (247). The serious issues of the novel seem to have
been exploded, and the sexual plot seems to have been exploded
too. It appears that "S." now stands for both "shunya" and "slut,"
and the entire book has been a kind of narrative trick to bring us to
this emptiness, a suggestion that the value of religious pilgrimages
is that they negate the routine, not that they lead the pilgrim to any
substantive enlightenment.

Such a vision does indeed seem to cut through the center of *S.;*
the book's lengthy theologizing about nothingness, its satirically
self-destructing plot, and its nonnarrative epistolary style all suggest that Updike, much like Art/Arhat in his tale of Kundalini, really
is using text to cross out text. If this is his purpose, Updike has done
well — but even more than in the other *Scarlet Letter* novels, he has
abandoned the *via affirmativa*.

Once again, though, there is an opposite movement here — in
fact, in this seemingly most negative of his books, I see one of the
most vigorous calls to embrace the ordinary world in the entire
Updike corpus. The story beneath the story of Sarah's discovery of
the fraudulence of the ashram and especially of the Arhat is her
implicit realization that the good, for her, is founded not on a
plunging into the nothingness but on a repetition of the flawed
reality that she has left in New England. She most dramatically
discovers the way New England follows her, of course, when she

finds—as Dorothy finds that the Wizard is really a chap from Omaha—that the Arhat is actually just Art from Massachusetts. His Jewishness, in fact, makes Art a repetition of Sarah's long-lost boyfriend Myron, who lingers in Sarah's memory with the fertilizing sweetness with which Edna lingers in Roger Lambert's. But we have already seen how difficult it would be to found a vision of substantive providence on Art; Art the horny semiotician is Updike's consummate Nothing- man. There are, however, other images and suggestions in Sarah's later letters and taped messages which suggest that the negative repetition of New England embodied by Art Steinmetz is accompanied by hopes for a more positive one.

Shortly before the exposure of Art, Sarah's description to her friend Midge of the two autumns—the desert autumn that now presents itself to her and the New England autumn that exists for her as an absence—shows signs of a lurking affection for the glory of the something. Of course, Sarah mostly focuses on the troublesomeness of the ordinary, and she claims to be enjoying the "almost nothingness" of the desert: "You get this feeling of vegetation that already lives in purusha [the realm of spirit], with just the tiniest delicate grip on the surface of prakriti [matter], without any of the turmoil and violence of our Eastern weeds and bushes and vines battling it out with all of their egos on every square foot that isn't absolutely rock. Here it's mostly rock, red rock and sand. . . . I love it, Midge, I love the freedom of the almost nothingness" (212). But the freedom of the desert somehow remains qualified, limited, by the image of New England autumns; fall in the desert, she tells Midge is "not fall like *we* have it, of course—nothing like all that glory of the leaves, the maples and sumac and ash, and the smell of burning applewood out of people's chimneys, and the ocean turning that almost vicious dark-gray greeny-blue color under the heavy autumn clouds" (211). And she follows her description of the two falls with a report that her marriage has seemingly reasserted itself, that Charles, her husband, has in a sense returned: "My dreams get more and more intense lately. It's frightening. And a lot of them are about, of all people, Charles. I've totally stopped thinking about him consciously . . . but in these dreams we're making love the way we did the first years we were married" (212). And whatever world-annihilating freedom she may be experiencing with the Arhat, it is from the dream image of Charles that she experiences "forgiveness and understanding": she says that in these dreams "I'm myself as I am now, and even know that sleeping with Charles is *wrong,* a betrayal of the ashram, but this sense of fatherly forgiveness and understanding enclosing me is coming from him, pouring from him" (213).

Such hints of a kind of redemptiveness to be found in the world of the ordinary, of marriage and suburbs rather than of adultery and desert, help explain the book's terribly ambiguous ending—an ending as ambiguous as that of *Rabbit, Run,* in which Rabbit Angstrom continues running away from the ordinary and yet the ordinary remains (not devouringly but providentially) poised to return, repeat. Similarly Sarah, unlike Tom Marshfield, does not end her story by going back to New England; rather, she goes to a more deserted desert—Samana Cay, an island in the Bahamas, "way out here on the edge of nowhere, where the Western Hemisphere thins out to almost nothing" (266). On the face of it, of course, this seems to represent a thoroughgoing negation of the ordinary and communal, a complete retreat to the nothing. But the true act of negation in *S.* is the initial withdrawal to the desert ashram; Sarah's move to Samana Cay is a negation of the negation, a double negative that affirms the positive—the flawed and toilsome "glory" of the New England suburbs. Indeed, the novel's final three letters, which Sarah writes in Samana Cay (to Myron the ex-boyfriend, to Art, and to Charles), show Sarah rejecting the nothing and if not embracing the something at least poised to do so.

Sarah's primary reason for writing to Myron may seem to be an act of negating: she wants him to mail letters to Art and Charles, so the letters will not have Samana Cay postmarks and will therefore allow her to remain absent, absconded. But her description of why she was drawn to Myron's Jewishness, "a blessed relief from the terrible *sparsity* in which I had been raised" (264), is a powerful affirmation of substance near the end of this novel that often seems obsessed with nothingness:

> It was not just you I was infatuated with, it was your family, tucked with all those others in this hilly wooden three-decker part of Boston I had never been to before, and that overheated long floor-through . . . so full of wallpaper patterns and kinds of plush and fat friendly knobby furniture and embroidered doilies and doodads still savoring of Europe, Europe as a place of actual living life. . . . [A]nd there was this *tumbling* feeling in your apartment—words, cookies, souvenirs, meanings crowded one upon the other with this cheerful exalting intimate (though of course you weren't rich) *abundance,* a sweet *crammed* feeling that made me feel crammed with my own existence, alive to all my corners and cherished or at least forgiven for being myself, my womanly self. (263)

Sarah's letter to Art is a key articulation of this embrace of the something. Sarah has, it turns out, concluded that Art is not a fraud after all; he really is "a jivan mukta, a living blank who simultaneously sustains the chittavrittis [eddies of consciousness] while locating his being beneath them, in the utter indifference which is purusha and the atman" (272). And Sarah announces that her response to Art/Arhat's blankness is a negation of his negation—"removal, denial, betrayal even: love's expression must become absence and silence" (273). While Fowles's Conchis, at the end of *The Magus,* withdraws from Nicholas and hence invokes the image (or nonimage) of the *deus absconditus,* in *S.* it is not the Magus but the pupil who absconds—and hence creates that double negative that becomes a positive. Sarah herself clearly tells Art/Arhat that, for her, life is the texture of particulars and that she rejects the blankness of the *via negativa:*

> I was never able quite to let go of my chittavrittis—I
> was afraid of the void beneath them. For what is life, this
> illusion which we live and wish to sustain, but this very
> same skin of fluctuating awareness, of unsteady and no
> doubt unworthy nibbles and glimmer and halted
> thoughts and half-sensations? Isn't this, this thin impal-
> pable skin of color and flicker, this and only this the ec-
> stasy of existence that we wish to prolong forever. . . ?
> The terrible unending stillness of samadhi [the ultimate
> contemplative state in yoga] was for me indistinguish-
> able from death . . .—I was terrified that moksha [en-
> lightenment] would swoop down and render me blank.
> (271–72)

And then in the letter to Charles, the book's final letter, the ordinary does return, albeit in a comically foolish way. We learn that Charles is, of all things, marrying Sarah's best friend Midge, that while Sarah was off in her desert the *Couples*-ish world of mundane carryings-on did not halt. On the surface, of course, this is neither positive nor revelatory, and Sarah's reflections on Charles and Midge are hardly an embrace of the sacred suburbs: "You and your roly-poly little suburban pudding can do whatever you want—retire to her rumpus room and leave adulterous stains all over the shag carpet" (279). And yet, there is a Molly Bloomish affirmation in this final letter: much as Molly, despite Leopold Bloom's emotional distance from her, is still able to affirm, imag-inatively, the "yes" that she sexily and substantively experienced on Howth Hill, so Sarah reminisces about a very sexy vacation she and Charles had: "Dear Charles, after the first nights I smelled of your semen all the time, my hands and face and between my breasts where you came that way once—nothing, not the saltwater at the beach or the soap in the shower could wash it off, this faint lingering semi-sour smell of *you* somehow worked into my pores" (281–82). She contrasts the gooey substantiality of their lovemaking with the sterility of her lovemaking with Art, who practiced the Eastern technique of nothing-sex, a withholding of sperm.

Sarah's memory of the vacation is not unambiguously positive, and the marriage with Charles has, after all, failed, but there is some sort of affirmation here of bodily presence as opposed to absence, of the need for something to return after an interlude of nothingness, and of the providential redemptiveness of such a return: "We shed our skins," Sarah says, "but *something* naked and white and amara [immortal] slithers out and is always the same" (284, my italics). And Sarah's next sentence is a statement of the potentiality that the novel ends with; Charles and Sarah's daughter Pearl has gone to Holland and become pregnant, and as often happens in Updike novels, it is a baby who draws the main character back to the messy stew of human circumstances: "I think," Sarah says, "I eventually will go to Holland and help Pearl bear our grandchild" (284).

S. remains, for all its comedy, one of Updike's most profoundly negative books. Despite its invocations of the world of ordinary human relationships and stories, it stays stubbornly in a desert, its main character removed from genuine human community (the ashram hardly counts) and its narrative form only a cluster of disconnected letters and tapes. *S.* is at best a series of shouts to the ordinary world from outside that world. Nonetheless, the context of these letters does increasingly reflect a yearning for the world they are cut off from; if the providential repetitions of marriage— to the world, to human others, to spouse—that mark many of Updike's books are absent here and, to a degree, in the other *Scarlet Letter* adultery books, these absent repetitions hang in the air as powerful potentials, as very *present* absences. It is as if Updike himself, in his *Scarlet Letter* books, has taken that drive south that Rabbit takes at the beginning of *Rabbit, Run,* searching for the pure freedom of a Gnostic absent God in narratives that cross themselves out. And yet Updike—who says in *Self-Consciousness* that human beings, as they age, "come again to love the plain world, its stone and wood, its air and water," and that "the act of seeing is itself glorious, and of hearing, and feeling, and tasting" (247)—cannot hold off substance; it creeps back into the holes in his text, a kind of literary Hound of Heaven.

So in the end, I maintain my initial assertion that Updike's tends to be a literary *via affirmativa* while Fowles's is a *via negativa.* The fact that I have found in my consideration of these later books that the theories and practices of the two novelists have been drawing more closely together does not after all overturn my explicit thesis about these novelists—or my implicit one about the novel genre.

Yes, Fowles in his later books seems to have become more Shelley than Sartre—as interested in a kind of ineffable spiritual vision as he is in pure existential freedom. But this does not make him any less a novelist who writes about absence rather than presence, who uses text to cross itself out rather than to affirm. It does, however, suggest yet another tension in Fowles—analogous to the tension between what J. Hillis Miller describes as two sorts of deconstruction. Miller argues that deconstruction can be a way of doing what William Carlos Williams tried to do when he wrote a cultural study of America called *In the American Grain:* rather than asserting dogmas about America, Williams tried to evoke "the strange phosphorus of the life, nameless under an old misappellation" (quoted in "Address," 282). Miller suggests that deconstruction—a concentration on what is deferred by a text rather than on what is present—can point toward the phosphorescent vision that conventional language (and all language is conventional) masks: "Good reading also is productive, performative. Naming the text rightly, it brings the strange phosphorus of the life, what Williams elsewhere calls 'the radiant gist,' back once more above ground" (282). But Miller goes on to say—in a throwaway comment that merits more extensive discussion—that Williams's "notion of a radiant gist" can be viewed either "as a deep insight or as an unfortunate residue of mystified religiosity" (282); deconstruction, in other words, can operate from either premise. Fowles has perhaps been moving from the latter position (which would tend to negate in order to invoke not a "radiant gist" but rather an absence, an existential void) toward the former (which would, in a Jungian way, cross out text to point toward the unnameable archetypes beyond linguistic specifics). As deconstruction becomes more familiar and less esoteric, it will, I think, become increasingly important to distinguish the Shelleyan/Jungian strands of deconstruction from the Sartrean ones. For the purposes of this study, though, it is Fowles's literary tendency to not-say rather than to say that is important. And while Fowles's later works, especially

A Maggot, do suggest that his philosophical basis for not-saying may be changing (and a movement toward a Shelleyan/Jungian grounding would bring Fowles a bit closer to the something, the world of saying), Fowles remains primarily a not-sayer.

And yes, Updike has in his later works become increasingly interested in the nothing, in the not-saying. Of course, as I have shown, nothingness has always lurked around the edges of Updike's fiction; the existential crises of his heroes almost always lead them to negate. But in his earlier works, the ordinary world providentially reasserts itself again and again; the textures of Updike's later books, however, and especially of the *Scarlet Letter* trilogy, are starker, and the narratives are more self-reflexive, always on the brink of annihilating themselves. Still, Updike displays a discomfort with the negative, even in these negative novels—and the fact that at the end of *S.* the humanly ordinary seems poised to return suggests that Updike himself has used these novels as a sort of religious retreat, a pilgrimage up Rabbit Angstrom's mountain, which will be followed by a return to, a literary (and theological) repetition of, the world's "stone and wood, its air and water."

Still, if the "something" and "nothingness" categories do end up somewhat blurred, what is the value, after all, of these categories for understanding Updike and Fowles and other novelists? In a sense, I have spent many pages using two contemporary authors to argue what Robert Scholes and Robert Kellogg said more economically in *The Nature of Narrative* (13): that the novel is an intersection of the fictional (in my terminology, this is something like the No, the removal from the ordinary into that romantic "*domaine*" of Fowles which I have called a kind of nothingness) and the empirical (which loosely corresponds to the Yes, the embrace of the ordinary, the historical, the something). Scholes and Kellogg assert that a novel is a union of both elements, the fictional and the empirical, that narrative which is only fictional is romance or fable, and that which is only factual is mimesis or history (14–15). I would argue similarly that a work which is all nothingness would at worst be a blank sheet of paper and at best be so removed from narrative that it crosses out not only its own text but its very designation as "novel" (Samuel Beckett's *The Unnamable* hovers as close to this borderline as any book I can think of). And I would assert that a work which is all something would probably be merely an unselfconscious, photographic duplication of external reality.

Nonetheless, I think—as do Scholes and Kellogg—that some novelists lean toward one pole and some toward the other; to deny this would be to obscure important differences between novelistic enterprises, to suggest that Daniel Defoe and Jane Austen and Charles Dickens and Nathaniel Hawthorne and Theodore Dreiser and Virginia Woolf and Ernest Hemingway were all up to the same thing. By arguing, in however qualified a way, that John Updike is a novelist of things and John Fowles a novelist of no-thing, I have shown the way makers of fiction do tend to gravitate toward one pole or the other.

In addition, I hope that my way of describing the dichotomy that constitutes the novel gives a new slant to the idea that Scholes and Kellogg articulate. By talking in philosophical and especially theological language about the tension between fiction which negates the world's "stuff" and that which affirms it, I want to suggest that Sören Kierkegaard and Karl Barth, Albert Camus and Jean-Paul Sartre, Emmanuel Levinas and Carl Jung can speak to students of literature as helpfully as the likes of Derrida, Foucault, or Lacan. To meditate on literature is to meditate on terribly significant realities—humanity, the cosmos, God—and entering into a dialogue with the wide range of humanistic thinkers who have also meditated on these things can, I think, only be helpful. If this makes me one of those right-wing traditionalists whom J. Hillis Miller castigated in his MLA Address—those who cry "that it is immoral to shift from a thematic concern with literature, a study of the way literature expresses the values of our culture, to a nihilistic and 'radically skeptical' concern with language, to get lost in the sterile meanderings of language playing with itself" (284)—then so be it. But I hope that instead I have complicated the too-simple dichotomy between traditionalism and postmodernism; by using such theological concepts as the *via affirmativa* and the *via negativa,* I have tried to show that literature about substance can be as complex and sophisticated as literature about absence, but that an interest in nothingness is not simply and unequivocally nihilistic. Two good contemporary novelists ought to help us see old truths about their literary genre in new ways, and I hope I have helped unveil some of these truths.

Works Cited

Index

Works Cited

Alain-Fournier. *The Wanderer* (translation of *Le Grand Meaulnes*). Trans. Lowell Bair. New York: NAL, 1971.

Bagchee, Shyamal. "*The Collector:* The Paradoxical Imagination of John Fowles." *Journal of Modern Literature* 8 (1980–81): 219–34.

Barth, Karl. *The Word of God and the Word of Man.* Trans. Douglas Horton. 1928; New York: Harper, 1957.

Beckett, Samuel. *Three Novels: Molloy, Malone Dies, The Unnamable.* New York: Grove, 1958.

Bellah, Robert N., et al. *Habits of the Heart: Individualism and Commitment in American Life.* 1985; New York: Harper, 1986.

Booth, Wayne. *The Rhetoric of Fiction.* Chicago: U of Chicago P, 1961.

Broyard, Anatole. "Letters from the Ashram." *New York Times Book Review* 13 Mar. 1988: 7.

Burchard, Rachael C. *John Updike: Yea Sayings.* Carbondale: Southern Illinois UP, 1971.

Camus, Albert. *The Rebel: An Essay on Man in Revolt.* Trans. Anthony Bower. New York: Vintage, 1956.

Coleridge, Samuel Taylor. *Selected Poetry and Prose of Coleridge.* Ed. Donald A. Stauffer. New York: Random, 1951.

Conradi, Peter. *John Fowles.* London: Methuen, 1982.

Crews, Frederick. "Mr. Updike's Planet." *New York Review of Books* 4 Dec. 1986: 7–14.

de Rougemont, Denis. *Love in the Western World.* Trans. Montgomery Belgion. 1956; New York: Harper, 1974.

Derrida, Jacques. "Force and Signification." Derrida, *Writing and Difference* 3–30.

———. "Violence and Metaphysics: An Essay on the Thought of Emmanuel Levinas." Derrida, *Writing and Difference* 79–153.

———. *Writing and Difference.* Trans. Alan Bass. Chicago: U of Chicago P, 1978.

Dessommes, Nancy Bishop. [Rev. of *A Maggot* by John Fowles.] *Southern Humanities Review* 21 (1987): 290–91.

Detweiler, Robert. *John Updike.* Boston: Twayne, 1984.

Dunne, John. *The Way of All the Earth.* New York: Macmillan, 1972.

Egan, Harvey D. *Christian Mysticism: The Future of a Tradition.* New York: Pueblo, 1984.

Fowles, John. Afterword. *The Wanderer.* By Alain-Fournier. Trans. Lowell Bair. New York: NAL, 1971: 208–223.

———. *The Aristos.* 1979; New York: NAL, 1975.

———. *The Collector.* 1963; New York: Dell, 1963.

———. *The French Lieutenant's Woman.* 1969; New York: NAL, 1970.

———. "Hardy and the Hag." *Thomas Hardy after Fifty Years.* Ed. Lance St. John Butler. London: Macmillan, 1977. 28–42.

———. *A Maggot.* 1985; New York: NAL, 1986.

———. *The Magus: A Revised Version.* 1978; New York: Dell, 1979.

———. *Mantissa.* 1982; New York: NAL, 1983.

———. "Notes on Writing a Novel." *Harper's Magazine* July 1968: 88–97.

———. *Poems.* New York: Ecco, 1973.

———. *The Tree.* 1979; New York: Ecco, 1983.

Freud, Sigmund. *A General Selection from the Works of Sigmund Freud.* Ed. John Rickman. 1937; New York: Doubleday, 1957.

Gado, Frank, ed. *First Person: Conversations on Writers and Writing.* Schenectady, N.Y.: Union College, 1973.

Galloway, David. *The Absurd Hero in American Fiction.* Austin: U of Texas P, 1981.

Honan, Park. *Jane Austen: Her Life.* New York: St. Martin's, 1987.

Huffaker, Robert. *John Fowles.* Boston: Twayne, 1980.

Hunt, George W. *John Updike and the Three Great Secret Things: Sex, Religion, and Art.* Grand Rapids: Eerdmans, 1980.

Hutcheon, Linda. "The 'Real World(s)' of Fiction: *The French Lieutenant's Woman.*" Ellen Pifer 118–32.

Jonas, Hans. *The Gnostic Religion.* Boston: Beacon, 1963.

Jung, C. G. *The Archetypes and the Collective Unconscious: The Collected Works of C. G. Jung.* Vol. 9. Part 1. Trans. R. F. C. Hull. Princeton: Princeton UP, 1968.

Kelsey, Morton T. *The Other Side of Silence: A Guide to Christian Meditation.* New York: Paulist, 1976.

Kesich, Veselin. "Via Negativa." *The Encyclopedia of Religion.* 1987 ed.

Kierkegaard, Soren. *Fear and Trembling* and *Repetition.* Trans. Howard V. Hong and Edna H. Hong. Princeton: Princeton UP, 1983.

Lehmann-Haupt, Christopher. "In John Updike's Latest, The Woman Called 'S.' " *New York Times* 7 March 1988. C16.

Levinas, Emmanuel. *Totality and Infinity: An Essay On Exteriority.* Trans. Alphonso Lingis. Pittsburgh: Duquesne UP, 1969.

Lodge, David. "Ambiguously Ever After: Problematical Endings in English Fiction." *Working with Structuralism: Essays and Reviews on Nineteenth- and Twentieth-Century Literature.* Boston: Routledge, 1981: 143–55.

———. "Post-pill Paradise Lost: John Updike's *Couples.*" *The Novelist at the Crossroads and Other Essays on Fiction and Criticism.* Ithaca: Cornell UP, 1971. 237–44.

Louth, Andrew. "Denys the Areopagite." *The Study of Spirituality.* Ed. Cheslyn Jones, Geoffrey Wainwright, and Edward Yarnold. New York: Oxford UP, 1986. 184–89.

Loveday, Simon. *The Romances of John Fowles.* London: Macmillan, 1985.

McDaniel, Ellen. "*The Magus:* Fowles's Tarot Quest." *Journal of Modern Literature* 8 (1980–81): 247–60.

MacIntyre, Alasdair. *After Virtue: A Study in Moral Theory.* Notre Dame: U of Notre Dame P, 1984.

McKenzie, Alan T. "'A Craftsman's Intimate Satisfactions': The Parlor Games in *Couples.*" *Modern Fiction Studies* 20 (1974): 53–58.

Mackey, Louis. *Kierkegaard: A Kind of Poet.* Philadelphia: U of Pennsylvania P, 1971.

———. "Once More with Feeling: Kierkegaard's *Repetition.*" *Kierkegaard and Literature: Irony, Repetition, and Criticism.* Ed. Ronald Scheifer and Robert Markley. Norman: U of Oklahoma P, 1984. 80–115.

Markle, Joyce. *Fighters and Lovers: Theme in the Novels of John Updike.* New York: New York UP, 1973.

May, John R. "The Art of Steering: Theological Criticism after Three Decades." *Religion and Literature* 21 (1989): 1–7.

Mellard, James. "The Novel as Lyric Elegy: The Mode of Updike's *The Centaur.*" *Texas Studies in Literature and Language* 21 (1979): 112–27.

Mill, John Stuart. *On Liberty.* 1859; Arlington Heights, IL: AHM, 1947.

Miller, J. Hillis. *Fiction and Repetition: Seven English Novels.* Cambridge: Harvard UP, 1982.

———. "Presidential Address 1986. The Triumph of Theory, the Resistance to Reading, and the Question of the Material Base." *PMLA* 102 (1987): 281–91.

Miller, Roger. "Updike says this year's will be the last Rabbit tale— but no promises." *Milwaukee Journal* 1 July 1990: E6.

Miller, Walter, Jr. "Chariots of the Goddesses, or What?" *New York Times Book Review* 8 Sept. 1985: 11.

Moynahan, Julian. "Fly Casting." *New Republic* 7 Oct. 1985: 47–49.

Olshen, Barry. *John Fowles.* New York: Frederick Ungar, 1978.

Pifer, Drury. "The Muse Abused: Deconstruction in *Mantissa.*" Ellen Pifer 162–76.

Pifer, Ellen, ed. *Critical Essays on John Fowles.* Boston: G. K. Hall, 1986.

Plimpton, George, ed. *Writers at Work: The* Paris Review *Interviews.* Ser. 4. New York: Viking Penguin, 1976.

Sartre, Jean-Paul. *Being and Nothingness.* Trans. Helen E. Barnes. 1953; New York: Washington Square, 1966.

Scholes, Robert, and Robert Kellogg. *The Nature of Narrative.* New York: Oxford UP, 1966.

Singh, Raman K. "An Encounter with John Fowles." *Journal of Modern Literature* 8 (1980–81): 181–202.

Taylor, Mark C. *Deconstructing Theology.* New York: Crossroad, 1982.

Updike, John. *Assorted Prose.* New York: Knopf, 1965.

———. *The Centaur.* 1963; New York: Fawcett Crest, 1964.

———. *Couples.* 1968; New York: Fawcett Crest, 1968.

———. "The Dogwood Tree: A Boyhood." Updike, *Assorted Prose* 151–87.

———. "Faith in Search of Understanding." Updike, *Assorted Prose* 273–82.

———. "The Future of the Novel." Updike, *Picked-Up Pieces* 34–40.

———. *Midpoint and Other Poems.* New York: Knopf, 1969.

———. *A Month of Sundays.* 1975; New York: Fawcett Crest, 1976.

———. "More Love in the Western World." Updike, *Assorted Prose* 283–300.

———. *Picked-Up Pieces.* 1975; New York: Fawcett Crest, 1978.

———. *Rabbit Is Rich.* 1981; New York: Fawcett Crest, 1982.

———. *Rabbit Redux.* 1971; New York: Fawcett Crest, 1971.

———. *Rabbit, Run.* 1960; New York: Fawcett Crest, 1960.

———. *Roger's Version.* 1986; New York: Fawcett Crest, 1987.

———. *S.* 1988; New York: Fawcett Crest, 1989.

———. "The Sea's Green Sameness." *Museums and Women and Other Stories.* New York: Knopf, 1972. 159–64.

———. *Self-Consciousness: Memoirs.* New York: Knopf, 1989.

Uphaus, Suzanne Henning. *John Updike.* New York: Frederick Ungar, 1980.

Vargo, Edward. *Rainstorms and Fire: Ritual in the Novels of John Updike.* Port Washington, NY: Kennikat, 1973.

Waldmeir, Joseph. "It's the Going That's Important, Not the Getting There: Rabbit's Questing Non-Quest." *Modern Fiction Studies* 20 (1974): 13–27.

Wood, Ralph C. "Karl Barth, John Updike and the Cheerful God." *Books and Religion* 16 (Winter 1989): 5, 26–31.

Index

John Neary received a B.A. from the University of Notre Dame and a Ph.D. from the University of California, Irvine. His dissertation dealt with the theme of marriage in the novels of Austen, Dickens, and Joyce, and he has published essays on Dickens's *Bleak House* and on the child motif in Dickens's novels. He has also published an essay on the religious vision of novelist Mary Gordon, as well as essays on Updike and Fowles. While working at Hampshire College in Amherst, Massachusetts, he developed a course on the fiction of Updike and Fowles from which this book grew. He is currently an assistant professor of English at St. Norbert College in De Pere, Wisconsin.

DATE DUE

PRINTED IN U.S.A.